# DotNetNuke® 5 U;

# DotNetNuke® 5 User's Guide

## Get Your Website Up and Running

Christopher Hammond
Patrick Renner

**WILEY**

Wiley Publishing, Inc.

# DotNetNuke® 5 User's Guide: Get Your Website Up and Running

Published by Wiley Publishing, Inc.
10475 Crosspoint Boulevard
Indianapolis, IN 46256
www.wiley.com

Published by Wiley Publishing, Inc., Indianapolis, Indiana

Published simultaneously in Canada

ISBN: 978-0-470-46257-7

Manufactured in the United States of America

10 9 8 7 6 5 4 3 2 1

For general information on our other products and services please contact our Customer Care Department within the United States at (877) 762-2974, outside the United States at (317) 572-3993 or fax (317) 572-4002.

**Library of Congress Control Number: 2009926383**

*I dedicate this book to my beautiful wife Natalie. Without her support, I wouldn't have the passion for DotNetNuke that allows me to enjoy my work every day.*

— Christopher Hammond


*For my family — Lauren, Rick, Shelley, Kate, Mike, Sallie, Christine, Scott, and Sunny.*

— Patrick Renner

# About the Authors

**Christopher Hammond** is a technical evangelist with Engage Software in St. Louis, Missouri. Chris has worked with DotNetNuke since its inception and been a DotNetNuke Core Team member for five years. Solidifying his role within the DotNetNuke community as a leading expert and evangelist on the platform, Chris is a part of the INETA Speaker's Bureau, which allows him to be a frequent presenter at conferences, user groups, and companies around the world. He's the founder of DotNetNukeBlogs.com, a site bringing in the best DotNetNuke blogs to one, easy-to-use location, as well as DNNVoice.com, a weekly DotNetNuke podcast. When he isn't busy working on DotNetNuke, he can be found wrenching on or racing cars with the SCCA. You can read more about Chris on his personal blog at www.chrishammond.com.

**Patrick Renner** is a project manager at Engage Software, where he oversees a variety of implementations primarily using the DotNetNuke framework. Over the course of numerous projects using DotNetNuke, he has seen the application used in organizations large and small for a multitude of uses. Patrick is excited about the versatility, flexibility, and rapid progression of DotNetNuke as a product and as a user community. Patrick has spoken at Tulsa Tech Fest, trains DotNetNuke portal administration, and consults on project planning and strategy for DotNetNuke implementations.

# Credits

**Associate Publisher**
Jim Minatel

**Development Editor**
John Sleeva

**Technical Editor**
Will Strohl

**Production Editor**
Kathleen Wisor

**Copy Editor**
Foxxe Editorial Services

**Editorial Manager**
Mary Beth Wakefield

**Production Manager**
Tim Tate

**Vice President and Executive Group Publisher**
Richard Swadley

**Vice President and Executive Publisher**
Barry Pruett

**Project Coordinator, Cover**
Lynsey Stanford

**Proofreader**
Dr. Nate Pritts, Word One

**Indexer**
Robert Swanson

# Acknowledgments

I would like to thank my parents for raising me to be the man that I have become; I hope I have done you proud. To anyone I have ever worked for and with in the past, thank you for helping me along my way. I've been blessed with meeting many people throughout my life whom I consider friends. Thanks to each and every one of you. Thanks, also, to the DotNetNuke Corporation, the Core Team, and, most importantly, the Community for helping to make DotNetNuke bigger and better every day. Thank you to everyone on the team at Engage Software for providing a great environment to work in and a wonderful group of guys to learn from and hang out with. Finally, thanks to Pat Renner. He stepped up when I needed help to get this book off the ground and has been there for the whole process.

— *Christopher Hammond*

I would like to thank my wife for her love and support, acting interested in my regular use of acronyms, and for not taking offense when I focus more on my computer screen than on her. I would also like to thank my family for encouraging me to rise to the challenges that I meet. Thanks to my coworkers at Engage for listening as I think out loud and volunteering ideas and solutions. Last, thanks to my coauthor, Chris, for challenging me to think critically and apply the powerful features of DotNetNuke simply and practically.

— *Patrick Renner*

# Contents

# Contents

# Contents

# Contents

# Foreword

Do you need a website? This question is as old as the World Wide Web itself and as the Internet has evolved to become an integral part of our everyday lives, websites have become critical requirements for almost every significant initiative we undertake today. Whether you have a product or service to promote, a social group you want to interact with on a continuous basis, or just a personal philosophy or stream of consciousness you wish to share with others, websites provide you with a virtual space which is highly available and accessible by people around the world.

Reducing the justifications for a website down to a few simple items may help make the benefits more obvious . . .  People will look for you online. Sooner or later, someone is going to type your name or organization into a search engine and it will be highly beneficial if they are able to find you. Websites are inexpensive. The cost of domain names, web hosting, and web publishing software makes a website a very economical, yet valuable, investment. Websites are great advertising. No other medium has the potential to reach so many consumers for so little cost. A website is a worldwide presence. On the Internet, it doesn't matter whether someone is next door to you or on the other side of the world, they can view your website just the same as anyone else. Your website can generate revenue. E-commerce has minimal overhead and there are a multitude of ways to make money online. Your website can save you time. Distributing information through traditional channels takes time and effort but since everything online is digital, the delivery is simple and instantaneous.

Perhaps you already have a website? If so, how often are you updating it? If the answer is "not very often", you very likely have an out of date website which is causing you more harm than good. Not only will visitors notice the stale content and lack of activity, they may judge "the book by its cover" which could result in damage to your reputation as well as reduced confidence in your products and services. Driving visitors and potential customers away from your website is only part of the problem; your overall search engine rankings will also go down as Google and other search engines will index your site less regularly. In light of the these issues, it's actually better to have no website at all than to have one that makes you look bad.

So what is the key to maintaining a healthy website? Well, creating and updating a website has traditionally been a complicated task. In the past you may have needed to pay an expensive web designer to publish your content changes to your website. Or, if you worked in a large organization, you may have needed to route all of your changes through the IT Department or internal Web Master who was responsible for updating web properties. Regardless, the overall process was cumbersome, which often resulted in the website being neglected for long periods of time, reducing its effectiveness.

However, things have changed dramatically in the past decade. The task of creating and maintaining a web site has become much simpler and you no longer need to be computer savvy or highly technical to get online. The innovation which has removed much of the early complexity of building websites is the emergence of low cost, highly functional software applications known as Web Content Management Systems (or WCMs).

Web Content Management Systems provide administrative tools through a standard web browser interface, eliminating the need for users to install or update sophisticated software on their desktop systems.

# Foreword

The administrative tools are simple and easy to use and allow users to make immediate changes to the content of their website anytime, anywhere. Advanced permissions are usually available as well that allow you to designate specific portions of the site for administration by specific groups of users and not others. WCMs typically use a templating system which provides standardization in the website appearance and helps keeps the content properly separated from the visual characteristics and graphics. Many WCMs also offer tools to manage search engine optimization to help make your site more discoverable by consumers. WCMs are generally quite economical which make them highly accessible to individuals and organizations of all sizes.

DotNetNuke® is a full-featured Web Content Management System for the Microsoft Windows platform. It is built upon a secure, extensible, high performance web application framework focused on addressing the broadest set of online business requirements and most innovative web trends. DotNetNuke® is an open source solution and is currently available in two editions: a free unsupported Community Edition, and a more feature-rich Professional Edition with commercial technical support provided by DotNetNuke Corporation.

In this book, Chris and Patrick have done a great job of explaining the rich functionality of DotNetNuke® from an end-user perspective. After a thorough explanation of system installation and setup, they dive into the details of how to build a variety of different websites each with varying business requirements — from a Personal site, to a League site, to a Small Business site. The book would not be complete without a solid discussion on Security and it is rounded out with an enlightening chapter on Tips and Tricks, most of which were discovered through real-world, hands-on experience by its authors. So, if you are interested in creating a new website, or migrating a legacy website to a modern platform, and you wish to utilize the highly versatile DotNetNuke® Web Content Management System, I highly recommend this book as I believe it provides the insight and guidance to allow you to achieve your goals.

Shaun Walker
*Co-Founder & Chief Architect*
DotNetNuke Corporation
http://www.dotnetnuke.com

# Introduction

In this day and age, there are a number of tools available to assist you in building a website. DotNet-Nuke (DNN) is an open source web application framework that is ideal as a content management system (CMS). The open source nature of the project means that DNN is continually growing, making it a powerful and robust system. Individuals, small organizations, and large businesses are all realizing the benefits of using DNN for their websites.

As DNN continues to grow, the number and types of websites built upon the framework expand as well. Websites using DNN vary from personal to corporate, from single portals to multiple enterprise implementations. DNN has been used for sites including:

- ❑ Personal websites
- ❑ Clubs and online communities
- ❑ Small businesses
- ❑ Magazines and newspapers
- ❑ Online social networks
- ❑ Schools
- ❑ Hospitals
- ❑ Not-for-profit organizations
- ❑ Government organizations
- ❑ Corporate intranets and extranets

Although a number of books about DNN are available, most of them are aimed at developers and designers. They are not written in terms that make sense to the common web user. With this book, we've taken the approach that anyone should be able to pick up the book and with its guidance build a website using DNN. With a firm understanding of the administrative tools and implementation choices available in DNN, we encourage you to branch out and extend your knowledge of the framework, but to make the most of this great tool it's important to understand all the features that make building websites in DNN easy and fun.

## Who This Book Is For

This book is for users of DotNetNuke 5 and primarily targets people interested in building a website for themselves or an organization. This book is for users with all levels of knowledge about DotNetNuke, from those first learning about the platform to those who have years of experience working with DNN. This book takes the powerful features of DNN and makes them easy to understand and apply for your needs. Along the way, you'll pick up a strong understanding of the administrative tools and options available in DNN.

# What This Book Covers

This book covers the implementation of DotNetNuke 5, from installation to completion and ongoing maintenance. We cover a number of the core modules, skins, and providers used to administer content on your DNN site. We discuss some of the changes from the previous versions of the platform, and then how to use the new and old features alike in building a website on the platform.

The first half of the book introduces you to the platform, the core DNN concepts, and the installation and configuration options for your website. The latter half of the book applies these concepts to common uses of DNN, utilizing some of the core modules provided with the platform. By the end of this book, you should feel confident with the tools provided with DNN and be ready to realize the opportunities it provides.

# How This Book Is Structured

The book follows the basic premise that you start off knowing little to nothing about DNN. As you read further into the book, we teach you more and more about the platform, building upon the previous chapters. By the time you've finished the book, you should have a complete website up and running on DNN, and understand what you should do with your website to keep things running smoothly.

❑ **Chapter 1: Introduction to DotNetNuke** — The first chapter introduces some of the common terms that will be used throughout the book. We explain what DNN is and some of the rich history behind the application. We also cover some of the core terms that will be used throughout the book and how these terms define the functionality that DNN provides. By the time you have read through the chapter, you should have a basic understanding of what DotNetNuke provides and be ready to move on to the installation covered in Chapter 2.

❑ **Chapter 2: Installing DotNetNuke** — This chapter walks you through the requirements for a DotNetNuke-powered website and the preparatory steps for the installation process. Once you have your web server configuration squared away, we will walk you through the installation process for both a local computer and a remotely hosted website. After making your way through Chapter 2 you should have DotNetNuke up and running.

❑ **Chapter 3: DotNetNuke Concepts and Host Configuration** — This chapter provides an overview of the core concepts of pages, modules, skins, containers, and various other definitions within the platform. Once you have a solid understanding of the terms, we'll jump into the security aspects of DotNetNuke, including the multi-portal functionality that DNN provides for you to be able to host multiple websites from a single installation. We finish off the chapter by covering the host settings and the management of extensions for the platform.

❑ **Chapter 4: Portal and Content Administration** — This is the chapter where we really dive into the administrative functionality that DotNetNuke provides. You'll get an overview of the various settings for your first portal, then a detailed discussion of how DNN handles security, through roles, within a portal and the ability to edit and create roles. Once you understand the role functionality, we will cover the users, and then the way that roles and users are given rights to content within DNN through the use of the permissions grid. Once you have the basics for permissions, we will get into adding pages to your website and content to those pages through the use of modules.

❑ **Chapter 5: Creating a Personal Website** — A personal website is often the first place people start to test a new tool or create their first website. This chapter reviews the goals, decisions, and considerations for creating a personal site in DNN. By walking through the steps to create a personal site, we build upon the administrative settings explained in previous chapters and apply these concepts to a personal website. We implement a number of modules and review the configuration options available when using these tools for your personal site.

❑ **Chapter 6: Creating a League Website** — The chapter looks at the process of creating a website for a small organization. By exploring the use of DNN for a softball league's website, we expose the power of permissions-based content and engage a user community in our websites.

❑ **Chapter 7: Creating a Small Business Website** — The need to establish a presence on the Web is nothing new for small businesses. Many small businesses most likely have a home on the Web, but after getting their initial site live, it can become apparent how hard it is to maintain a static website without a full-time web administrator. Using DNN, you can create a robust website and keep your content current with a number of modules. Chapter 7 looks at the process of creating a small business's e-commerce site using the Store, FAQ, and Feedback modules.

❑ **Chapter 8: Advanced Portal Administration** — DNN has an extremely attractive and powerful feature that allows you to manage multiple websites under a single application. Understanding the power of a multi-portal environment can help you to maximize your DNN implementation. Along with added sophistication comes greater complexity. In this chapter, we'll review at a high level the structure of websites built in DNN to gain a better understanding of the implications to creating multiple websites, or portals, in a single installation of DNN.

❑ **Chapter 9: Your Website Is Up And Running, Now What?** — By this point, you should have a good understanding of how you can implement various types of websites using DNN. To follow up on that knowledge, we provide you with information on how to maintain your DNN sites, as well as some additional advanced administrative functionality that DNN provides.

# What You Need to Use This Book

To use DNN, you will need to have website-hosting capabilities, either through the use of an installable web server on your own computer or through a third-party hosting provider. Because DNN runs on the Microsoft .NET platform, you will need Microsoft's IIS web server software, as well as Microsoft's SQL Server, either SQL Server 2000, 2005, or 2008 or one of the free Express editions.

# Conventions

To help you get the most from the text and keep track of what's happening, we've used a number of conventions throughout the book.

> **Boxes like this one hold important, not-to-be forgotten information that is directly relevant to the surrounding text.**

*Notes, tips, hints, tricks, and asides to the current discussion are offset and placed in italics like this.*

As for styles in the text:

❑ We *highlight* new terms and important words when we introduce them.

❑ We show keyboard strokes like this: Ctrl+A.

❑ We show filenames, URLs, and code within the text like so: `persistence.properties`.

❑ We present code in two different ways:

```
We use a monofont type with no highlighting for most code examples.
We use gray highlighting to emphasize code that's particularly important
in the present context.
```

# Errata

We make every effort to ensure that there are no errors in the text or in the code. However, no one is perfect, and mistakes do occur. If you find an error in one of our books, such as a spelling mistake or faulty piece of code, we would be very grateful for your feedback. By sending in errata you may save another reader hours of frustration, and at the same time you will be helping us provide even higher-quality information.

To find the errata page for this book, go to `www.wrox.com` and locate the title using the Search box or one of the title lists. Then, on the book details page, click the Book Errata link. On this page, you can view all errata that has been submitted for this book and posted by Wrox editors. A complete book list, including links to each book's errata is also available at `www.wrox.com/misc-pages/booklist.shtml`.

If you don't spot "your" error on the Book Errata page, go to `www.wrox.com/contact/techsupport.shtml` and complete the form there to send us the error you have found. We'll check the information and, if appropriate, post a message to the book's errata page and fix the problem in subsequent editions of the book.

# p2p.wrox.com

For author and peer discussion, join the P2P forums at `p2p.wrox.com`. The forums are a Web-based system for you to post messages relating to Wrox books and related technologies and interact with other readers and technology users. The forums offer a subscription feature to e-mail you topics of interest of your choosing when new posts are made to the forums. Wrox authors, editors, other industry experts, and your fellow readers are present on these forums.

At `http://p2p.wrox.com`, you will find a number of different forums that will help you not only as you read this book but also as you develop your own applications. To join the forums, just follow these steps:

1. Go to `p2p.wrox.com` and click the Register link.

2. Read the terms of use and click Agree.

3. Complete the required information to join as well as any optional information you wish to provide, and click Submit.

4. You will receive an e-mail with information describing how to verify your account and complete the joining process.

*You can read messages in the forums without joining P2P, but in order to post your own messages, you must join.*

Once you join, you can post new messages and respond to messages other users post. You can read messages at any time on the Web. If you would like to have new messages from a particular forum e-mailed to you, click the Subscribe to this Forum icon by the forum name in the forum listing.

For more information about how to use the Wrox P2P, be sure to read the P2P FAQs for answers to questions about how the forum software works as well as many common questions specific to P2P and Wrox books. To read the FAQs, click the FAQ link on any P2P page.

# 1

# Introduction To DotNetNuke

The first web pages were created in the early 1990s, and since then managing the content of those web pages has been key to the acceptance and expansion of the World Wide Web. In the early days, this information was not managed in a specialized editor, as it was later in the 1990s, but by the web browser itself.

As the web expanded, this editing functionality became more restrictive, limited only to the owners of a web page or server. Early web pages were limited to text-based content, and the editors were rudimentary as well, providing simple text entry formatted with the Hypertext Markup Language (HTML) syntax. HTML is the syntax used to code a web page, and web browsers, such as Internet Explorer or Firefox, parse the code to display content.

A lot has changed in the nearly 20 years since the first pages launched. Every person on the Internet has the ability to create and manage his or her own web page, or a collection of pages forming a website. The tools used to manage these pages have evolved over time into extremely powerful and easy-to-use applications, enabling people with all levels of knowledge the ability to manage and create pages.

This chapter provides an overview of some of the common tools, called content management systems, available to aid in the creation of a web page, and how DotNetNuke provides those tools.

This chapter answers the following questions:

- ❑ What is a content management system?
- ❑ What is open source?
- ❑ What is DotNetNuke, and what is the history behind it?
- ❑ What does DotNetNuke provide and how?

# What Is a Content Management System?

Before we get into discussing what a content management system (CMS) is, let's cover some of the basics about web pages and how they are assembled and managed. The contents of a web page are usually stored on a web server as files. These files consist of HTML code to control the formatting of the web page. In order to view a web page, a request must be made through a web browser. A web browser will present the HTML information returned from the web server in a formatted manner to the visitor of the website. You can also view the source of the page to see the HTML content that is returned from the web server.

The tools used to manage HTML have progressed over the years, from simple text editors to full-blown applications that do most, if not everything, for the user when creating a web page. A CMS can be a mix of both of these extremes, providing you with a simple way to edit the text that makes up the HTML code for a web page, or to manage all your web page(s) in an automated fashion.

A CMS is an application that allows for the editing, publishing, and management of websites. In general, a CMS will provide you with the basic tools to create a new web page and manage the content on that web page. Most websites will consist of multiple web pages, and a good CMS will provide an organizational structure for these pages and allow you to manage that structure and provide navigation options to your website's users.

There are many other benefits to using a CMS. Most CMSs will provide dynamically generated content, meaning that they store the content that makes up a web page in a predefined format, usually using a templating system to display the content and a database to store the content. The content is retrieved from the database and then displayed to the visitor of the website by applying a template to that content prior to sending the information back to the browser.

This is an important part of a CMS because the separation of the content and the layout allow flexibility in the design and layout of your websites. Most CMS systems will allow you to change the look and layout of a web page through the selection of a new theme, sometimes known as a *new skin*. Applying a new theme to your page or website allows you to change the branding of a site without having to redo all the content contained on the pages. Being able to change the look of a single web page, or even your entire website, with a theme is an important feature to look for in a CMS.

As a CMS, DNN provides the ability to change the theme of a website or page through the use of skins. We will cover skins more in Chapter 3.

Another important feature of some content management systems is their extensibility. Extensibility within a CMS can mean a number of things. In regard to the topic of this book, we will refer to extensibility as the addition and customization of functionality for a website, such as adding the ability to have a weblog (blog), host a survey, or even an e-commerce application.

There are a number of CMSs available for use in building a website, among those are a number of open source solutions such as Joomla! and Drupal that run on Linux Apache, MySQL and PHP, or otherwise known as LAMP. There are even a few open source CMSs for the Microsoft .NET Framework other than DotNetNuke.

# What Is Open Source?

DNN is the largest open source project built using Microsoft-based technologies. Open source, in simple terms, refers to an application — be it a web application such as a CMS, a desktop application that runs on a computer, or even an operating system for a computer that controls everything a computer does — that has the source code available, in most cases for free. Source code for a software program consists of the code written in a computer language that defines functionality to a computer and then tells the computer how to execute that functionality.

Open source has become very popular in recent years with the increased acceptance and use of the Linux operating system. Linux initially was a hobbyist's toy, but it has grown into an enterprise application that is used widely in business. Generally, open source projects are developed by volunteers, usually organized into a team that customizes, tweaks, and helps to promote the product. In most cases, these developers are not paid for the modification and enhancements put into open source projects. Although they might use that application in their business, and thus get paid by other means, the work for the application itself is not paid for by any general entity or business.

As Linux proved that the open source model for software could work, more and more applications were developed with open source in mind. Some notable examples of successful open source projects include SugarCRM, JBoss Portal, and Alfresco, all of which have received acclaim from the press and high acceptance in the business marketplace.

## Software Licenses

Almost all software packages have a software license associated with them. These licenses generally define the terms of ownership and what the users of a software package are entitled to in regard to the software. In the early days, software licenses were included within the packaging, sometimes on the installation disks themselves.

Now software licenses tend to come into play during the installation process. The installation will usually provide a review of the license and require acceptance before the installation will complete. The next time you're installing a piece of software and see a message prompting you for acceptance, try reading the license, at least some of it; they can be quite long.

### Common Retail Software Licenses

The source code for most retail software is not available and is closely guarded as intellectual property by the application's creator/owner. Software licenses for retail software generally limit you as to how you use the application, the number of computers you install the application on, and the liability that the creator/distributor of the software has. In most cases, these licenses will also include terms that define the software as owned by the creator and only available for you to use, not to own yourself.

### Common Open Source Licenses

Open source applications, on the other hand, generally differ in many ways from their retail software counterparts. Software that is truly open source and freely available generally comes with very liberal software licenses. These liberal licenses allow for a wide range of scenarios for use of the open source software, from simply being able to use the software without charge to having the right to modify, rename, and redistribute or even sell the software without having to pay the creators or team that manages the software.

A permissive license in open source is considered fairly liberal in its terms because it usually allows you to modify and redistribute the code, and doesn't restrict you to using the same license in future iterations of the code. The BSD license is a commonly used permissive license, originally named after an open source operating system called Berkeley Software Distribution (BSD). The primary restriction with a BSD license is that the included copyright in the source code must remain in future iterations. This copyright is usually held by the owners of the open source project.

Another common type of open source license is known as a *copyleft license*. A copyleft license usually gives the same type of licensing as the BSD but has restrictions as to how the open source code can be redistributed and licensed. The GNU General Public License (GPL) is a common copyleft license. The primary restriction for open source projects released under the GPL is that any modifications and enhancements to the source code must also be released under the same software license. In other terms, any company making changes or enhancements to an open source project released under the GPL must also release that package under the GPL.

# What Is DotNetNuke?

DotNetNuke (DNN) is an open source web application framework that can provide CMS functionality. Where DNN differs from other CMSs is the extensibility that it provides through the use of add-ons, known as extensions. DNN can be used for many different types of websites, from the simplest of personal websites to the most complex enterprise internal and external sites. Later in the book we will go into how to configure DNN to work in some common website scenarios.

DNN runs on Microsoft .NET, a platform designed to allow a variety of programming languages to be used for developing applications that can run on Microsoft-based operating systems. DNN is written in the VB.NET language, the latest iteration of Microsoft Visual Basic. DNN is the largest and most utilized open source project running on the Microsoft platform, with more than 700,000 registered users at DotNetNuke.com.

Because DNN runs on the .NET Framework, you can configure the application to run on web servers powered by Microsoft operating systems, including Windows XP, Windows 2000, Windows 2003, Windows Vista, and Windows Server 2008. DNN is a database-driven application, storing most of the pertinent information for the content and settings for a website in a defined database structure running on Microsoft's SQL Server, a database server. In most cases, the database server software can run on the same computer as the web server. Websites that receive a lot of traffic can experience performance issues, so putting the database on a standalone server is a common practice.

It is also possible to configure DNN to run on free tools that Microsoft provides. These tools can run on multiple versions of Windows but are mainly useful for versions such as Windows VISTA Home edition that don't provide the ability to install a web server as part of their core offering. These tools include a free version of the database server, web server, and other components necessary to run a web application. You can find these tools available from Microsoft's Web Platform Installer by visiting www.microsoft.com/Web/downloads/application.aspx.

The combination of a Microsoft operating system and database server is a very common configuration in website-hosting businesses. This availability can provide you with many different options for website-hosting services, if you are not comfortable hosting your own website. We will cover these free tools and hosting providers in Chapter 2 when we go through the installation procedures for DNN.

## Who Uses DotNetNuke?

DNN is flexible enough as an application that it is used both by individuals and by companies to build just about any type of website imaginable.

For an individual, DNN provides a number of easy-to-use modules that can be configured to run a weblog, family sites, photo galleries, community websites, and even sites for a small business. Both authors of this book use DNN to power their own personal websites. We also have experience configuring DNN to run in a wide variety of business scenarios, including retail sales, education, and healthcare markets.

From an enterprise level, DNN provides many of the tools necessary to manage an intranet website, as well as the flexibility and ease of use to develop and manage customer-facing websites. The tools we will cover in this book will provide you the basic functionality for enterprise websites. Another strength of DNN, although the topic is outside the scope of this book, is the ease of development for new extensions. Developers within business organizations can easily develop new extensions for DNN to meet specific business requirements.

## What Does the License Allow?

DNN is released under a BSD license, meaning that it can be modified and redistributed in any number of ways, the only requirement being that the original copyright statements in the source code remain. This license has allowed many individuals and companies to utilize DNN in a variety of markets and projects. Many of these companies choose to rebrand DNN into a product of their own to fit into a vertical market. Doing so is completely legal because of the BSD license.

In addition to the license, there are a few other restrictions to the DNN brand. The terms "DotNetNuke" and "DNN" are trademarked entities owned by the DotNetNuke Corporation. The DNN Corp. has fairly liberal usage requirements for these brand items, the main restriction being that offshoots of the DNN code base cannot be branded as DotNetNuke or DNN. You can make changes to the source code and release it as another open source application; you just can't call this application DotNetNuke. We'll cover more later in the chapter about why it is in the DNN Corp. and the project's best interest to prevent such actions from occurring.

## A Brief History of DotNetNuke

DNN has had an interesting history, most of which we have had the pleasure of experiencing. In 2001–2002 Microsoft was ramping up the marketing machine for their latest platform for software developers, the Microsoft .NET Framework. In order to gain acceptance for this new platform, Microsoft commissioned the development of some free tools for the development community. Now known as *starter kits*, these tools were sample applications to demonstrate the ease of use and power of this new platform.

One of these applications, the IBuySpy Portal, was a sample web portal that could be set up to run on ASP.NET and be used to create and manage a simple web portal. The application was distributed as a best practices implementation for software developers to use in designing their own application on the new .NET Framework. There were two versions of the IBuySpy Portal released, one written in VB.NET and one written in another .NET language, C#. Essentially, both applications were the same; they were just written in different languages to highlight best practice code for a wide range of developers.

> *ASP.NET is the Web side of the .NET Framework, providing the tools necessary for a web server, such as Microsoft's IIS, to execute code written in various .NET languages.*

> *VB.NET is a popular programming language, the latest iteration of the popular Visual Basic language that was a foundation for the beginnings of Microsoft. DotNetNuke is written in VB.NET.*

> *C# is another popular programming language. Although it's not the basis for DNN, there are a number of extensions for DNN written in C#.*

From these initial releases of code, many developers jumped on the .NET bandwagon. On December 24, 2002 Shaun Walker released an enhancement to the IBuySpy Portal. He announced this in the forums located at www.asp.net, the primary community website where ASP.NET developers interacted, discussing changes and enhancements to the IBuySpy Portal. The enhancement, called IBuySpy Workshop (IBSW), included many changes and customizations of the original application to provide a more rounded and functional application.

It didn't take long for the application to gain steam within the Microsoft developer community as people realized the functionality that IBuySpy Workshop provided far exceeded the functionality of the standard IBuySpy Portal. Over the next few months, developers continued to make enhancements to IBSW and submit those enhancements back to Shaun, as well as post them in the forums for others to see. As these enhancements continued to roll in, a core group started to form as influential developers in the community.

Shaun, and others, realized that this free application could turn into something more. It was decided that the application was named too similarly to the IBuySpy Portal and should be renamed. After much discussion it was decided to name the product DotNetNuke, after the many other open source portal systems running on technologies other than Microsoft .NET. At the time, the other prominent portals were PHPNuke and PortalNuke, as well as a few others.

## Who Develops DotNetNuke?

With a new name, it was time to form a team to help extend the functionality for DNN; thus, the Core Team was founded during the summer of 2003. The Core Team helped to provide the final few releases of what was then known as DotNetNuke 1.0.10 in the fall of 2003. They then began working on the next major version of DNN, a version that would be pivotal for a number of reasons.

DotNetNuke 2.0 was released in March of 2004 and promptly took the portal package to a whole new level. Some of the new features and flexibility added into this release included a totally new skinning engine, a very flexible extension installer, and a new backend model that allowed DNN to work with different types of databases. We'll go into more detail on these features later in the chapter as we discuss the different types of functionality that DNN provides.

DotNetNuke 3.0 came out just short of a year later, in March of 2005. This release had a number of enhancements targeted at extension developers. These enhancements provided methods for developers to access and modify information within the DNN framework, allowing for more functional extensions, empowering better websites using DNN and these extensions. This release of DNN also provided user integration with a new technology that Microsoft was preparing to release later in the fall. This integration with the technology prior to the official release provided Microsoft with some real-world testing, and provided DNN with some great promotion and support.

The 3.0 release of DNN also provided the abstraction of some of the key functionality provided by DNN into individual extensions. Prior to version 3.0, DNN provided a broad range of functionality, in a lot of cases more functionality than most websites needed. This functionality was built into the framework and was not easily removed for websites that didn't need this functionality. By abstracting these functional items into extensions, it was now possible for website administrators to remove unnecessary functionality from a website. This is an important item to note. As an administrator of a website, you might have multiple content authors working on your site. Limiting the amount of information and functionality that authors have access to can be an important part of maintaining a website. By limiting the tools available to authors, you will likely minimize the amount of work that administrators have to do cleaning up mistakes that result from authors' not knowing how to properly use some of the tools.

These abstracted extensions each turned into projects of their own. The DotNetNuke Core Team divided up these functional pieces into individual extensions that were then managed by smaller teams, called *project teams*. Each project team within the DNN open source project managed a particular extension, usually represented by at least one DNN Core Team member. These project teams provide the development, testing, and release of these extensions outside of the normal DNN release cycle. We spend the last half of this book covering some of these individual extensions and how you use them to build various types of websites.

## *Multiplatform Support*

The fall of 2005 brought the release of two versions of DNN, DotNetNuke 4.0 and DotNetNuke 3.2. While numbered differently, in theory the two releases provided the same functionality. The difference between the two versions was the technology they ran on. Until this point, DNN had run on Microsoft's .NET Framework version 1.0 and 1.1, the version of .NET that DNN 3.2 ran on. In the fall of 2005, .NET 2.0 was released. DNN wanted to capitalize on the marketing behind the new .NET Framework, so DotNetNuke 4.0 was compiled for the new framework and released the same day that .NET 2.0 was released.

For the next year, two different versions of DNN were released in tandem, a version for .NET 1.1, and a version for .NET 2.0. In the fall of 2006 the final 3.*x* version of DNN was released as DNN 03.03.07. This ended the support for the .NET Framework 1.1, and all releases since have supported .NET 2.0. In the future, it is likely that .NET 2.0 support will be sunsetted, as the DNN platform moves to utilize features of .NET 3.5 that aren't available in 2.0. As of this writing, however, all current releases of DNN run on .NET 2.0. You will find .NET 2.0 support from nearly every hosting provider when you start looking for a company to host your website.

*We'll talk more about configuring DNN in a hosting environment in Chapter 2.*

Another change for the DNN projects came in the fall of 2006. While the project had always been managed by Shaun Walker and three or four individuals on the board of directors, the copyright, trademarks, and other materials for DNN were owned by Shaun's consulting company, Perpetual Motion Interactive Systems (PMIS). Although this provided a great background for the project in its infancy, as the project grew and more individuals and businesses started to rely on DNN on a larger scale, there were discussions of what would happen to the project if something were to happen to Shaun. Being the sole owner of PMIS, if he were to get hit by a bus, the common what-if scenario in the IT world, what would happen to DNN as a whole?

To prevent this potential scenario, the members of the board of directors on the DNN Core Team formed a corporation licensed in the state of Delaware, the DotNetNuke Corporation. The process of transferring the ownership of the copyrights and trademarks for DNN to the DNN Corporation started at this time. Now if something were to happen to one individual, DNN can live on due to the management of the DNN Corporation.

## The DotNetNuke Corporation

The DotNetNuke Corporation is tasked with managing the DNN project, continuing the growth and development of the project, and protecting the trademarks and copyrights associated with the project. This is a necessary and important role in an open source project. Due to the open license that DNN is released under, it is possible for anyone to take the source code and re-release that code in just about any way they deem fit. However, they are not allowed to utilize any DNN trademarks in doing so; the corporation is responsible for policing and protecting this usage.

As we've discussed, the DNN project has been around for a number of years and has quite a bit of brand recognition/value within many circles. If someone were to take the source code for DNN and re-release it under the same name, the value of the brand would become diluted. The potential for confusion exists within the community if there appear to be two projects called DotNetNuke.

Another potential issue that the DNN Corporation is tasked with is to the prevent something known in the open source world as a *fork*. A fork is when an individual or group decides to take the source code for an existing project and start up their own open source project based on that code. Although this is completely legal based on the license for DNN, it has the potential to fragment the strong community that has been built around DNN.

Since its inception the DotNetNuke Corporation has been working to secure funding to help continue to drive the DNN project. As of the time of this writing the DNN Corp has recently secured a round of venture capital funding that will allow them to continue to grow. For a more thorough history of DNN and the funding process, check out *Professional DotNetNuke 5* (Wiley, 2009).

## DotNetNuke Professional and Community Editions

The DotNetNuke Corporation recently announced and released a new product called DotNetNuke Professional Edition. This product is a licensed application sold and supported by the DNN Corporation. At the same time, the free version of DNN was rebranded as the DotNetNuke Community Edition.

There are a few differences between these two editions, the biggest being the cost associated with a license of the Professional Edition. The Community Edition remains free. The Professional Edition has a few enhancements over the Community Edition, as well as services provided with purchase, such as a year of free upgrades and product support provided by the DotNetNuke Corporation.

The Community Edition remains the most adopted and widely used version of DNN and will continue to grow just as it always has. The content in this book applies to both the Community and Professional versions of DNN. In most cases, you will find that the Community Edition provides everything you need.

If you work for a company that is opposed to using open source software, the Professional Edition might provide your management team with the assurances that DNN can be used in enterprise environments.

# What Is the DotNetNuke Ecosystem?

DNN has a very extensive community that has grown with the project since its inception. That community includes individuals and businesses that provide a lot of information, services, and products for DNN. Because of DNN's extension model, it is very easy for administrators to plug new extensions into their website. Combined with high developer acceptance of the platform, this has allowed an extensive ecosystem to spring up around the platform. It is easy for individuals and businesses to find support and products for DNN though the members of this ecosystem.

Some of the strength of this ecosystem is the availability of thousands of modules and skins for DNN, in addition to the modules and skin packages that come with the packages available from dotnetnuke.com. Some of these modules and skins are offered for free, whereas others have a price associated to them. A lot of the individual developers/businesses sell these modules on their own websites, but many of them can also be found at the DotNetNuke Marketplace (http://marketplace.dotnetnuke.com).

This ecosystem didn't form over night; it has taken time to grow and continues to grow today. Most members of the ecosystem got their start in the DotNetNuke Forums (http://forums.dotnetnuke.com), assisting other customers and learning as much about the platform as they were able to. Because of the continual growth of the platform, it is important for those providing products or services to keep a finger on the pulse of the project and users in the community, so you will still find those community members/vendors posting frequently in the forums.

One of the strengths of DNN is the breadth of knowledge available from its community members. As the project has grown, so has the community itself. You will find great blog posts from active members in the community that provide insight into the platform and how best to use the different tools that DNN provides. You can find blog posts at DotNetNuke.com as well as DotNetNukeBlogs.com, a website run by this book's coauthor, Chris Hammond. In addition to the helpful blog posts, you will find a great group of people that provide support to DNN users in the forums. If you run into a problem with DNN, that is the first place you should look for an answer.

# What Does DotNetNuke Provide and How?

DNN enables you to create web pages and add content to those pages through the use of extensions. There are a few types of extensions; the one we will primarily use through this book is the module extension. DNN provides an extensive list of modules out of the box, offering a wide range of functionality that you can choose to implement on your website. There are 25 modules available for installation, either during the DNN installation process or after your website is up and running. Chapter 2 covers the DNN installation process.

> With the advent of DotNetNuke version 5, the term extensions has been entered into the vocabulary of a DNN website. In previous versions of DNN, there were many different types of extensions, but they were not grouped together to be called extensions.

DNN's modules range from the Text/HTML module, a simple module that provides the most basic CMS functionality within DNN, to the Store module, which provides a very capable e-commerce solution for your website. Before we get into this extended functionality, however, it's important to have a basic understanding of how DNN works.

When someone visits a website, the information is downloaded from the web server to the user's web browser for display. How that page is actually generated depends on the type of web server it is running on and what, if any, CMS is being used to manage the website. Some CMSs will generate individual files for each web page; these files are known as *static files* and are stored as files on the hard drive of the web server. They are static because once they've been generated by the CMS, they exist entirely on the server. In the future, the CMS may update the files, but that depends on the requirements of the CMS system.

Other CMSs will actually create the web pages dynamically when requests are made from visitors of the website. In most cases, the information used to generate the web pages is stored in a database. This database may be located either on the web server itself or on a specific database server. CMSs that dynamically generate the web pages returned to visitors allow for websites that can be highly flexible in the layout and formatting of the content to be displayed on the web pages.

DNN is a CMS that generates the web pages using this dynamically driven model. Almost all the content that is entered through the web browser interfaces for DNN will end up being stored in a database. The primary database that DNN supports is Microsoft SQL Server 2000/2005/2008 or SQL Server Express. It is possible to get DNN to run on other databases such as MySQL, but that discussion is beyond the scope of this book.

When managing your DNN website, you will provide most of the maintenance through your web browser. Only rarely will you have to maintain anything outside of the browser — for example, installing DNN (see Chapter 2). The following sections provide a brief overview of the basic functionality that the DNN framework provides to website administrators. This will give you a better understanding of how things will fit together over the next few chapters.

## Security

Before we talk about the content on your website, it is important to understand that DNN provides administrators with the ability to define multiple levels of permissions for their websites. You can create a website that is completely open to the public for viewing or one that requires users to register and log in, in order to view it. Once you have users logging in to your website, you can take the security further and provide individuals or groups with the ability to view or edit content. DNN's security model is extremely flexible, even allowing you to limit users or groups to edit only parts of a web page instead of the whole thing. Chapter 3 covers the security functionality within DNN in more detail.

## Pages

Most websites you run across on the Internet have multiple pages, different files on the web server that provide different content for each of the pages that are loaded by request. DNN is no different. As a site administrator, you can create and manage pages within your website. As you'll see in Chapter 3, adding pages is easy to do through the web interface. You can choose a predefined template for the page that consists of a defined layout, skin, and even already populated content. Pages within DNN, sometimes referred to as *tabs*, have multiple properties, such as title, layout, descriptions, keywords, as well as permissions. These can be defined at or after creation. Another important aspect to pages within DNN is the impact that they have on the navigation and organizational structure of your website. We'll cover all these aspects in more detail throughout the book.

The final thing to keep in mind with your pages is that they do not actually store content, other than the items discussed earlier in this section. Pages have a skin applied to them that defines either a single pane or multiple panes for use on the page. A *pane* is part of a DNN skin that provides a location for placing content.

## Extensions, Modules, and Skins

Extensions enable you to add functionality to your DNN website with minimal effort. Although there are multiple types of extensions, we will be focusing primarily on the skin and module extensions. Extensions are installed using compressed ZIP files, known as packages, which you upload through the browser through the extension installer. Chapter 3 covers installing extensions in more detail.

Skin packages provide the layout and design for your DNN pages. Because of the flexibility built into DNN, it is possible to completely overhaul the look of your website simply with a few clicks of the mouse. Beside the graphical and style elements of a skin package, the important aspect of skins is the number of panes they provide. A skin for a DNN page controls the number and placement of panes on a page.

A simple skin might contain a single pane in which all of the content for that page resides, whereas a more complex skin can have multiple panes with different formatting applied to each pane to control the look and feel of the content within that pane. Chapters 3 and 4 cover how to utilize skins on a portal and page level, as well as how to arrange content within your skins. We will not get into the development of custom skins in this book. If you are interested in custom skin development, check out *Beginning DotNetNuke Skinning and Design* (Wiley, 2007).

The Module type of extension provides the functionality and content on your DNN website. There are numerous types of modules available for DNN, providing countless ways to configure and manage different content on the site. DNN comes with a selection of modules that you can install during the initial setup or after your website is up and running. Modules, like the other extensions within DNN, are uploaded through the browser in a compressed ZIP file. DNN extracts the file in this ZIP folder and runs any database scripts necessary to install the module on your instance of DNN. Once a module has been installed, it will be available for placement on a page. We'll cover this process for using modules in Chapter 4 and then cover specific modules in detail in the later chapters of the book.

The primary focus of this book is on using the available resources that DNN provides. The following table lists the modules that are included in the download of DotNetNuke 5, along with a brief description of each. We will cover a number of these modules and their usage throughout the book.

## Available Modules

| Module Name | Description |
| --- | --- |
| Adsense | The Adsense module enables you to easily set up and configure Google's Adsense advertising tools on the pages of your website. |
| Announcements | The Announcements module is a simple module that allows you to enter a title and description, and link to another resource. The module provides a list of recent announcements with the ability to restrict them by date, as well as archive the content. |
| Blog | The DotNetNuke Blog module provides an easy-to-use blogging tool. It can be configured to provide a single weblog or multiple weblogs to users, depending on the needs of your website. |
| Documents | The Documents module is a useful tool if you are providing downloadable documents to visitors of your website. The module can be configured to provide download links to users, as well as track the metrics from those downloads. |
| Events | This module can be used to provide a list of events, in either a calendar format or a listing format. Events can have registration and notification options created for them as well; this is useful for managing websites for organizations that schedule meetings for groups of people. |
| FAQs | The FAQ module enables you to create a list of frequently asked questions and answers for users of your website. |
| Feedback | The Feedback module is a useful module for providing users with the ability to send administrators an e-mail with by providing a simple form on the website. It also has some useful reporting tools. |
| Form and List | The Form and List module is a very useful, yet complex, module that enables you to create forms in which data can be entered, and then display that data in a formatted manner for display to your website users. This module can be useful for reporting scores from events, or other statistical information. |
| Forum | The Forum module provides advanced community features such as thread posts and replies, thread status, e-mail notifications and a number of other functions. This module is a must for a community website. |
| Help | The Help module is useful for creating documentation on a website. You can create nested categories and organize content in a formal structure. |
| Text/HTML | The Text/HTML module is one of the most used modules for DNN. It provides you a simple What You See Is What You Get (WYSIWYG) editor that provides a rich text entry interface, easily allowing users to style content with basic HTML tags without having to know HTML syntax. |
| IFrame | The IFrame module enables you to use an HTML feature to display the contents of another website in a frame on a different web page. You can control the width, height, title border, and scrolling of the frame. |

| Module Name | Description |
|---|---|
| Links | The Links module provides an easy interface to display a list of links in multiple formats. You can choose a list or a drop-down list. You also get an easy entry and maintenance screen for the links without having to know HTML to generate the lists. |
| Map | The Map module allows for simple mapping functionality within DNN and can be useful for tracking meeting locations. |
| MarketShare | The MarketShare module enables you to link to content at http://marketplace.dotnetnuke.com while earning referral credit ($) from any sales generated from your links. |
| Media | The Media module enables you to display images, videos, and audio files on a website without having to know the HTML necessary to include such content. |
| NewsFeeds | The NewsFeeds module enables you to easily display and format RSS streams from other websites; these generally consist of latest news or blog feeds from the sites that distribute them. |
| Reports | The Reports module enables you to generate reports using SQL queries against the website's database. These can be useful for seeing the statistics of your website and its visitors. |
| Repository | The Repository module is a complex module that allows for a number of different configurations. In general, it is a way to manage a collection of items, such as contacts, photos, videos, and even articles. |
| Store | The Store module is DNN's e-commerce component; it can be configured in a variety of ways and can track products and purchases. |
| Survey | The Survey module enables you to configure and track results for surveys on your website. |
| User Defined Table | The UDT module is the basis for what has become the Form and List module. The module allows you to setup simple and complex HTML tables, allowing for data entry and display of this customized data. |
| Users Online | The Users Online module allows you to track and display the current user activity on your website. |
| Wiki | The Wiki module provides basic wiki functionality to the visitors of your website, allowing for user-generated and -moderated content. |
| XML | The XML module enables you to display the contents of an XML file, applying style to it through the use of an XSL file. It is not a commonly used module but can be very flexible for someone with familiarity in Extensible Stylesheet Language (XLS). |

In addition to the modules provided with the core package for DNN, thousands of third-party modules are available; some of these are free and some are for sale.

## *Upgrades*

DNN is built to be very flexible, enabling you to implement upgrades to new versions of the framework, as well as to upgrade the extensions installed on a website. Upgrading extensions follows the same process as installing them. The framework checks to see if an upgrade is being performed and completes the appropriate actions. Chapter 9 covers upgrades to the platform in more detail, and Chapter 9 discusses upgrading the functionality of modules and skins.

## *Users Management*

Users on your website can interact with content and functionality in different ways. Some of these interactions will require users to be logged in, whereas others will not. DNN provides a customizable registration system, allowing you to define user profile fields that must be filled in during the registration process.

# Common Misconceptions

Because DNN is an open source project and available for free, there are quite a few common misconceptions about the software and its use. As mentioned previously, the ecosystem around DNN is quite active and healthy. Because of the open source nature of the project, many people expect everything regarding DNN to be free, including support, customizations, implementation, and training. As with most things in life, that is just not the case. Although you can find a lot of great free products for DNN, and free support on the DNN Forums (forums.dotnetnuke.com), in most cases you will find that businesses supporting or providing services for DNN are not free, and why should they be? These companies are providing services and products; the fact that they are for an application that comes with a free license doesn't mean that they have to release their products and services for free.

Keep that in mind when you are getting into a project that requires work above and beyond the scope of what DNN provides out of the box. With that in mind we lead on to another common misconception. While DNN provides a whole world of functionality out of the box, with the core functionality and core modules, you won't necessarily be able to accomplish all the tasks your website needs with these free tools.

The ecosystem for DNN exists to provide the knowledge and products necessary to accomplish tasks with DNN that are not provided with these out-of-the-box tools. While it is often possible to accomplish a whole host of functionality with unique configurations for free tools, it will likely save you time, and ultimately money, to invest in third-party extensions or services.

# Summary

We've covered a lot of information about content management systems, open source projects, licenses, and DotNetNuke in this first chapter. The community and developers behind DNN have worked hard to make it a very functional product. While we will be the first to admit that it does contain some things that are not always the easiest to comprehend, we hope that this book will make using DNN easier for everyone. We hope this chapter has whetted your appetite for using DotNetNuke, as well as for the rest of our book. In Chapter 2, we will cover the basics of installing DNN so that you can get your website up and running.

# 2

# Installing DotNetNuke

To get started with DotNetNuke (DNN), you must first install it on a web server. Installing DNN can be challenging for those who have never completed the process before. However, after using DNN for a number of websites, you likely will become comfortable with the tools and be able to get a new website up and running in a matter of minutes. A number of other books about DNN go into more detail about the installation process; however, the aim of this book is to cover the basics to get your website up and running.

There are several different ways to install DNN. This chapter walks you through a few of the simple ways: using free tools provided by Microsoft, using tools you may already have installed on your personal computer, and, finally, using a hosting provider's tools to install your website on an external web server.

This chapter discusses the following topics:

- ❑ Web server basics
- ❑ Pre-installation considerations
- ❑ Installation options and resources
- ❑ Installing DNN
- ❑ Common hosting installation options

## Web Server Basics

In order for a website to exist, it must be hosted on a computer known as a *web server*, which is accessible to the outside world via the Internet or accessible to a local network of computers (for example, in an office environment) for an intranet site. Literally thousands of companies provide services revolving around website hosting; picking the right one to host your website is an important decision. We will cover some of the deciding factors you should consider when looking for a website hosting service.

It is not always necessary to have your website hosted by a company; in today's world, where broadband access is available to a large percentage of homes, it is not uncommon for people to host their own websites on computers within their household, even if they only have a single computer available. The installation processes that we go through later in this chapter will cover scenarios for hosting your own website and setting up DNN on a hosted web server. In general, we recommend installing DNN locally for testing purposes and using a dedicated web server or hosting company for a production website.

# Pre-Installation Considerations

Before installing DNN, you need to figure out a few things regarding your website. We will help you try to define some goals so that you can properly plan your DNN implementation, although from a business perspective there is a lot more planning that goes into a website. An important aspect of these goals will be to define exactly what type of hosting you are going to need for your website.

To plan properly for your website, you should have an idea of a number of things. It is beyond the scope of this book to cover all the various topics relating to the planning of a website, but we will cover some of the most important topics. The first section will cover the content of your website, and the second some audience-specific questions, all the while focusing on how this will impact your DNN installations.

## What Kind of a Website Will You Be Building?

One of the most important factors in planning the installation of your website is to determine what type of website you want to build. This book covers four types of websites:

❏ Chapter 5 describes the basics of setting up DNN as a personal or family website, including the basic settings necessary for this type of website and some of the functionality that DNN provides for such a site.

❏ Chapter 6 walks you through some of the modules commonly used for setting up a community website — for example, one for a softball league.

❏ Chapter 7 gets into a more business-like approach by focusing on functionality for a small business website.

❏ Chapter 8 discusses some of the functionality necessary for an enterprise-level website.

Figuring out what type of content your site will provide will help you to plan the hosting requirements for your site.

## How Much Content Will Your Website Have?

To answer this question, it is important to define what content is on a website. In general, content can be constrained by pages and the information contained in those pages. Depending on what type of site you are building, content might also include media and documents, such as images, videos, audio files, and other files. If you are going to have a lot of media and documents on your website, you will want to be sure that your web server has plenty of disk space. A typical DNN website will use 20 to 50 MB of space. Once you start uploading files, though, the amount of space used will increase. You will likely find that 500 MB of storage is sufficient, unless you start uploading a large number of videos and images to your site. In most cases, even the cheapest of web hosting plans will come with more than enough storage for a standard website.

## How Much Traffic Will Your Website Receive?

Another important aspect of website planning is trying to gauge how much traffic your website will receive. Everyone loves having traffic on a website, but in all honesty, we recommend that this be the least of your concerns when setting up your first website. Traffic is a good problem to have, so if you approach the limits of the bandwidth available in your web hosting package, you are likely to be generating enough business though your site that you will have more money to dedicate to your hosting. When you reach this point, you can upgrade either with your current hosting provider or by moving to another provider.

## Who Is Your Intended Audience?

Will your intended audience be employees within a company? If so, are they all in the same location, accessing the website on a local computer network? If that is the case, perhaps you don't need to use an external hosting provider but can simply host your DNN website in-house, saving you the cost of a third-party hosting service.

Are you hosting a simple personal website that will only be accessed by your close friends and family? You might be able to set up hosting on your own personal computer. Otherwise, you will likely be hosting your website on a web server with a third-party hosting provider, meaning someone you pay specifically for hosting services.

## Will Your Website Have Its Own Domain Name?

This is an important question to ask so that you can figure out how your users will be accessing your website. If your website will not have a unique domain of its own, it will have to be accessed in some other way, such as by computer name over a local network. The examples in this book use the name of the computer that the website is running on, DNNBOOK. This will allow you to access the website by going to http://DNNBOOK/, but only when you are on the same internal network as the computer. If you wanted to access it from the outside world, you would need to have an Internet address with the Domain Name System (DNS) that points users and computers to your web server. This is usually handled through the use of a domain name.

A domain name is used to identify a computer, or multiple computers, on the Internet. Domain names can be purchased from a wide variety of domain name registrars with an annual subscription for each domain name. The cost for domain name registration will vary by the registrar used, as well as by the top-level domain (TLD) used. A TLD is the last portion of a domain name, such as .com or .org. When a domain name is registered, you define an IP address for that domain name through the use of domain name servers, which tell other computers how to locate computers on the Internet. When you sign up for a hosting account with a third-party hosting provider, they will provide you with a list of domain name servers that you can associate with your domain name through the registrar you used to purchase the name.

If you are using an existing domain name, you'll have to make sure that the domain name is pointed to your new web server by changing the DNS entries. In most cases when you use a third-party hosting service for a website, they will provide you with a temporary domain name that you can use to configure the website. Once you have your website ready, you can switch the DNS records to point to your new web server. If your website will be sharing a domain name of an already existing website, you will most likely be setting up your site in a virtual directory. Virtual directories, or applications, are folders configured on the web server to run as a separate application from the primary website located at the root URL of the domain. An example of a virtual directory site is `http://www.dotnetnukeausersguide.com/chapter1/`, where `www.dotnetnukeausersguide.com` is the primary domain name and `chapter1` is the virtual directory in which DNN is running. This is well within the functionality that DNN supports, but it is important to understand that you still need to take into account the hosting requirements for DNN in order to provide this. Be sure to pay attention to the "Installation Requirements" section of this chapter to make sure that your web server will provide the tools necessary to run DNN.

Whether you choose to host your website yourself or to pay a hosting company for their services, there are some common requirements for DNN, which we will cover in the next section.

---

### Purchasing a Domain Name

A number of domain name retailers are available on the Internet. One of the most common is GoDaddy.com, which also provides some basic DNN hosting for a very low price. Domains can vary in cost depending on which extension (`.com`, `.net`, `.org`, etc.) you choose, but in general you should be able to find something in the range of $10–20 per year.

---

# Installation Requirements

Before installing DNN, we will cover some of the requirements for installation. We will provide the steps necessary to install DNN on your own computer and also discuss what you must look for in a hosting provider if you use a third-party to host your website. If this is your first website, you will most likely be doing just that, having someone else host and manage the web server that delivers your website to the world. So, we will cover a common approach to getting DNN installed on remote servers.

## DotNetNuke Requirements

Because DNN is built on the Microsoft .NET Framework, there are some common tools necessary for a web server to be able to host a DNN website. Most hosting providers today will support these tools with even the lowest-priced hosting plans. In the early days of .NET hosting support, that wasn't always the case. In order to run your website on DNN, you need to find a hosting provider with Windows-based hosting services. As mentioned previously, nearly every hosting provider out there nowadays will provide Windows hosting of some sort. Before you place an order, make sure they support the approaches discussed in this chapter.

### Operating System and Web Server

In order to host a DNN website, the web server must be running Internet Information Server (IIS) 5.0 or higher on a Windows operating system. There are a number of operating systems available from

Microsoft that provide support for IIS. The following table lists the operating systems that provide IIS, along with which version of IIS is available.

**Windows Operating Systems and Versions of IIS**

| Operating System | Version of IIS |
|---|---|
| Windows 2000 / Windows Server 2000 | 5.0 |
| Windows XP Professional | 5.1 |
| Windows Server 2003 | 6.0 |
| Windows Vista | 7.0 |
| Windows Server 2008 | 7.0 |
| Windows 7 | 7.0 |

Which version of the Windows operating system you choose to host your website on will generally be left up to your hosting service, be that dependent on the computers within your home or internal organization, or the third-party hosting service you choose to use. It is most common to find a web server running Windows Server 2003 or Windows Server 2008.

## Microsoft .NET Framework

DNN is developed in the Visual Basic .NET (VB.NET) programming language; because of this, the application requires the .NET Framework to be installed and available on a hosting environment. There are two .NET Frameworks that you will find commonly installed on Windows-based computers. Older computers may have both the 1.1 Framework and the 2.0 Framework available. Newer computers may only have the .NET 2.0 Framework available. For versions of DotNetNuke 4.0 or greater, we will be using 5.0 as our focus in this book; you need to have the .NET 2.0 Framework available. As we are finishing up writing the book, there is discussion that, starting with version 5.1, DNN will require .NET 3.5sp1; take that into account if you are working with the 5.1 release of DNN, which is scheduled for late spring 2009.

The .NET Framework versions are available as free downloads from Microsoft.com, if you do not already have a version installed. You can also get them through the Windows Update process.

## Database Requirements

As discussed in Chapter 1, DNN is a dynamic content management system (CMS), which means that the pages and content for DNN-based websites are stored within a database and loaded by the software when requests to the website are made. This leads to a database requirement for running a DNN website. The most common configuration for DNN is to run against Microsoft's SQL Server database platform. A number of versions of SQL Server are available. DNN currently supports SQL Server 2000, SQL Server 2005, and SQL Server 2008, as well as the free versions of the latter two, SQL Server 2005 Express and SQL Server 2008 Express.

In addition, other implementations of DNN are available to run against other database servers, such as MySQL or Oracle, but for the purposes of this book, and in general, we recommend that you use Microsoft's SQL Server software, as most of the modules and other extensions available for DNN run against SQL Server without requiring custom code to be developed.

Many web hosts that provide Microsoft platform hosting services will provide SQL Server database support within their hosting plans. If you are going to use the local installation process, as opposed to the hosted installation, you will have to install Microsoft SQL Server in order to run DNN. We will be using the SQL Server 2008 Express version for simplicity's sake. If you haven't yet installed SQL Server 2008, when you do go through the installation and are prompted for what type of authentication to use, choose Mixed Mode and be sure to remember any password information you might provide.

### Necessary File Permissions

In order to run DNN as a framework for your website, the account in which the IIS web server is running the website will need to have read/write access to the folder on the file system where the website is installed. This is an important requirement because without read/write access DNN will not be able to function. We will walk you through the process of configuring permissions in the upcoming "Configuring Security Permissions" section, as well as which users typically need access, depending on the operating system.

## Third-Party Hosting Considerations

If you are going to be hosting your own website, we will walk you through the process of installing DNN on your computer or on a server that you have remote access to. If you are going to be using a third-party hosting service, we will walk you through a basic installation process as well. However, there are a number of ways that hosting providers will enable access to their servers, far too many variances to be covered within the scope of this book. In most cases, the scenario we will use will suffice; however, you should contact any hosting companies you are considering for hosting prior to purchase.

You might find they will install DNN for you, or they may have automated tools that will provide the installation of DNN. If you find a host who does provide such services, there are two important questions to ask: what version of DNN will they install, and is it possible to upgrade the version they install to a newer version? In most cases, upgrading a DNN website is a simple process, although there have been cases where web hosts have limited the ability for users to upgrade to newer versions of DNN. Having the ability to upgrade DNN will allow you to keep current on features and bug fixes with each release of DNN. Chapter 9 discusses when and how to upgrade in more detail. Another important aspect of the ability to upgrade DNN is that upgrades will provide patches for security issues as they are found. While DNN has a very good track record of being a secure application, it is always possible that an issue will be found. Being able to upgrade to resolve the issue is an important benefit of the DNN platform.

# Which Version of DotNetNuke?

Before beginning the installation process, you must decide which version of DNN to install. Typically, a number of versions are available for downloading from DotNetNuke.com. As of this writing,

DotNetNuke 5.0.1 is the most current. With frequent updates, however, it is not always easy to decide which version of DNN to use.

Sometimes a new release will have new features that might not be completely stable in the initial release. It is our recommendation that you do some research to see which is the most stable version of DNN at the time of your installation; this may not always be the latest released version. If you have a question about which version to install, we recommend posting in the forums on DotNetNuke.com to ask which version is currently the most stable. You will find a highly active support community that will gladly answer that question before you install DNN. If you are unable to find out a recommended version, feel free to contact the authors for advice.

To download a version of DNN, you first must create a user account on DotNetNuke.com. Once you have registered and logged in, go to the Downloads page at `http://downloads.dotnetnuke.com/`. You will find multiple packages that you can download for the available version(s) of DNN.

For the purposes of this book, we recommend that you download the Install package. You might also check out the Documentation (docs) package, as well as the Upgrade package if you do look at upgrading an instance of DNN to a newer version. For now, go ahead and download the Install package of the version of DNN of your choosing. Be sure to remember where you save the downloaded ZIP file.

# The Local Installation Process

In order to install DNN, there are a number of requirements that must be met on the machine on which you will be installing the framework. If you happened to skip over the earlier "Installation Requirements" section of this chapter, it is recommend that you read and understand the requirements prior to trying to complete a DNN installation.

To begin the process of installing DNN manually, you must configure your file system for the application.

---

### Web Platform Installer

Microsoft has been launching new initiatives lately aimed at making hosting on the Windows operating systems easier. One of these initiatives is the Web Platform Installer, which will provide you with some of the common tools necessary for web applications, including IIS and SQL Server 2008 Express. Recently Microsoft announced a new version of the Web Platform Installer that will actually setup and configure a number of open source applications, including DotNetNuke. You can download the Web Platform Installer for Windows Vista and Server 2008 from `www.microsoft.com/Web/downloads/platform.aspx`.

---

# *File System Configuration*

To get your website up and running, you need to create a folder on your computer's file system in which you will place the contents of the DotNetNuke Install package you downloaded previously. For the purposes of this book, we will locate the files in a common website directory within Windows. Although using this location is definitely not a requirement, it will make following along with the book easier if you do the same.

## *Creating a DotNetNuke Folder*

To create the folder, perform the following steps:

1. Right-click on the Start menu button, and choose the Explore option (see Figure 2-1).

2. After the Windows Explorer opens, navigate to the following directory:

   ```
   C:\inetpub\wwwroot\
   ```

   If that folder does not exist, you should verify that you have IIS installed. If you can confirm that IIS is installed, you should create the folders necessary to navigate to that path.

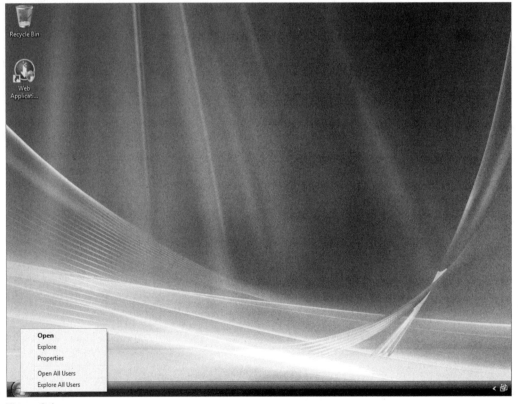

Figure 2-1

3. Once at the \wwwroot folder, create a new folder named DotNetNuke. Your Windows Explorer should look something like Figure 2-2.

Figure 2-2

## *Placing the DotNetNuke Files*

Now that you've created a folder for your DNN website, locate the DotNetNuke_*xx.xx.xx*_Install.zip file that you downloaded previously from DotNetNuke.com, where *xx.xx.xx* is the version number that you downloaded. We're using 05.00.01. You should copy the contents of this ZIP file into your c:\inetpub\wwwroot\dotnetnuke\ folder, as shown in Figure 2-3. Your view might differ if you do not have the Details option selected in Windows Explorer, but the files should generally be the same no matter which version of DNN you are installing.

## *Configuring Security Permissions*

Now that you've extracted the contents of the DNN package into your website folder, you need to configure the file permissions on this folder for the Windows account under which IIS is running. To do so, perform the following steps:

1. Right-click on the DotNetNuke folder in Windows Explorer, and choose the Properties option, as illustrated in Figure 2-4.

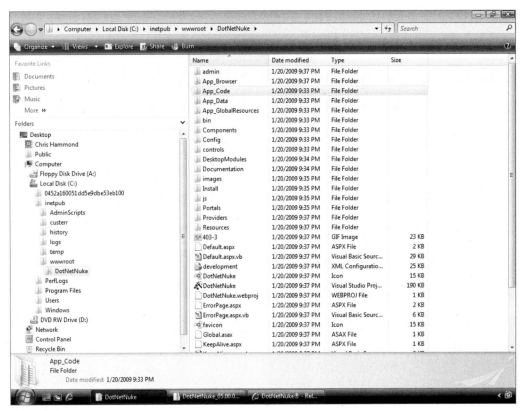

Figure 2-3

2.     From the properties window that will open, click on the Security tab.

If for some reason you do not have a Security tab, you will need to cancel out of this window. (This is a common problem on Windows XP.)

You should see a menu at the top of the Windows Explorer screen. To enable the permissions in Windows XP, click Tools ➪ Folder Options, and then click on the View tab within the options window. From there, scroll down to the bottom of the advanced options and uncheck the "Use simple file sharing" option. Accept the changes to the folder options screen.

3.     Once you're on the Security tab, you should see a list of users available with the permissions for those users on this folder. You need to add the appropriate permissions for your website account to be able to read and write to this folder. Which account this will be for depends on which version of Windows you are running. If you are using Windows XP or Windows 2000, you will be configuring the user known as ASPNET. If you are configuring Windows 2003/Vista/2008, you will be configuring the NETWORK SERVICE account.

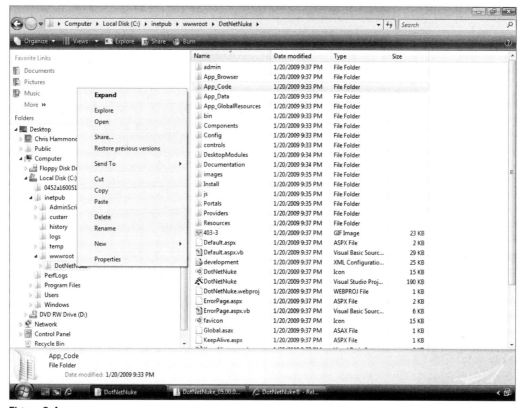

Figure 2-4

To configure these permissions in Windows Vista, click on the Edit button. In Windows XP you will be able to edit the permissions from the first screen. Once there, click on the Add button. You should see the Select Users or Groups dialog box, as shown in Figure 2-5.

**4.** In this window you can type in the ASPNET or NETWORK SERVICE account name. If you're on your home computer, this is likely all you need to do within this screen, However, if your computer is on a domain, you will need to first click on the Locations button and then select your computer name as the location you are searching. By default, on a domain it will be searching within the domain. Once you've typed in the name of the account, either ASPNET or NETWORK SERVICE, click on the Check Names button to be sure that the account is properly located. You should see a result similar to that in Figure 2-6.

**5.** Click on the OK button. Your user should now be listed in the accounts with permissions on this folder.

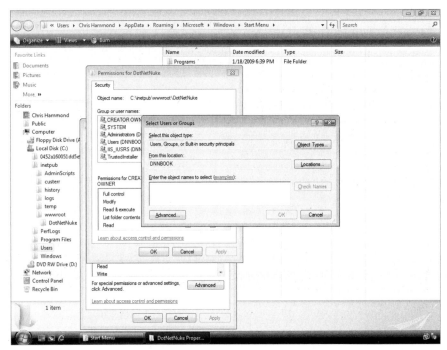

Figure 2-5

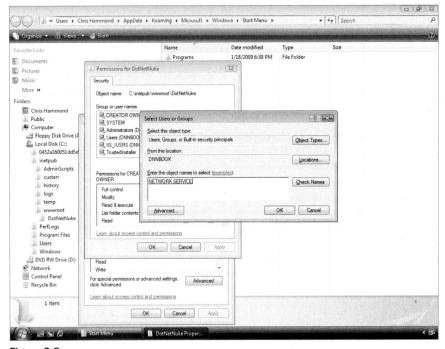

Figure 2-6

6. Click on the newly added user, and then click on the Full Control checkbox in the grid down below. The end result should be similar to that in Figure 2-7.

7. Now that you have these permissions configured, click OK to accept all the changes for the security screens.

---

**File Permissions Not Propagated**

It is common on some Windows machines that the file permissions won't be propagated to all the files within a folder. If you run into permissions problems when using your website, you might need to reset the permissions by using the Advanced option on the Security tab. From there, you can reset the permissions on all child objects.

---

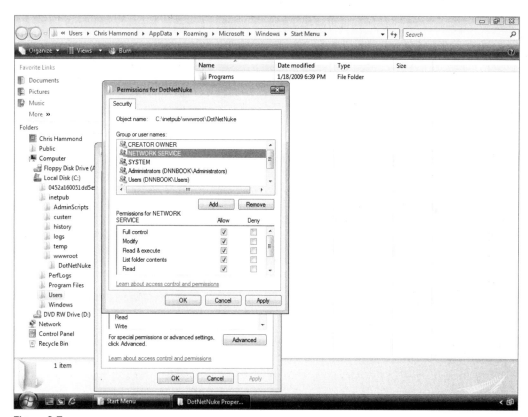

Figure 2-7

# Setting Up Your Web Server

Now that you have your files configured for your DNN installation, you must configure a website, or web application, within your local web server. If you are running Windows XP on the computer that you will be installing DNN on you will be limited to configuring DNN as a virtual directory/application on the machine, or replacing the default website available in XP. In Windows 2000/2003/Vista/2008, you actually have the ability to configure multiple websites in IIS, which means that you can configure DNN in its own website.

The difference between a website and a virtual directory/application is pretty simple. A website can be thought of as a domain name or computer name, such as `http://www.dotnetnuke.com` or `http://computername/`, whereas a virtual directory generally has the format of `http://computername/dotnetnuke/`. For the purposes of this book, we will be configuring DNN as a website.

## Configuring Your Web Server

Microsoft's web server software is Internet Information Server, otherwise referred to as IIS. IIS comes with various versions of the Windows operating system. If you have Windows XP Professional or Windows 2000/2003/Vista/2008, you should have the ability to install and configure IIS. In Windows XP/2000/2003/2008, you can find the IIS Manager tool by clicking on Start and then on the Run option. In the Run window, type **INETMGR** and then click OK, which should load the IIS Manager. If you are using Windows Vista, simply click on Start, and then type **INETMGR** in the search/run option at the bottom of your Start menu.

Depending on which version of Windows you are running, and thus which version of IIS you have installed, your screens may differ slightly from the screens shown in the following sections, but the overall functionality will be similar. We are writing this book using Windows Vista and will walk through the process of creating a website within our IIS Manager. If you are using Windows XP, you will need to create a new virtual directory for your website.

For this demonstration, we are going to create a website with the name of our computer as the URL. Our computer name is DNNBOOK. This will enable you to access the website from your local web browser by going to `http://dnnbook/`. If you like, you can rename your computer so that it is called DNNBOOK by going to the properties screen from the My Computer icon on your desktop. Otherwise, we recommend that you use your own computer name in place of DNNBOOK for the following references. If you don't know your computer name, simply right-click on My Computer on your desktop, or on Computer in your Vista Start Menu, and choose properties. You should see the computer name listed on the properties screen.

## Creating Your Website

After opening IIS Manager, navigate through the tree view on the left, expanding down through the nodes until you arrive at the Sites node. By expanding the Sites node, you should see at least one listing, the Default Web Site (see Figure 2-8). You are going to add another listing here for your DNN website.

To create a website here, right-click on the Sites folder, and then choose the Add Web Site option. Figure 2-9 shows the resulting Add Web Site screen within which you will provide the necessary information to create your site.

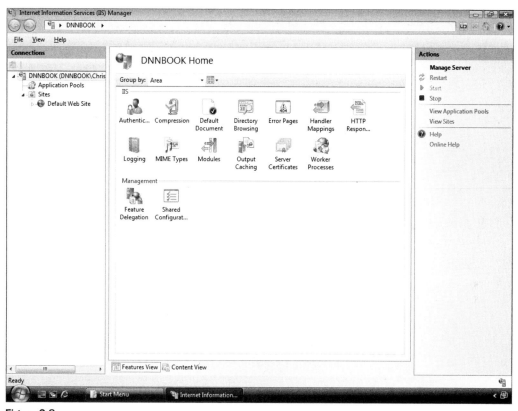

Figure 2-8

For the Site name, use DNNBOOK. The application pool will automatically be populated based on our site name. For the Physical path option, choose the DotNetNuke directory that you created during the file system tasks in the previous section. For the Binding section, the only information you really need to provide is the host name. Enter DNNBOOK in the Host name field, as this is how you will load your website (http://dnnbook/).

### Configuring a Virtual Directory/Application in Windows XP

If you're using Windows XP for your web server, you cannot create multiple websites within IIS, so you will likely need to configure your DNN website as a virtual directory/application. If you've placed your DotNetNuke folder within the C:\inetpub\wwwroot\ path, you can expand the Default Web Site: right-click on the DotNetNuke folder, and choose Properties. In the Application settings section of the resulting window, click the Create button. This will turn your DotNetNuke folder into a virtual directory from which the website can run.

*Continued*

You must also check the ASP.NET tab and be sure that the ASP.NET Version setting is 2.0 or greater. Also make sure that the Enable Default Content Page section of the Documents tab of this properties window lists Default.aspx. You should also click on the Directory Security tab and verify the settings for Anonymous access and authentication control. Click on the Edit button for the section and make sure that Anonymous access is enabled, as well as Integrated Windows authentication.

After setting up your website in this manner, you can access it with the URL http://localhost/dotnetnuke/.

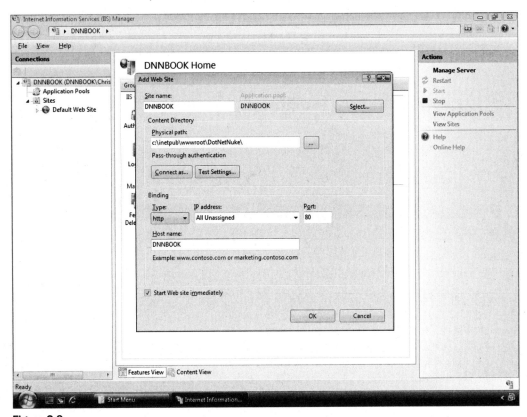

Figure 2-9

## Configuring Your Database

To make the installation process easier, for this book we are going to configure DNN using Microsoft's SQL Server 2008 Express. If you don't already have it installed, you can download it from `www.microsoft.com/express/sql`. After downloading the installation file, go ahead and run the program. The default settings should be sufficient for the purposes of this process.

Once you've confirmed that SQL Server Express is installed, you are done with the database portion of the installation. DNN comes configured with a SQL Server Express option, so you don't need to go through the normal database-creation process. The database ultimately will live in the App_Data folder within your DNN website's folder.

If you are a more advanced user, comfortable with creating databases and not limited to using SQL Server Express, you can manually create a database for your DNN website to use. We will define the database connection information in the "Using the DotNetNuke Installation Wizard" section of this chapter.

This concludes the local installation process for DNN. If you are interested in reading about installing DNN on a hosted web server, read the following section; otherwise, you can skip ahead to the "Installation Wizard" section in which we will actually walk through the DNN Installation Wizard that will configure our database, and ultimately load our first web page within DNN.

# The Hosted Installation Process

If you are installing DNN on a web server hosted by a third-party company and do not have remote access to the machine through which you can log in to Windows, as you might on your own personal computer, you likely will have a hosting control panel of sorts that will allow you to perform the steps necessary for DNN installation. We will walk through the process of installing DNN using the Helm control panel. A control panel is usually provided by your hosting company to allow you to configure the aspects of your website from a web browser interface, as opposed to having remote access to the server. Helm is not the only control panel you may come across; another common one is Plesk.

Generally, a control panel will provide you with some of the same functionality that we configured in the previous section, only with a web front end attached to it. In most cases, using a control panel ends up being easier than trying to configure the application manually, as we did previously.

## Adding the Domain

Depending on the configuration of your hosting account, you will likely be adding a domain to your account. This assumes that you aren't configuring DNN as a virtual directory under an existing website in your hosting account.

You will need to log in to the control panel provided by your hosting provider. Once there, you need to find a page similar to the one in Figure 2-10.

From this screen, click on Add New to start the process of creating your new website within the control panel. You will be prompted to enter a domain name for your website; we've used `www.dnnusersguide.com`. You'll likely be able to change this later, but you should already have your domain name purchased.

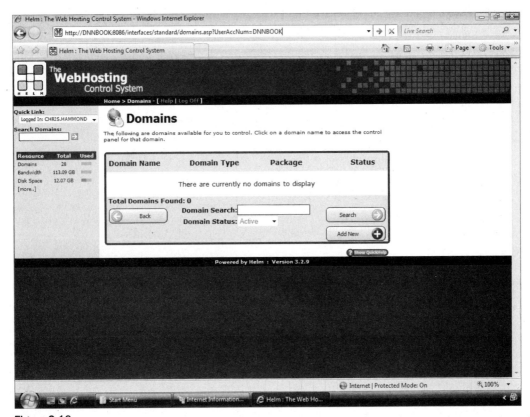

Figure 2-10

## Configuring the Settings

Once you've created your domain in Helm, you can go through the process of configuring the necessary properties for the website and DNN. Helm provides you a list of domains associated with websites on your hosting account. Click on the domain that you are configuring for DNN. This should bring you to the Domain Menu page, shown in Figure 2-11, from which you will configure and manage the properties for your website.

Click on the Web Site Setting icon. The resulting Web Application Settings page will include some of the same settings that you configured in the manual process for IIS. Default.aspx should be listed in the Default Docs section, and you will need to choose Version 2 for the ASP.Net version (see Figure 2-12).

Click on Save in order to save the changes made to the website Settings page.

The last step you will need to perform in the Helm control panel is to create the database for your DNN website. Click on the Database Manager option. On the Database Manager page, click the Add New button to begin the process of creating your new database. What you name the database is up to you, but we generally recommend naming the database something that resembles the domain name — for example, DNNUSERSGUIDE.COM. An important thing to remember on this screen is to be sure to choose the Microsoft SQL Server option, as shown in Figure 2-13.

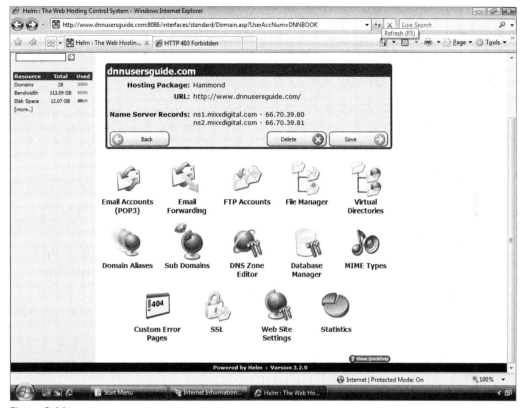

Figure 2-11

Once you've created the database, you will land on an Update Database page, where you can create a new database User. Click on the Add New button to go to the user creation screen. Here you will choose a username and a password for your database. Be sure to remember this information, as you will need it during the DotNetNuke Installation Wizard (discussed later in the chapter).

## Configuring the Files

After configuring your website, you need to upload the DNN installation package to your web server. When setting up your hosting account, your provider should have supplied you with FTP information for your site. If you weren't provided with FTP information, you can create an account through Helm by clicking on the FTP Accounts option on the Domain Menu (refer to Figure 2-11). From the FTP Accounts page, you should see a list of FTP users. You can create a new account by clicking on the Add New button.

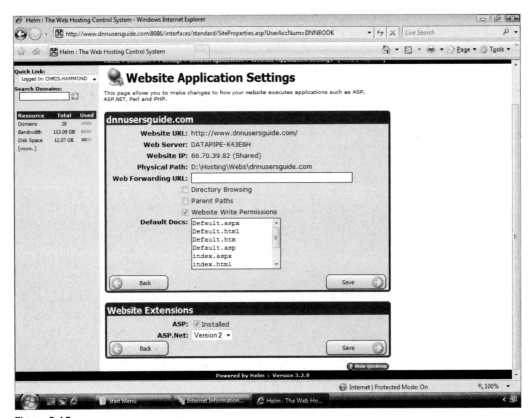

Figure 2-12

When configuring a new FTP account, or editing an existing account, you should be able to define the FTP username, the password, and which folders the FTP user has access to within the website. You should allow this FTP user to be able to read and write to the WWWROOT folder; this is the folder you will be uploading the DNN files to for the website. Once you have configured your FTP account, you can connect to the FTP server by using the information that should be provided by your hosting service, or from the FTP Account page in Helm.

Uploading the files is fairly simple, but you will need to have an FTP application in order to access this folder structure on the server. A number of free FTP applications are available, including an open source application called FileZilla, which you can download from FileZilla-Project.org. Each application will be configured a little differently, but the basic premise for all FTP applications is that you will need to provide the FTP server address, usually something like ftp.domainname.com, and the username and password for accessing the server. Once you've connected to your server via FTP, you will need to upload the contents of the DotNetNuke_Community_XX.XX.XX_Install.ZIP file. We recommend extracting the contents of the ZIP file locally, before trying to upload them via FTP to your website. It is not likely that you will be able to extract and upload them through the FTP application.

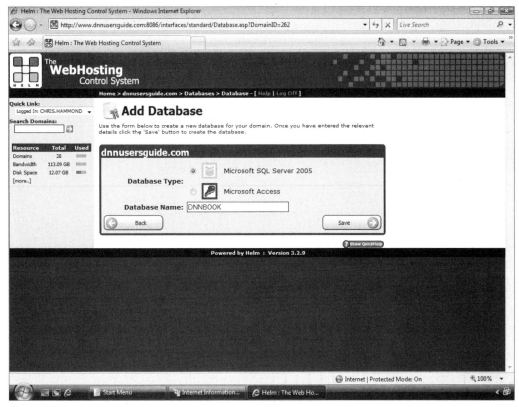

Figure 2-13

Once you've uploaded the files necessary for the DNN installation, you can continue on to the next section, "Using the DotNetNuke Installation Wizard."

# Using the DotNetNuke Installation Wizard

Once you've gone through one of the previous processes, either configuring your local environment or configuring a third-party web hosting account, you should be ready to walk through the DotNetNuke Installation Wizard. This process will configure the database for your DNN website, as well as two default user accounts for the website.

To access the DotNetNuke Installation Wizard, you must open your favorite web browser and then access the URL for your website. Depending on the configuration process you followed in this chapter, it will be one of the following URLs.

### Website URLs

| Installation Method | URL |
| --- | --- |
| Manual IIS Configuration | `http://MACHINENAME/` |
| Third-Party Hosting Configuration | `http://www.DOMAINNAME.com/` |

When you access your website for the first time, if everything has been configured properly, you should see the DotNetNuke Installation Wizard, as shown in Figure 2-14. This screen lists three primary installation choices: Custom, Typical, and Auto. This section focuses on the Typical installation process.

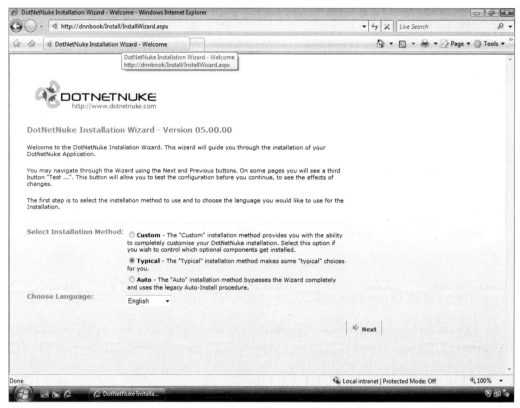

Figure 2-14

The Custom Installation Wizard will walk you through a highly detailed set of installation options for DNN. You will be able to choose which extensions and skins are installed, as well as a number of other options. The Automatic installation option will force DNN to install using the most basic settings and default usernames and password configurations. This is generally not recommended. As a measure of security, at a minimum, you should customize the passwords used when you install DNN for the first time.

## File Permissions Check

After choosing the Typical option on the first page of the DotNetNuke Installation Wizard, you should come to a File Permissions page, where you will be able to verify that the permissions are configured on your DNN file system. This is an important step in the process, as you can prevent some common problems with a DNN installation by verifying that the permissions are configured properly before proceeding. To verify the permissions, simply click on the Test Permissions option at the bottom of the page. If the permissions check is successful, you will receive a message at the bottom of the screen that looks like the one in Figure 2-15.

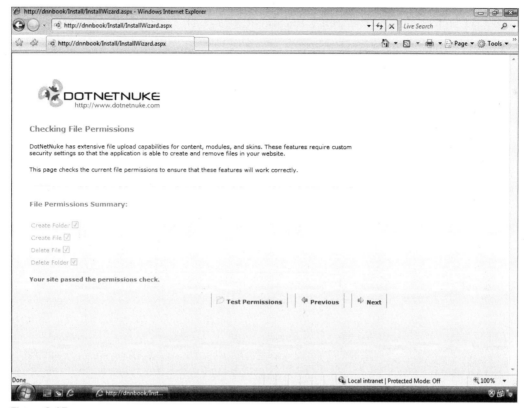

**Figure 2-15**

If the check for permissions isn't successful, take a step back and ensure that you set up the proper file permissions during the installation process. It is common to configure the wrong user account with permissions on the DotNetNuke folder. You can turn back a few pages in this chapter and see what account you should have been using based on your web server's operating system. If you're using a hosted website solution, you may need to contact the service's support team to make sure that the permissions are configured properly.

Once you have confirmed the proper file permissions, you can move on to the next step in the wizard.

## Database Check

The Configure Database Connection page enables you to make any necessary changes to the database options for DNN. If you are using SQL Server Express installed with the default options, you should be able to simply choose the Test Connection option at the bottom of the page to verify that your database connectivity is working properly. Figure 2-16 shows the default settings and the result of a successful check.

If you are not using SQL Express you can configure your database information on this page, you will first need to choose the SQL 2000/2005 Database option. You will then need to configure the name of your database server, likely the same name as the web server in which your site is hosted, or the name provided by your hosting provider. You will also want to configure the security option by un-checking integrated security and entering the username and password you configured for the database. Once you have this information configured you can use the Test Connection option and continue with the next steps in the installation process.

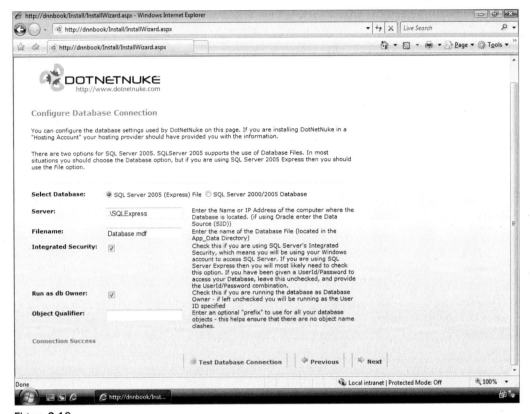

Figure 2-16

After verifying the database portion, click on the Next link. The Run Database Installation Scripts page will appear, and DNN will execute all the required database scripts. This will effectively create all the tables and other objects that are stored in the database for a DNN website. If this process is successful, you should see a page similar to the one in Figure 2-17.

## User Configuration

After completing the database installation portion of the wizard, you can move on to the final few steps for the installation. The next page you will see should look similar to Figure 2-18. The Configure Host Account page is used to manage the "Host" or super user account. Chapter 3 goes into more detail about the difference between the super user account that you will create on this page and the administrator account on the following page. For now, however, you should define a password for the Host account. The password should be something that you will remember easily, as this account will be used heavily during the next chapter. You will also have to enter a valid e-mail address in the Email Address field; otherwise, DNN will not allow you to proceed.

Figure 2-17

Figure 2-18

For now, you can skip the SMTP Server Settings portion of the wizard. We will discuss it in more detail in Chapter 3 when describing how to configure your website to be able to send e-mails.

After clicking on Next, you will be taken to the Portal Title page, where you can configure another user account, the Administrator, also with a valid e-mail address (see Figure 2-19). At the bottom of this page, you can define two Portal Properties, the Title and Template. The Portal Title will be the name of your website. Do not worry about having to define this immediately. It is something that we will be changing when we look at all our portal settings in Chapter 3.

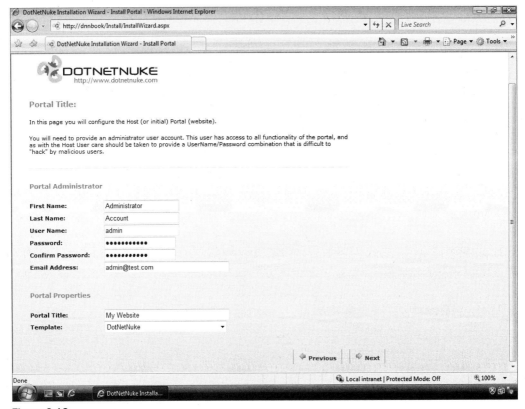

Figure 2-19

The template is an advanced feature you might look to implement in future installations of DNN. In this case, you will see that there is only one template available in the drop-down menu. Templates within DNN provide a way to define some basic pages and content for those pages when you create a portal, predefining a website's layout and content.

After you configure both the Host and Admin accounts, along with the portal title and template, you have completed all the necessary steps in the DotNetNuke Installation Wizard. You can click Next, and you should see a confirmation page that tells you DNN was set up successfully and provides you with a link to your newly created website. When you click on this link, you should see the standard landing page for a DNN website, as shown in Figure 2-20. Congratulations! You have completed the DNN installation process.

Figure 2-20

# Summary

Now that we've covered the installation process and set up our first website using DNN, we will spend the next couple of chapters getting you ready to manage your website. Chapter 3 will cover the basic administration functionality provided by DNN for managing your newly installed website, and then in Chapter 4 we will get into the details of how you manage the pages and content on your website.

# 3

# DotNetNuke Concepts and Host Configuration

Installing DNN is just the first step in setting up your website. Once you have your website loaded in a browser, it's time to look at the key concepts around the functionality that DNN provides. There are a number of common terms that we will define in more detail, and we will discuss how those items relate to the application as whole.

Once we have the concepts out of the way, we will jump into the Host Settings and other features provided to super users. We won't cover the process of administering content or users in this chapter; we will cover content administration aspects of DNN in Chapter 4, and target content maintenance in the remaining chapters of the book.

This chapter discusses the following topics:

- ❑ Common DNN terms and concepts
- ❑ Administrator and super user access
- ❑ The Host Settings
- ❑ Managing and installing extensions

## Definitions

This section defines some of the key terms within DotNetNuke (DNN) in greater detail than in previous chapters. Knowing what these terms mean will help your understanding of how to build and administer a DNN website come together as we reference them throughout the rest of the book.

# Portals

DNN provides the ability to host multiple websites on one installation, or instance, of the software. These individual websites are known as *portals*, so your DNN instance can have a single portal, or multiple portals, depending on your configuration. We will talk more about portals later in this chapter, as well as in Chapter 8.

# Pages

With any website, you will have pages. These pages are generally files located on the web server and returned by the server to the user's browser. With a dynamic content management system such as DNN, these pages are not individual files stored on the file system but dynamically generated files that are built with information from the database and returned to the browser. Each page generated within DNN will have its own unique address, or URL (Uniform Resource Locator).

---

### Tabs and Pages

In DNN, the terms "page" and "tab" are interchangeable. We primarily will use "page," but there will be a few references to "tabs." Just understand that when we are talking about a tab, we are talking about a page.

---

# URLs

A URL is basically an address that a browser and web server use to locate the information requested by a visiting user. A URL generally consists of a domain name, such as www.wrox.com, followed by a directory structure, and then a page (file) — for example, http://www.wrox.com/WileyCDA/ or http://www.wrox.com/WileyCDA/Section/Home.id-105001.html. In most cases, files of the type .htm and .html are static, as they actually exist as an individual file on the web server.

Many dynamic content management systems will build URLs that use what are known as *query string parameters*, which are name/value pairs that are passed after a filename in a URL. For example, previous versions of DNN would build their URLs as follows: http://www.dotnetnuke .com/default.aspx?tabid=825, where default.aspx is the filename and tabid=825 is the query string parameter. This parameter tells DNN to load page number 825 from the database and return the content for that page to the user.

DNN uses query string parameters in a number of ways, more than just for the page ID. In the past, these parameters generally were not thought of as being a good practice. The generally accepted theory was that search engines treated pages that had query string parameters with less weight than pages that appeared to be a static file. It was assumed that search engines would pick up on the fact that a page was being loaded dynamically and treat the content on that page with less respect than they might a static HTML page. Although engineers from Google have debunked this theory, it is still generally recommended to avoid using query string parameters where possible.

The recent versions of DNN avoid using query strings in URLs by using what are known as *friendly URLs*. Friendly URLS can take many forms, but the default in all basic DNN installations will be of the following format. The URL we looked at earlier, http://www.dotnetnuke.com/default.aspx?tabid=825, would become `http://www.dotnetnuke.com/tabid/825/default.aspx` using the friendly URL formatting. To the search engines and individual users, this looks like a static page that exists on the server, when in fact there is no directory with the path of `tabid/825` and a page called `default.aspx` within that directory. DNN dynamically parses the URL to figure out which page is being loaded and still treats that URL as query-string-based. It is possible to change the formatting of the URLs on your DNN website by plugging in a new friendly URL provider. These providers are developed by individuals or companies usually not directly affiliated with the DNN project.

## Skins

There are a number of ways to manipulate and control the layout of the content of your DNN website. The primary layout configuration is handled through the use of a skin. A *skin* is a file consisting of HTML and other code that provides formatting and styling information for your site. A skin also provides the location(s) available for placing content on a page. These locations are called *panes*. All skins have at least one pane, called *ContentPane*. Beyond that, it is up to the skin developer to provide additional panes.

Skins generally are constructed with HTML code, although they may also have VB.NET or C# code embedded within them to provide additional functionality. The important thing to realize with skins in DNN is that a website will have a default skin defined, but this setting can be overridden at the page level, meaning that you can control the look and feel of individual pages.

The flexibility of DNN and its skinning engine lets you change the look and feel of your website by choosing a new skin through the page settings. Changing skins is a pretty straightforward process that requires only a few mouse clicks to change a few settings.

DNN comes with one skin package by default, the MinimalExtropy skin. While there are no other skin packages currently available on your DNN site, you can use the Extensions page to install skins that you have developed, gathered, or purchased from other sources. Any skin that is installed from the HOST/Extensions page will be available to all portals within an instance of DNN.

## Modules

In addition to the layout and styling, the other basic component of a DNN web page is the page's content. As content is generally key to having a good website, it is an important aspect of any web page. In DNN, content is provided through the use of modules, mini-applications that are one of the key strengths of DNN's flexibility. Although there are thousands of modules available for DNN, we will focus on the modules available with the basic installation package downloaded from DotNetNuke.com. (Refer to Chapter 1 for a brief description of each module's functionality.)

To provide content and functionality to a page, a module must be placed on the page in one of the available panes. You can have multiple modules within a pane and multiple panes on a page, so effectively you are not limited in the number of modules you can place on a page, although good web practice would lean toward not weighing a page down with too much content.

We will discuss how modules are installed later in this chapter, and then, in Chapter 4, we will cover the basics of using modules within your DNN pages.

# Containers

A container is to a module what a skin is to a page. Containers are HTML snippets that wrap around modules within a pane and define any borders, a title for the module, and other design elements for modules on a page. At the portal level, you can define a default container for all modules on your website, which can be overridden at the page level, defining a default for the page and then again at the individual module level.

Containers also have an HTML section, called `ContentPane`; the difference between a container and a skin, however, is that a container can have only one of these panes, not multiple ones. The `ContentPane` within a container provides the location for the content and functionality of a module to be displayed. Although containers typically provide some other basic functionality to all users, such as links to syndication data (RSS), to a printer-friendly view, and to the actions a module can perform, the most important functionality is reserved for users who have edit rights to the module.

You can administer modules by selecting a menu or buttons within the container that link to the actions available for that module. Although a number of actions are common to all modules, some actions are specific to the individual module. Chapter 4 describes the common module actions in more detail and then subsequent chapters cover actions available to specific modules, as we walk through various scenario-based websites.

> **Hiding a Container**
>
> Chapter 4 describes how to turn off a container on an individual module. This effectively removes any of the styling and images that a particular container provides to a module. As an administrator, one thing to keep in mind is that the container will always remain visible when you are in Edit mode. In order to preview what the page would look like without the container, you must switch to View mode. This is necessary so that you can access the edit functionality for the modules.

# Actions Menu

Another common section of a DNN web page that you see when you are logged in as an administrator is the Actions menu for each of the modules. The Actions menu enables you to access the administrative capabilities for individual modules as well as some settings that apply to all modules. It is up to each module to provide specific functionality from within the Actions menu. Although not all modules utilize this functionality, a majority of the modules do. We'll show you the Actions menu later in this chapter.

# Control Panel

When you're logged in to a DNN website with certain editing permissions/rights, you will find a control panel section on the top of all the web pages. The control panel provides access to some of the administrative functionality we will be covering within this chapter. For now, however, you can ignore this particular portion of your DNN pages. We will highlight specific functionality provided by the control panel as we cover the primary location of this functionality in Chapter 4.

# Providers

A lot of the flexibility that DNN provides to a site administrator is due to the fact that the platform is built on a provider model. This means that it is possible to plug in new functionality for your website by swapping out a provider. A provider is similar to a module in that it offers precompiled functionality that can be used to extend DNN, the difference being that a provider generally affects the website as a whole, whereas a module affects only individual content.

A number of DNN's features can be extended through the use of providers, including the formatting of the URLs that DNN generates. Getting into the provider functionality is outside of the scope of this book but is definitely worth looking into as you get into more advanced DNN site administration.

# Dissecting a DotNetNuke Page

DNN websites and their pages share a number of common features. This section looks at the basic default home page for your DNN website, as shown in Figure 3-1. This is the page created when you use the default settings in the DotNetNuke Installation Wizard. Although not all of these elements will be found on all pages — which appear will depend on the skin, page content, and other configuration options — this is a good representation of some of the elements most DNN pages will have.

Figure 3-1

## *Logo*

Most skins designed for DNN will have placement for a logo. The logo is a configurable option within the Site Settings found underneath the Admin navigation item; we will look at the Site Settings in Chapter 4.

If you choose to implement the logo setting, the image you choose will be displayed within the skin for your DNN pages. This logo is hyperlinked and will take visitors to your website's home page.

## Navigation Elements

Many DNN websites have a horizontal navigation structure. It is not necessary to include the navigational elements within a skin, but it is common practice to do so, as they represent an important aspect of a website. As you create pages within DNN, you will have the ability to control where the navigation elements reside — at the top level (as shown in Figure 3-1) or as a submenu item. DNN comes with some common navigation providers, and the flexibility to implement custom navigation in a variety of ways, all of which are usually handled within the skin package.

## Search Functionality

DNN provides basic search functionality for modules and their content. Although not fully featured like a search application, such as Google.com or Live.com, DNN's search functionality can be an effective way to allow visitors to search your site. This particular search functionality is provided within DNN's default skin; you can also add it to a page through the use of the Search and Search results modules.

## Register/Login Links

Most DNN skins enable website users to create an account and log in to the website, although as the administrator you can turn off that functionality. Although Register and Login are two separate links, DNN skins commonly place them near each other. After users log in to a website, these links will change. The Register link will enable a user to manage his or her profile, and the Login link will change to Logout and allow the user to log out of the website.

## Breadcrumb

Another common navigation element provided within most DNN skins is the notion of a breadcrumb. This can be seen in the default DNN skin just under the navigation elements. The breadcrumb portion of a skin generally displays the current location of the page a user is browsing in relation to the navigation structure of a website, providing links within the page hierarchy. This makes for a better user experience because it allows users to easily navigate back to other pages within the site.

## Page Content

The primary concern for any website is the content of its pages. As mentioned previously, DNN websites handle content through the use of modules. By default, a DNN home page has three modules. There is a single module visible in Figure 3-2, and the two different modules in Figure 3-3 are visible if you were to scroll down on the default DNN home page. In Chapter 4, we will discuss the modules more directly, but the content on the home page is being provided by the three instances of the Text/HTML module.

Figure 3-2

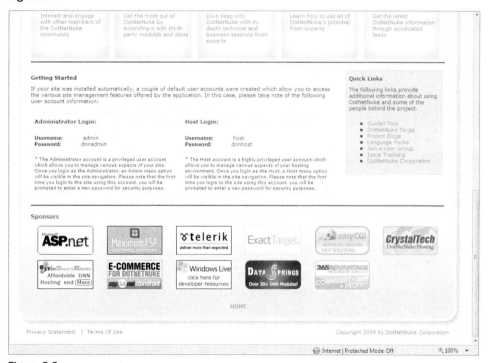

Figure 3-3

# Content Positioning

The layout and position of content on a DNN page is controlled through the use of panes. Within a DNN skin, there will always be at minimum one pane in which you can place modules. This default pane is called the *ContentPane*. Beyond the requirement for this pane, skin developers can create as many panes as they wish to house content on a page. It is common for DNN skins to have multiple panes, and in many cases you will find that you do not need to place content into each pane in order to manage the content and layout of your website. Figure 3-4 shows the default home page in Layout mode, illustrating the available panes within the skin.

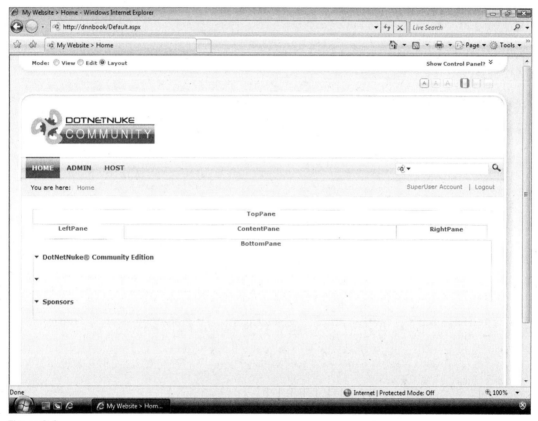

Figure 3-4

As you can see, five panes are available in this skin: TopPane, LeftPane, ContentPane, RightPane, and BottomPane. As mentioned previously, the default home page has three modules, all of which are placed in the BottomPane for layout purposes.

# Privacy Statement, Terms of Use, and Copyright

Privacy Statement and Terms of Use are dynamic links to content that DNN provides on your site. This content is stored in language resource files, allowing you to customize the content for these two pages.

We don't cover editing language resource files in detail in this book, but you edit them through the language editor available on the Extensions page underneath the Admin navigation item.

The Copyright values are populated for each portal in a setting on the Site Settings page, which we will cover in more detail later in this chapter.

# Overview of Administration within DNN

The DNN installation process creates two different user accounts for your website. It's important to understand what these two users are used for in regard to DNN functionality. The first account, the super user account, has a default username of Host. The second account, the administrator account, has a username of Admin. What's the difference between a super user and an administrator? To answer that question, we need to clarify the concept of portals within a DNN website.

## The Super User Account

DNN differs from other CMS systems because it enables you to host multiple websites (portals) out of the same set of files and a single database. This flexibility is what causes the need for super user and administrator accounts. The super user, or Host, account has the ability to create new portals within a DNN instance. This account has access to everything within a DNN instance; it can manage all the content and users of a website, as well as add new extensions. This chapter will cover a majority of the information you need to know about the super user account. The important thing to remember is that a super user can do anything on any portal.

## The Administrator Account

So, if the super user account has the ability to manage everything with an instance of DNN, what does an administrator have the rights to do? An administrator account is tied to one portal within a collection of portals in a DNN instance. An administrator can manage all the content and users within a single portal, as well as utilize the modules installed within that portal, but he or she cannot install modules or skins.

The reasoning for this is twofold. First, because a Host/super user account is set up to be the manager of everything, he or she is likely to be the person who set up and configured the database, the website in IIS, and other hosting-specific information. The Host account is generally someone who will be doing the upfront homework of investigating modules and skins before they are installed to ensure that they are from a trusted source.

The second reason is that when a module or skin is installed, it can impact all portals in a DNN installation. Because modules and skins can, and most likely do, contain computer code that is executed on the server, it is possible for code to be malicious. Even if a module or skin is not malicious, changing the functionality that a skin or module provides can easily impact more than just an individual website. For this fact alone, the super user account is the account that has the ability to install modules and skins.

This is a little different from previous DNN versions. In prior versions of DNN, it was possible to allow administrators to install skins for their portal. Because of the potential for code to live in the skins, however, DotNetNuke 5 restricts this to only super user accounts.

It is possible for a DNN instance to have multiple super users and multiple administrator accounts for a portal. In general, it is recommended that you use the administrator accounts when logging in to a website and managing the content. You should use super user accounts only when you need to access the extended information provided to them. We'll cover some of that super user information after we talk about logging in to a DNN website.

# Logging In to Your Portal

Before getting into the specifics of user accounts and their rights within DNN, we should talk about how you log in to a DNN portal. In general, you can log in to a DNN website simply by clicking on the Login link provided by most skins. This will take you to a page that looks similar to Figure 3-5. Logging in from here is pretty straightforward; simply enter the username and password you configured during the installation process. For the purposes of this chapter, it is assumed that you are logging in with the Host account.

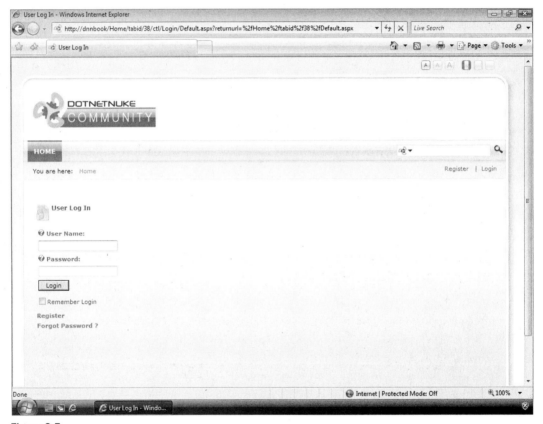

Figure 3-5

You might find that some DNN websites have removed the Login link. This is definitely something you might consider for your website. You can remove the Login link by configuring a simple modification to the skin in use on your site. Once you have done this, however, you will need to know how to access the login page.

In order to do that, you will need to know the URL for the page. You can access this in most DNN sites by modifying the URL of any DNN page in your browser. For example, you might access this book's sample website by going to `http://dnnbook/`. To log in to that site, though, you could simply visit `http://dnnbook/?ctl=login`. You might recognize that as a query string parameter from our earlier discussions in this chapter. This parameter tells DNN to load the login page. You could do this from any page on your website by adding the parameter onto the URL with the format of `?ctl=login`. However, if other parameters already are being passed to the current page, you will use `&ctl=login`. To tell if other parameters are being passed, look for the question mark in the URL.

# Administrative Modes

As a super user of a DNN website, you will have access to the site in ways that the individual portal administrators don't. The first time you log in to your DNN website with either the Host or Admin account, you should see some changes to the way the pages appear. For example, compare Figure 3-1 with Figure 3-6.

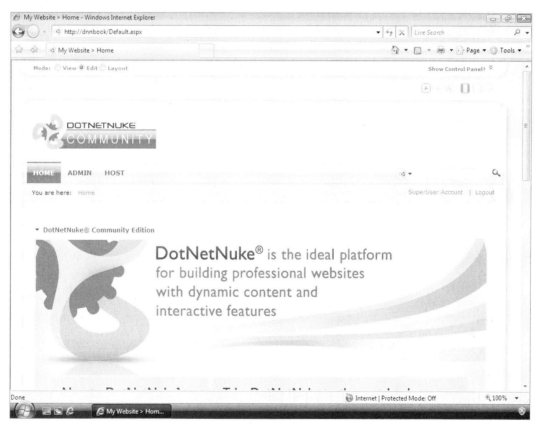

Figure 3-6

In Figure 3-6, notice in the upper-right corner of the page a new link called "Show Control Panel?" As shown in Figure 3-7, the control panel provides shortcuts to basic site administration functionality, as well as options for placing modules on your DNN page.

Figure 3-7

## *Page Mode Selection*

Before we get into the details of the items in the control panel, it's important to take a look at a few of the other options you see when logged in to the website with an account that has edit rights to the portal. The Mode radio buttons are located at the top-left side of the control panel: View, Edit, and Layout. These mode options are an important concept to comprehend within DNN, as they can cause confusion among users.

❑    The View option is the best way to preview what a DNN web page will look like to a user who does not have permissions to make changes to the content on the page. We will talk about permissions for a DNN website in Chapter 4, but the basic premise is that users can be given access to view a page or edit a page, or they can be denied access to a page completely. For most websites, users will only be able to view the site, not to make changes to it. The View mode is a way to let users view what a page will look like if they were logged out, without having to log out of the site.

❑ The Edit option enables users to edit the content of the web page. When you are in Edit mode, and on a page you have rights to, you should see that you have more functionality available to you than you do in View mode. This functionality is mainly provided through the use of the Actions menus for the modules on a page (see Figure 3-8). To expand a module's Actions menu, simply mouse over the icon. In the default skin, this icon is the downward-pointing triangle next to the modules. Chapter 4 goes into more detail about the functionality that Edit mode and a module's Actions menu provide.

❑ In previous versions of DNN, the Layout option was known as the Design option. As shown previously in Figure 3-4, the Layout mode displays an outlined view of the panes available on a DNN page, as well as any modules placed in the panes. You might notice that this mode does not have any content within the modules. This is by design. Layout mode is useful if you are trying to quickly move modules around on the page. We will go into more detail on moving modules in Chapter 4.

*When working with your DNN website, it is important to remember which Mode radio option is selected. It is very common for users to think that they have lost the content on their DNN website simply because they were in Layout mode and DNN was not displaying the content because of this. Another common mistake occurs when a user is in View mode and doesn't have access to edit the content in the modules because the Actions menu for each of the modules isn't displayed.*

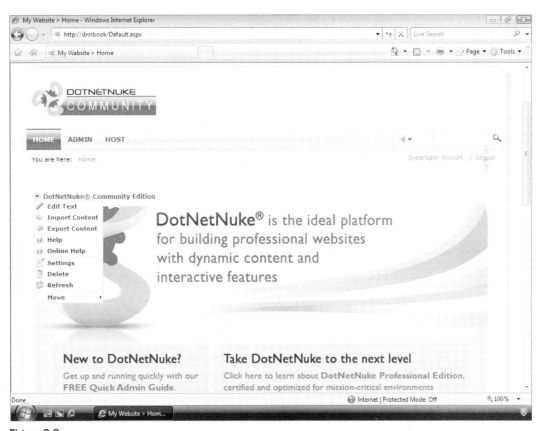

Figure 3-8

# ADMIN and HOST Menu Items

When you are logged in with administrator or super user access, you will notice another major change to your DNN website: additional items in the navigation portion of your pages. Depending on whether you've logged in as an administrator or super user, you may notice that one or two items (ADMIN or ADMIN and HOST, respectively) have been added to the navigation menu. These two items are not actually pages that you can click on, but if you mouse over them, you will see that they have a hierarchy of items underneath them, which are pages that you can click on (see Figure 3-9).

Figure 3-9

The following sections describe some of the key items on the HOST menu.

## The Host Settings Option

Once you have a basic understanding of the layout of a DNN website and how to log in and out, you can start to configure your site. The first things to configure are the host settings. Clicking on the Host Settings link under the HOST menu will take you to the Host Settings page, as shown in Figure 3-10.

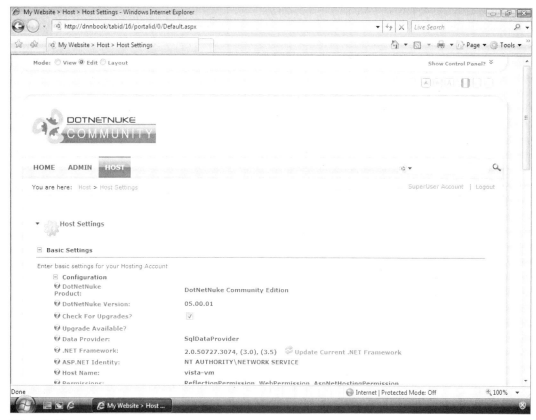

Figure 3-10

---

## Help Text

Many of the settings on the administration side of DNN will have a label with the name of the setting, and a small image of a question mark that provides more detailed information about the setting. By either moving your mouse over the image or clicking it, you can see this additional help text for the setting in question. Figure 3-11 highlights the help text for the DotNetNuke Version label, which is the first item on the Host Settings page.

Unfortunately, however, not all this help text will be useful. The nature of an open-source project tends to mean that documentation is lacking. You will find this to be demonstrated in the lack of help text for some of these labels. In most cases, however, you will get at least a little bit more information about the settings you are configuring by viewing the help text.

---

| Product: | |
| --- | --- |
| DotNetNuke Version: | |
| The DotNetNuke application version you are running | 05.00.01 |

Figure 3-11

## Configuration

The first portion of the Host Settings page, Configuration, provides you with some basic information about your DNN instance. Understanding most of this information isn't necessary for basic DNN administration, but we will point out a few items in this section. If you are unsure of which version of DNN your site is running on, you can access this information here. You can also enable the ability for DNN to check for upgrades. This service will check for the latest recommended version of DNN. If a new version is available, a message will be displayed that will link you to the downloads page at DotNetNuke.com so that you can access the latest release. The other portions of the Configuration section simply provide you with information relating to your DNN instance, such as which version of the .NET Framework your site is currently running on. Note that this is not something that will commonly be changed.

## Host Details

The Host Details portion of the Host Settings page provides some basic information about your DNN instance that will really only be used if you are in the custom scenario where you are allowing people to create their own portals within your DNN instance. These details could be used in skins on each of those individual sites, giving hosting credit back to the primary website in this DNN instance. For now, we recommend that you provide the domain information for your website such as the Host Title, Host URL, and Host Email, as shown in Figure 3-12. The e-mail address setting will be used in a few places but is generally not an e-mail address that a website visitor will ever see; only website administrators will see this being used.

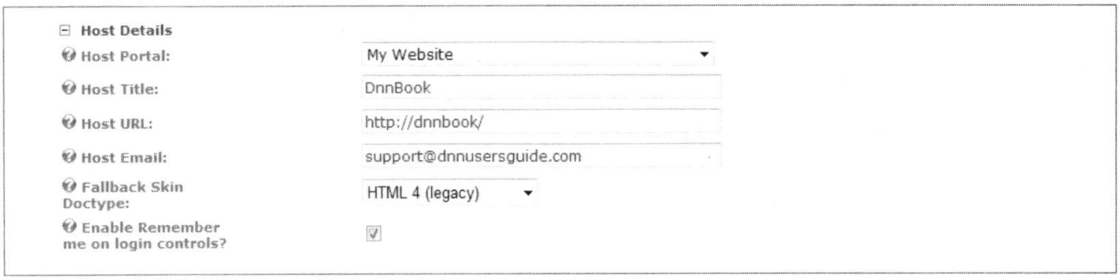

Figure 3-12

### Fallback Skin Doctype

The Fallback Skin Doctype setting is new to DotNetNuke version 5. This is a skin setting that can generally be left in its current state. If you need to define a different default doctype for your pages, this setting will allow you to define the default doctype that DNN will provide for skins that don't have their own settings defined. In most cases you will not be changing this information, as it should be handled by your skin.

### Enable Remember Me

The final option in the Host Details section is the Enable Remember Me on the login controls check box. This option enables or disables the display of the Remember Me check box on the login page. If this is enabled and a user checks the Remember Me box when logging in, they will remain logged in to your site through the use of a cookie placed on their computer. For most sites, it is recommended that you leave this enabled. For the most secure of sites, you might disable it so that people don't remain logged in if they close their browser without first logging out.

## Appearance

The Appearance section, as shown in Figure 3-13, controls some of the basic appearance information for your website. You will see a similar section in Chapter 4 when we look at the Site Settings, which are the settings for a specific portal. Some of the settings in the Host Settings page will control the Host/super user pages only.

**Figure 3-13**

### Show Copyright Credits

The first option in the Appearance section is Show Copyright Credits. The copyright credits this setting refers to are based in HTML code that is entered into the source code of the application pages generated by DNN (see Figure 3-14). Although this option is enabled by default, we recommend that you disable it. Although the copyright credits are visible only to users who look at the source code of the page, you don't need to broadcast the fact that you are using DNN for your website framework.

---

**Security Notice**

Although DNN strives to deliver a secure application, there are times when security exploits are found within all applications. The DNN project handles patching these exploits quickly when possible, but one of the safest ways to avoid having your site exploited is to not broadcast the platform and version of said platform that your website is running on. This prevents hackers from having an easy way to know that your site is vulnerable to any known exploits.

---

### Use Custom Error Messages

The Use Custom Error Messages option is also enabled by default, and it is our recommendation that you leave it that way. This option controls whether DNN will handle application errors or whether the ASP.NET process on the web server will handle the errors. Leaving this option enabled will allow DNN to catch any errors and store them in the database for the administrator/super user to access later. This will also display a friendlier message to the visitors to the site when a page has a problem and a more descriptive error message to the super user account to enable tracking down any errors.

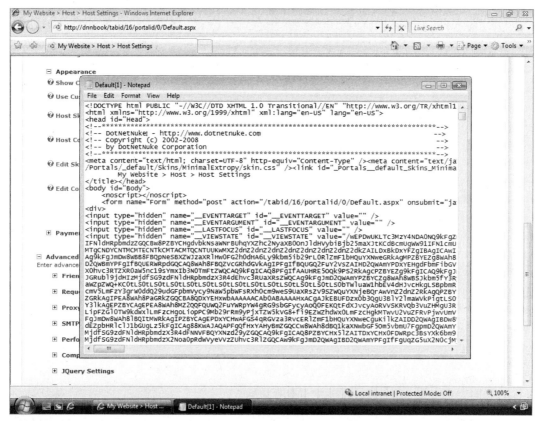

Figure 3-14

## Skins and Containers

The next four options in the Appearance section are the options for the default skins and containers that a portal within this DNN instance will use. Each portal can have its own skin defined. We will cover how to do that in Chapter 4, but if this hasn't been defined, a portal will use the Host Skin setting. Essentially, this means that you can define the skin that all sites should use by default within your DNN instance and then override skins at the portal level. You can further override the default skin at the page level, as described in Chapter 4.

### Host Skin

The Host Skin option allows you to choose the primary skin that a DNN instance will use. By choosing either the Host or Site radio button, you will populate the drop-down list with skins. Skins at the host level are available to all websites within a DNN instance, whereas skins installed at the site level will be available only for the individual portal. We will look at skin installation in Chapter 4. For now, you won't have any skins installed other than the four skins provided by default from the DNN installation (see Figure 3-15).

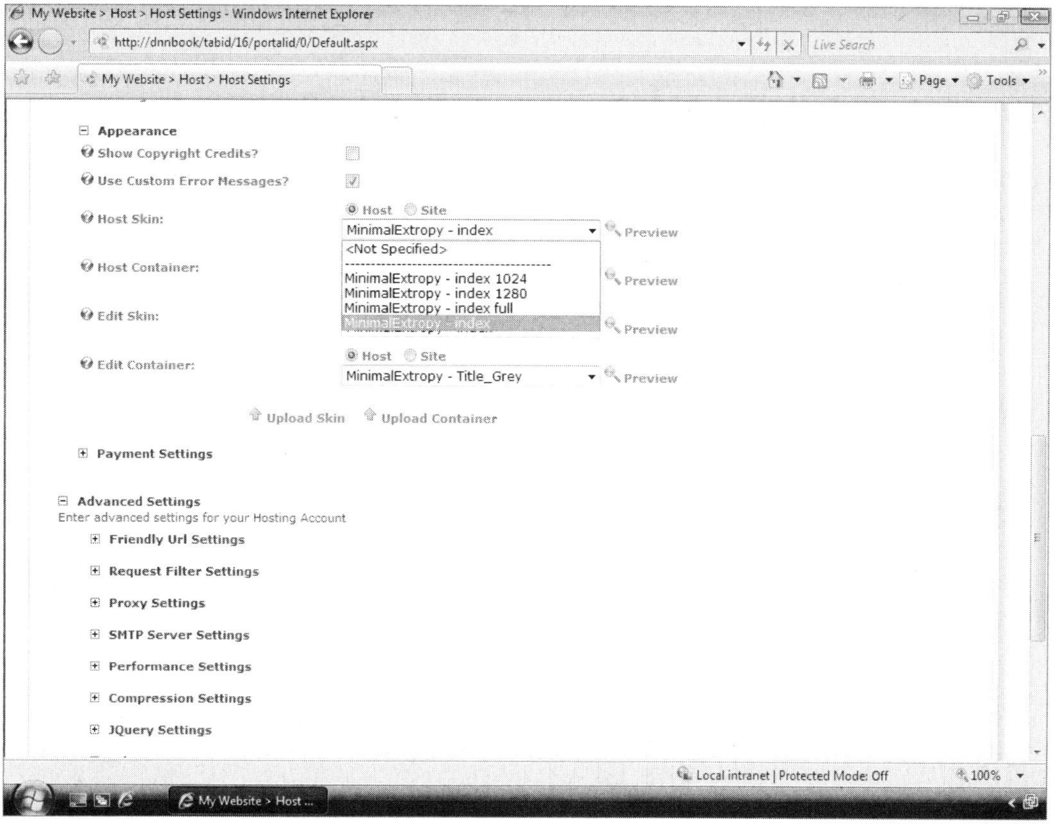

**Figure 3-15**

The Preview link next to the drop-down list will take you to a page previewing the skin selected in the dropdown list. A quick tip regarding the preview mode; this does not save your changes. You still need to change your settings by clicking on Update at the bottom of the Host Settings page to save the skin change, or any other changes you've made to the page.

### Host Container

The Host Container setting is similar to the Host Skin setting in that this selection will be the default container for all portals in the DNN instance. The container, as we discussed earlier in this chapter, is HTML code that wraps around modules on a page. Chapter 4 discusses containers in more detail.

### Edit Skin and Edit Container

The Edit Skin and Edit Container settings are like the Host Skin and Host Container, except for where these skins/containers will get loaded. For many DNN modules there will be a singular view for specific functionality. That is, when that portion of the module is loaded, usually by clicking on a link, only the content for that portion of the module will be loaded on the page; all other modules on the page will not be loaded. This can cause some skins to have display issues because of the lack of content being loaded on a page. It is sometimes useful, though not always necessary, to define a specific skin for these types

**61**

of pages, a skin that is designed to load only one section of content, generally this skin would consist of only a single pane. If you're just getting started with DNN, you can ignore this type of scenario for now. The Edit Skin and Edit Container settings, just like the Host Skin and Host Container settings, can be overridden at the individual portal level.

## Advanced Settings

The Advanced Settings section contains some of the custom information you can configure as a host. Some of this information is applicable to new portals that are created, and some of these settings you will see again in Chapter 4 as we look at the Site Settings. We will touch on each of the sections here in advanced settings, although we won't go into great detail on some of the settings that are not completely necessary for all websites.

### Friendly URL Settings

The Friendly URL Settings option allows you to enable or disable friendly URLs. As we discussed earlier this chapter, DNN has friendly URLs enabled by default, which will effectively transform query string parameters into the path of the page request. Most websites will not require any changes with the Friendly URL Settings option.

### Request Filter Settings

The Request Filter Settings option allows you to block specific types of web requests, such as malicious traffic from a particular IP address. This is a topic outside the scope of this book, but there are a number of blogs by DotNetNuke community members that cover the Request Filter Settings option.

### Proxy Settings

The Proxy Settings option enables you to configure a web server that sits behind a proxy server for Internet access. Without these settings, a DNN site running on a server that is behind a proxy server would not be able to see the outside world and access critical update information. Most third-party hosting environments don't use proxy servers in front of the web servers, so you likely won't have to worry about these settings. If you believe your site is behind a proxy server, you can get these settings from your hosting company or network administrator.

### SMTP Server Settings

The SMTP Server Settings option enables you to configure information about your outgoing e-mail server. This information, provided by your web hosting provider or network administrator, is required if you want to configure your DNN website to be able to send e-mails. Once you've provided the necessary SMTP server information, you can click on the Test option and DNN will send a test e-mail to the Host Email defined earlier on the page in the Host Details section. If the test is successful, you will receive a confirmation message on the screen and an e-mail at that address. Be sure to save the updates you've made to the Host Settings page, as simply clicking on Test and moving on to another DNN page will not store your changes.

Configuration of e-mail server information can be tricky. In a number of cases, SMTP servers will be set up so that they can only send e-mails from a specific domain, IP address, or even e-mail address. If you are having trouble configuring your SMTP settings make sure that your Host Email setting is using an address that has been allowed proper access to the SMTP server.

## Performance Settings

Figure 3-16 shows our recommendations for the Performance Settings section. These values have proven to be the optimal settings for most DNN applications and should help to increase the performance of your website. If this is your first site, you are likely not going to be too stressed on performance, as you will be more concerned with getting traffic to your site. For information on each of the settings in the Performance Settings section, you can click on the Help Text to get a more detailed explanation of the setting.

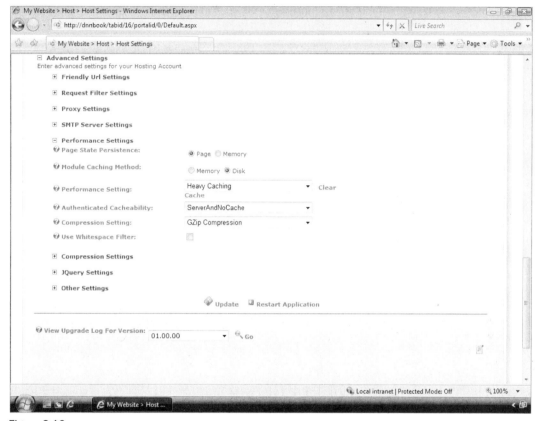

**Figure 3-16**

## Compression Settings

The Compression Settings section controls options for the final two values of the Performance Settings from the previous section. The Excluded Paths option allows you to configure a list of paths that will not be compressed by the Compression Setting option of the Performance Settings option. This list of paths are locations to files or pages on your site that shouldn't be compressed; to create the list simply put each additional path on a new line in the text box. In some cases, compression on specific files, usually JavaScript files, can cause problems. You can directly exclude those files by listing them here. The Whitespace Filter is a string of characters, known as a regular expression, that provides information for the Use Whitespace Filter option of the Performance Settings. It is our recommendation that you always use the Compression Setting option in the Performance Settings. This makes the Whitespace Filter setting within the Compression Settings section obsolete, as using compression removes all of the whitespace in the content that is sent to the user's browser. You should never need to modify this setting.

### JQuery Settings

The JQuery Settings section is an advanced configuration section that allows you to replace the default JQuery libraries that DotNetNuke 5 includes. This is a section that is new from previous versions of DNN and, in most cases, will not need customization except by developers. JQuery provides common JavaScript libraries for web developers to implement and utilize within their modules to provide a unique user experience to visitors of a website. The settings in this section allow you to use a hosted JQuery library such as the JavaScript libraries provided by Google. Doing so will minimize the bandwidth your web server uses, as your site visitors will download the JQuery files from Google, rather than from your web server. It is also likely that they have those files already cached, thus improving performance for the user.

### Other Settings

The Other Settings section, as shown in Figure 3-17, allows you to control some of the various properties for your DNN installation. We recommend leaving them configured in the manner that DNN provides out of the box. One setting you may want to configure differently, though, is the Allowable File Extensions setting. This setting provides a list of file extensions that DNN will allow users to upload; there are a few common file types that are missing from the default settings that DNN provides. If you want to allow your users to upload MP3 or WAV files to your site, you will need to add those extensions to the list (see Figure 3-17).

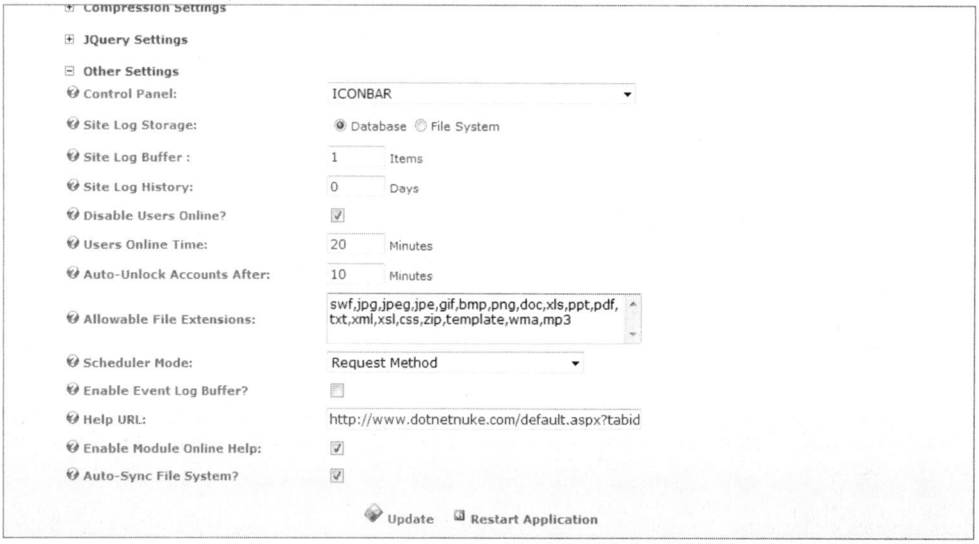

Figure 3-17

## Saving the Host Settings

After making changes to the Host Settings page, you need to save those settings to the database. To do that, simply click on the Update link at the bottom of the page. There is another option next to the Update link, called Restart Application. This setting will prompt DNN to restart the application on the web server. The restarting of the application occurs by DNN making a minor change to a file, known as the `web.config` file, in the website's root folder. Restarting the application can be useful for trying to track down issues with cached information on your website during development but is not an option most website administrators will utilize on a consistent basis.

## *The Module Definitions/Extensions Options*

Much of DNN's power comes through its flexibility — the ability to install and modify content and functionality through the use of extensions. The primary extensions we will be handling in this book are modules and skins. As a super user, or host, you have the ability to install new extensions for DNN that can be used on the various portals in the instance. Whereas in previous versions of DNN, the installation of skins and modules was handled through two different pages, in DotNetNuke 5.0, the installation is handled through the Extensions page.

You can access the Extensions page by placing your mouse cursor over the HOST in the navigation and then choosing the Extensions option from the menu. The Extensions page provides a list of all the currently installed extensions on your DNN instance. As you can see by visiting the page on your own DNN instance, a large number of extensions are available. Near the top of this page you will see two drop-down lists, one for Type Filter and another for Language Filter.

These filters allow you to narrow the list of items on the Extensions page to only the types of content you are looking for. The primary option we will be using is the Type Filter to show you the available types of extensions, as illustrated in Figure 3-18. As mentioned earlier, this book will primarily focus on the Module extension type, but we will make brief mention of the Skin extension type as well.

## Locating Extensions

Before you can upload/install a new extension, you need to have one ready to use. As we discussed in Chapter 1, a large ecosystem has built up around DNN, so there are a number of resources that provide extensions. The best location to find extensions is the DotNetNuke Marketplace at `http://marketplace.dotnetnuke.com`. You can find a large selection of skins and modules available from the DNN Marketplace from the leaders in module and skin development. You can also find skins and modules available directly from the developers of those modules, sometimes even for free.

Extensions within DNN can consist of programming code, much which will access restricted parts of your web server, the file system, and the database for your website. Therefore, you should ask the following questions before purchasing or installing an extension:

❑ Do you trust the developer of the extension? Have they been in the DotNetNuke ecosystem for a while, or are they new to the scene?

❑   Is the source code for the extension available? If the original extension goes away, are you stuck with functionality that cannot extended further or bugs? This used to be a larger concern in the early days of DNN but is still a relevant question.

❑   Are there any special requirements for the extension? Does it require a specific version of DNN or a specific hosting configuration in order to run? It is common for DNN extensions to be configured for specific versions of DNN.

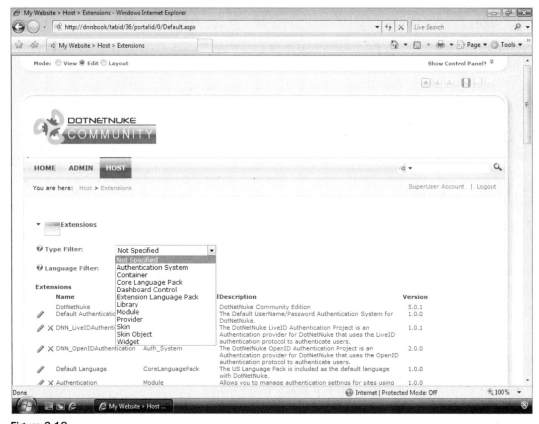

Figure 3-18

## Installing Extensions

The Extensions page, just like any other page within DNN, has a module on it. Remember, modules provide specific functionality. In this case, the Extensions module provides a listing of available extensions, the ability to filter those extensions, as well as some additional functionality such as the ability to install new extensions. This added functionality is available through the module's Actions menu, as shown in Figure 3-19. To install an extension, you use the first option in the Actions menu, Install Extension Wizard.

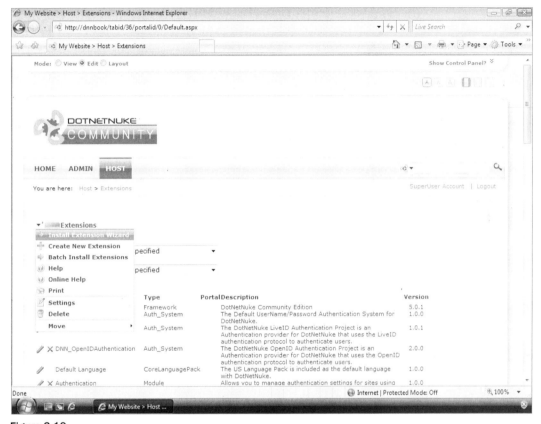

Figure 3-19

The Install Extension Wizard will walk you through the process of installing a new extension into your DNN instance. This process involves uploading a ZIP file of the extension. DNN will walk you through the selection of the ZIP file from your local machine, the acceptance of any license information provided with the package, and an overview of any release notes available with the package, followed by the installation process log. The wizard's interface is similar to that of the Installation Wizard, with information to review on each page followed up with a Next and Cancel button. Figure 3-20 shows the first screen of the installer.

Figure 3-20

### Restricting Access to Modules

The module installation process is fairly straightforward; you can follow the Install Extension Wizard process from the previous section. After installing a module on a DNN instance, you can control whether the module is available to all websites or only to particular websites within an instance of DNN. To control this accessibility, go to the HOST/Extensions page and from the list of available extensions, click on the pencil image next to the module you would like to restrict. For example, if you click on the pencil next to the Banners module, you should be taken to a page that looks like Figure 3-21.

If you scroll down slightly on this page, you'll find a setting called Is Premium Module. By enabling this setting, you restrict which portals within your DNN instance have access to this module. In most cases, you will find that you don't need to limit the modules available to portals (although if you're hosting multiple websites out of your DNN instance, you may need to limit the availability to some modules).

## The Portals Option

We've mentioned previously that DNN has the ability to host multiple websites, portals, out of a single instance of DNN, one set of files, and one database. This can be useful if your hosting budget is limited and you have website requirements that are similar across multiple sites. To configure additional portals within DNN, you need to access the HOST/Portals page from your main navigation. The Portals page will provide you with a list of the available portals for this instance of DNN.

From this page, you can edit the Site Settings for a portal; we will be covering the site settings in Chapter 4 in detail, as this is information that an administrator of a portal has access to as well. The Actions menu for the Portals module will show you a few other options for portals. For example, the Add New Portal option enables you to populate the new portal information, and the Export Portal Template option provides you with an XML document and content for your portal to allow you to easily re-create a portal. Chapter 8 describes adding a new portal and exporting/consuming portal templates in greater detail.

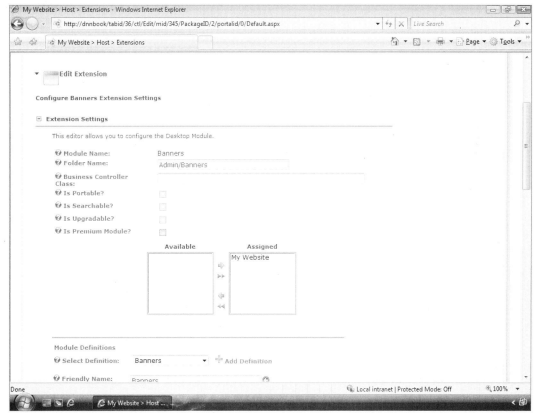

Figure 3-21

# Summary

Most of the information in this chapter will apply to every instance of DNN that you come across. Having a basic understanding of how DNN works, with pages, skins, modules, containers, and panes, is important before getting into the more administrative nature of functionality that will be covered in the rest of this book. Chapter 4 will dive right into the specifics of managing a website within DNN, while the subsequent chapters cover various scenario-based configurations of content for your website in more detail.

# Portal and Content Administration

Now that you've installed DotNetNuke (DNN) and configured the Host Settings for your website, you can start working on your site from an administrator's perspective. In this chapter, we will get into the daily administrative functionality that DNN provides, the ability to create pages and put modules on those pages.

Before getting into the daily administrative functionality, we will cover the basic settings for your portal. These settings are specific to each portal you create within your DNN instance. After we talk about the Site Settings, we will get into security roles, user management, page creation, and, finally, module implementation and settings.

This chapter discusses the following topics:

- ❑ Site Settings

- ❑ Roles and users

- ❑ The permission model

- ❑ How to create and manage pages

- ❑ How to put modules on a page and configure their settings

## Administrative Functionality

All the administrative functionality covered in this chapter will apply to a website's administrator, the Admin account created during the installation process. We will highlight a few things on the Site Settings page that are specific to the super user accounts, but in general the content administration and user management within your DNN portal will be handled, or delegated, by the administrator(s).

The first section we are going to cover for the administrator is the Site Settings page, the first menu item underneath the Admin menu in the site's navigation. To access the Admin menu, log in to your portal with the Admin account you created during the installation process, most likely with the username Admin.

# Site Settings

To access the Site Settings page, move your mouse over the Admin navigation item and choose Site Settings from the drop-down menu. Alternatively, you can use a link in the control panel at the top of your page. If the control panel is not expanded, click on the image next to the text that says Show Control Panel to expand it. You can also collapse the control panel by clicking on the same image. On the right side of the control panel, you should see a Common Tasks section that provides you six icons/links. Click on the Site icon to go to the Site Settings page. We will address more of the control panel functionality later in this chapter.

Once you've navigated to the Site Settings page, you will see that it, like the Host Settings page from the previous chapter, is broken up into multiple sections: Basic Settings, Advanced Settings, and the Style Sheet Editor. These sections have their own subsections beneath; we will spend the next few pages going through the settings that are most relevant to configuring your website.

## Basic Settings

The Basic Settings section provides you with some of the key information about your DNN portal. The following sections discuss the three subsections within the Basic Settings section: Site Details, Site Marketing, and Appearance.

### Site Details

The Site Details section provides some of the key descriptive information for your portal (see Figure 4-1). This information, and all the information on the Site Settings page, can be modified at any time. If you need to skip over a section during the initial configuration process, you can always come back and update the information later.

---

### SEO – Search Engine Optimization

Throughout the book, we will mention the term "search engine optimization," otherwise known as SEO. SEO is the theory and process of optimizing the content of your web pages and website for better indexing by the various search engines, such as Google, Microsoft's Live Search, and Yahoo! This is done to try to make your pages show up higher in the search result listings, thus driving more traffic to your site. SEO is an art of its own, but we will try to point out elements within DNN that can assist you with better optimizing your website for the search engines.

---

#### Title

The first setting you will see, Title, is used to define the name of your website. The Title will be used in a number of locations on the site, including for e-mail messages generated from the site, and within DNN settings to identify the portal if you have multiple portals defined in your DNN instance. Defining a Title is an important part of the SEO process for any website, as the Title of your portal will be used as part of the Browser Title on DNN web pages. There are certain cases where the Portal Title will not be used in the browser title of a page; we will point out these cases when we talk about creating and maintaining pages later in this chapter.

Figure 4-1

## Description

The Description field should be a broad description about your website. This information will be used as the META Description HTML element on the pages of your website. The META Description element is important for SEO purposes and is only visible to search engine spiders, search results, and users who view the HTML source for a web page. The META elements of a web page are HTML tags within the HEAD tag of the page. The site description will be used as the default description for all the pages on your DNN site; however, you can override the site's description at the page level. The Site Settings Description will be used on all pages that don't have their own description provided in the page settings.

## Keywords

Keywords are another META element in the HTML source of a webpage that can be important for the SEO of a website. There is debate about how much search engines will pay attention to keywords, as they can be abused, but we will treat them as if they are still an effective element for SEO purposes. The Site Settings Keywords will be used on every page in your DNN website. Like the description, these keywords are overridden by the page-level keywords. If you don't define page-level keywords, then the site-level keywords will be used. Keywords should be a comma-separated list of words that are descriptive of topics on your website. Good SEO practice would recommend that you not overload the keywords on any page with information that cannot be found elsewhere in the content found on the page.

## Copyright

The Copyright element allows you to define a copyright statement for your portal. This setting will be used in DNN skins that utilize the COPYRIGHT token. You can define the value of this setting, or you can leave it blank. If you leave this setting blank, DNN will generate a copyright statement dynamically using the current year and the Title of your portal.

---

**Tokens**

DNN skins can consist of dynamic elements called tokens. These tokens are simple text such as [COPYRIGHT] that are replaced with coded elements when a skin is parsed from an HTML file and turned into an ASCX file for use in DNN. There are a number of tokens defined by DNN. You can find more about these tokens in books dedicated to DotNetNuke skinning.

---

## GUID

The GUID element of the Site Details section stands for globally unique identifier. A GUID is simply a string that is generated randomly and has an extremely low probability of being duplicated. For your purposes, you can ignore this identifier, as there is not any functionality that allows administrators to utilize this ID.

## *Site Marketing*

The Site Marketing subsection of the Basic Settings, also shown in Figure 4-1, provides functionality relating to search engines and getting your site indexed. You don't have to use any of this functionality to configure your website; in fact, you should likely skip over this section until you have your site ready to be launched, and then come back and use these settings and options.

### Search Engine

The Search Engine feature in Site Marketing allows you to submit your site to three search engines, Google, Microsoft (Live.com), and Yahoo! This process will add your website to a queue that the search engine will use to index new sites. There are more effective ways to get your website listed in the search engines, such as being linked to from other websites, but this is a good start for a beginning website. There are no guarantees as to when the search engines will add your site to the index; don't expect to see your site in the results immediately.

### Site Map URL

The Site Map URL is not actually a setting but a value that you can use to submit the location of your sitemap to the search engines that accept sitemaps. Google provides a service in which you can register with their program called Webmaster Tools. Once registered, you can submit a sitemap that Google can use to help index your website. By providing a sitemap, you essentially provide a listing of pages and their order of relevance to Google for indexing.

### Verification

The Verification setting applies to the Google Webmaster Tools functionality. In order to verify that you are an owner of a website when registering for Google's Webmaster Tools (www.google.com/webmastertools), you will be asked to upload/create a document on your website that Google will then try to access. Google will provide the name of the file, which you then must place in the root of your website. This Verification setting allows you to take the unique name that Google requires for your site (for example, google53c0cef435b2b81e.html) and create the document through this web browser interface. DNN will use the setting to create the document in the root of your site for Google to access. Once Google has found this file to exist on your website, you will be given access to the Webmaster Tools in which you can add a sitemap for your site, as well as other functionality.

### Banners

It's debatable if the Banners setting actually belongs here in the Site Marketing subsection, but nonetheless that is where it can be found. DNN enables you to display banners within your skin or as individual modules on your pages. The setting here on the Site Settings page allows the site administrator to choose where these banners should be populated from. You choices are: None, in which no banners will be used on the site; Site, in which only banners from this particular portal will be displayed on the site; or Host, in which banners from the host level will be displayed on the site.

While it is not very common that banners will be used in these terms, this functionality can be a very powerful way to rotate content on your website without having to develop custom modules to do so. The Vendors section, under the Host menu enables you, as a super user, to configure banners that should be displayed on all websites; or, at the site level, you can configure banners specific only to an individual website. As an administrator, you can create vendors within your own site from under the Admin menu. Once you have vendors created, you can add banners to each vendor. Chapter 9 takes a more in-depth look at banner functionality.

## *Appearance*

The Appearance subsection provides a way to manage the basic appearance of your website, from the image used as your logo to the default skins and containers.

### Logo

The Logo setting for your website allows you to define the image that DNN will use for your site. The only place this setting will come into play is in the skin(s) for your website, assuming that the skin uses the Logo token in its design; most skins will do so. When choosing a logo you are given the ability to choose a File Location, a folder where the image exists on your portal's directory, and then a File Name option, which shows a list of files within the selected folder (see Figure 4-2).

**Figure 4-2**

If you have not already uploaded a logo for your website, you can choose the Upload New File option. This will provide you with a different interface in which you can browse for the file on your local computer to upload to the web server, as shown in Figure 4-3. When you press the Browse button, your browser will load a file selection window in which you can locate the image you would like to upload to use as your logo.

DNN will not resize the image, so you must be careful with the size of the image that you upload. Some skins are designed for smaller logos, whereas others are designed for larger logos. See the associated documentation for the skin your website is using to figure out what size Logo will work best.

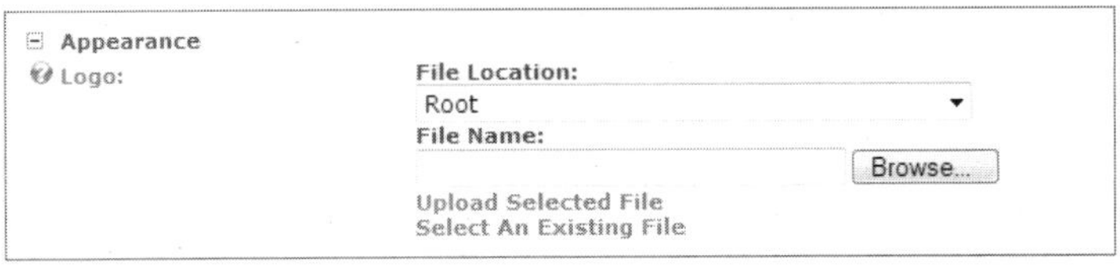

Figure 4-3

## Body Background

The Body Background setting is a holdover from the initial days of DNN, before the skinning engine was implemented. It is still possible to choose a body background, using the same file selection interface that you found in the Logo setting, although we don't recommend that you use this setting. Your skin should have a background image or color defined. If it does not, we recommend using a different skin. If you set up the Body Background setting, you may not see any difference in your site; however, if you later change to a skin that doesn't have a background, the image will likely show up.

## Enable Skin Widgets

New to DotNetNuke version 5 is the introduction of widgets, bits of Web 2.0 functionality that can be included in a skin to provide more dynamic functionality for the end user of a website. Widgets generally consist of JavaScript functionality that is executed by the user's browser, as opposed to modules that provide functionality that is executed in code on the web server side before being returned to the user's browser. You can turn off the widget functionality on DNN sites at the site level, although we haven't found a need at this point to turn it off in our experiences with DNN 5.

## Skins and Containers

The settings for the default portal skin, portal container, edit skin, and edit container all use a similar interface, as you can see in Figure 4-4. We'll explain it once and talk about each of these settings individually afterwards. The first options you will see in the selection process are the Host and Site radio buttons. These options allow you to select where the skin/container your site will use can be found. Host means that the skin/container is at the host level, meaning that all portals in your DNN instance can use the skin. This is good for shared skins that are common across multiple websites, such as the default DNN skin, MinimalExtropy.

Figure 4-4

The Site option allows you to select from skins that are configured only for this particular portal. Skins must be installed by a Host/Super User account, but they can be installed either for all portals in an instance of DNN or for an individual portal. If you haven't installed any additional skins to your site, you will likely only have the MinimalExtropy options under the Host selection, and no options available under the Site selection.

Once you've chosen a radio button selection, the drop-down list beneath these buttons will be populated with the skins available based on the selection. Figure 4-5 shows the skins that came with this version of DotNetNuke. In the list, you will see the name of the skin package (for example, MinimalExtropy) and then you'll see the actual skin file, such as index or index 1024.

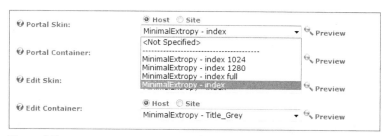

**Figure 4-5**

It is common for a skin package to have multiple layout options available with different pane configurations. Containers can also have multiple configurations. Although they won't differ in the number of panes, as a container can only have one pane, they can be configured with differing borders, images or even colors. If you have a skin or container package that includes multiple skin/container files, it is recommended that you choose the one that will be used on the majority of your web pages and modules. By choosing a widely used default skin/container, you can minimize the amount of work necessary to configure individual pages and modules later in the process.

If you aren't sure which skin you want to use, click on the magnifying glass or the Preview link (they both go to the same place). This will take you to a new URL, which will be the current page but with a parameter passed in, forcing the page to load using a different skin. Be careful with the preview functionality. If you've changed any of the settings on the page before clicking on the Preview link, those changes will be lost when you click on Preview. It would be best to only use the preview functionality when you're not making any other changes to the Site Settings page. You can always come back to the Site Settings page and change these skin/container defaults.

## Portal Skin

The Portal Skin setting defines the default skin that your portal will use. Defining the default portal skin is an important part of the configuration process, as this is the skin that will be used on all pages of your website that don't have their own skin defined in the Page Settings. (Page Settings are discussed later in this chapter.) You should choose the most common skin that pages on your site should use. This will allow you to save on the amount of work necessary because you won't have to configure most pages on your site manually, only the skin settings for pages that don't use the portal skin.

## Portal Container

The Portal Container setting defines the default container that the modules on your portal will use. This setting will apply to all modules on your site, although you can override this setting in a couple of places. On individual pages, in the Page Settings, you can set a default container for the page; this would override the default container from the Site Settings. For individual modules on a page, you can also override the container in the Module Settings. We will cover Module Settings later in this chapter.

### Edit Skin

The Edit Skin setting is definitely one of the most misunderstood options in DNN. In previous versions of DNN, this setting was called the Admin Skin. Although the name has changed, the functionality provided is still the same. To understand this, first consider how DNN handles and loads modules. In most cases, DNN will load multiple modules on a page, either into a single pane or into multiple panes. Every module has a View control, the default interface that users will see when they load a page that has the module on it. Most modules will also have a Settings control, in which you can configure the settings for the module, as well as an Edit control, in which you can interact with the content/functionality that the module provides.

When you edit the module or go to the settings for a module, DNN will load only that particular control on the page. You will notice when you do this that all the other modules that were on the page go away. You can tell when your DNN site is loading an individual control by looking at the URL of the page; you will likely see "CTL" in the URL. For example, in the default configuration, DNN will load the Login control using this functionality when you click on the Login link on your page. When we are on our home page, if we click on the Login link, we get a URL of the following format:

```
http://dnnbook/Home/tabid/38/ctl/Login/Default.aspx
```

Notice the /ctl/login/ section of the URL. This is a query string parameter telling DotNetNuke to load the Login control. You will notice similar functionality if you click on the Register link from your home page; DNN will load the Register controls.

```
http://dnnbook/Home/tabid/38/ctl/Register/Default.aspx
```

The edit and settings functionality for modules, along with the login and register controls, are loaded in the Edit skin, defined with the Edit Skin setting. In many cases, having the Edit Skin and the Portal Skin be the same is perfectly acceptable, although in other cases you might find that you want a cleaner, more concise (less graphics, panes, etc.) skin when you are editing or changing the settings for a module. You will also see this Edit Skin when you add/edit pages within DNN later in this chapter.

### Edit Container

The edit container, like the edit skin, is used in the case where DNN is loading only a particular control. In most cases, this is only something administrators will see; however, as we've pointed out with the Login and Register links, it is possible that other users will see this container as well.

## Advanced Settings

The Advanced Settings section contains a number of subsections. If you are logged in with a Portal Administrator account, you will see Security Settings, Page Management, Payment Settings, Usability Settings, and Other Settings. If you're logged in with a super user account, you will see those subsections as well as Portal Aliases, SSL Settings, and Host Settings.

## Security Settings

The Security Settings subsection has one setting, the User Registration options for your portal. The options are None, Private, Public, and Verified.

The **None** option is pretty self-explanatory. There will be no registration options on the website, the Register link from the main skin will not be visible, and if people click on the Login link, there will not be a registration link on the Login control as their normally would be.

The **Private** registration option allows people to register on the website, but they won't be able to log in with their newly created account until they have been approved. We'll cover the approval process (authorization) later in this chapter.

The **Public** option allows anyone to register on the website and immediately login.

The **Verified** option is our recommended configuration. This option allows users to register on the website, but they cannot successfully log in to the site until they receive an e-mail from the site with a verification code. When they attempt to log in the first time, they will be prompted for this verification code. Once they've successfully verified their account, they login as normal with a username and password. In order for the Verified option to work properly, you must have the SMTP settings configured on the Host Settings page; otherwise, the website will not be able to e-mail the user's the verification information. This option is useful when you want to validate that people enter their own valid e-mail address into the site when registering.

## Page Management

The Page Management subsection of the Site Settings page allows you to configure some extended functionality for a few specific features of your DNN website. All the settings in this section, except for the Home Directory, have drop-down lists associated with them that are populated with a list of the pages on your DNN website. It is important to configure a page before selecting it from the drop-down list. We'll cover exactly why in regard to each of the settings.

### Splash Page

The Splash Page setting allows you to define the very first page that visitors will see when they access your website, assuming that they come directly to the root of your site, such as browsing to www.dotnetnuke.com, as opposed to browsing to a page on your site by going to www.dotnetnuke.com/home.aspx. Splash pages are commonly used for an animation or welcome image of some sort that users see when they first visit a website. Once users have navigated into your website, you generally don't want to send them back to the splash page, which is where the Home Page setting comes into play.

To configure a splash page, you can choose a page from the drop-down list. The configuration of such a page is up to you, but as we mentioned previously, the splash page will likely contain an animation or some other message. You should place this on the page before setting up the Splash Page setting. Another common feature of a splash page will be a minimalist skin file, with very few of the common elements found on a skin, only providing the animation for the user to view and click on.

### Home Page

The Home Page setting is actually already defined for you as the page that was created during the installation process called Home. The Home Page setting controls the default page that loads on a website, if the Splash Page setting is not defined. It also controls where people are sent when they click on the logo of a DNN website. In most cases, you won't find a need to change the Home Page setting.

## Login Page

The Login Page is not configured by default, and as previously mentioned, should not be configured until you've properly set up a page to be your Login page. This means that you have to put the Account Login module on a page. There are two common scenarios for using the Login Page setting. One is to put the Account Login module on the Home page and choose that as the Login page. The second is to create a page called Login and put an Account Login module on that page. The latter scenario can be useful if you are trying to provide more information to your website's users before they log in to the site, perhaps some instructions for logging in and navigating through the site. You might also create a login page that needs to use the SSL settings available to DNN pages if the host has configured SSL for your portal. Whatever you decide, you must be sure that you have an Account Login module on the page you choose in this drop-down list.

When you define a Login page, DNN will no longer use the URL /ctl/login/ to load the Login control. When users click on the Login link, they will be directed to the page defined in this setting. Another thing to watch out for is to not make your Login page require permissions to be visible. They should be visible to All Users. We will describe how to configure this permission at the page level later in this chapter.

## User Page

The User Page option is like the Login Page option, in that you must select a page that has the User Account module on it. The User page is where users will go to register when they first sign up for the website, and also where they will go when they want to update their profile information and change their password. If you don't put the User Account module on this page, users won't be able to register or update their profile information.

In previous versions of DNN, the User Account module was a separate module that could be placed on a page. Now it is part of the Users and Roles module. You should read later sections of this chapter covering the use of modules before attempting to configure a user page. Once you are comfortable with managing modules on pages, you can get to the User Account definition by putting the Users and Roles module on the page and then deleting two of the three modules that are installed, the Security Roles and User Accounts module, leaving the User Account module on the page.

### Home Directory

The Home Directory option is not a setting you can configure after the creation of a DNN portal, but it is something you can change during the portal-creation process. For your purposes, the Home Directory setting tells you where the files for this individual portal exist, from the root of your DotNetNuke folder. In Chapter 2, we created our DNN site in this directory:

```
c:\inetpub\wwwroot\DotNetNuke\
```

The Home Directory shows our portal's directory is in Portals\0\, which equates to the local web server path of:

```
C:\inetpub\wwwroot\DotNetNuke\Portals\0\
```

## Payment Settings

The Payment Settings section allows you to configure payment information if you have a portal on a DNN instance that requires payment for the portal. It can also be used to require payment for special role access to the website. In all our years of using DNN, we haven't had a need for the settings, so we are going to skip over this section, as it is highly unlikely that you will need them either. However, if you do need payment information for your portal because of hosting or role access, the settings are fairly straightforward.

## Usability Settings

The Usability Settings subsection provides a few options that you can turn on or off that control some of DotNetNuke's usability features. Figure 4-6 shows the recommended configuration. It is not common to need to change these settings for most portals.

**Figure 4-6**

### Inline Editor Enabled

The Inline Editor functionality within DNN is limited in its implementation, but it can allow you to make changes to certain parts of your website without having to go into an edit mode. This functionality can be found with the Module Titles for most containers in DNN, allowing you to change the Module Title without having to go to the Module Settings page. You can also find inline edit functionality using the Text/HTML module. Some administrators find this inline edit functionality to be obtrusive and would rather turn it off. You can turn off the functionality for Module Titles and the Text/HTML module by unchecking the Inline Editor Enabled check box.

### Control Panel Mode

The Control Panel Mode setting allows you to select the default mode for the control panel, either View or Edit. In most cases, we recommend leaving this in Edit mode, as it makes it easier to get to the administrative functionality for the individual modules. Once users have changed their mode, a cookie will be stored on their machine, saving the state. They can always change the mode back later.

### Control Panel Visibility

The Control Panel Visibility setting allows you to configure whether the control panel should be expanded or collapsed by default. It is possible for users to control the state of the panel themselves by expanding or collapsing the control panel, using the Show Control Panel option. Once users have expanded or collapsed the control panel, it will remain in that state, based on a cookie placed on their machine.

### Control Panel Security

The Control Panel Security setting allows you to configure who has the ability to view the control panel on a page: users with Page Edit rights or users with Module Edit rights. In general, we recommend that you leave this set at the Module Editors.

## *Other Settings*

The Other Settings subsection allows you to define a few key items that relate directly to the portal.

### Administrator

The first setting is the Administrator; this is the default administrator account for your portal. This drop-down list is populated by users in the Administrators role. It is possible to have multiple people in this role, as you will see later in this chapter. The Administrator setting essentially defines the primary Administrator for a website. The e-mail address that is defined for this account is the address that e-mail notifications from the website will come from. It is common for a site to set up a default administrator account that uses a specific e-mail address, such as support@dnnusersguide.com, and have this be the account selected here in the Administrator setting, rather than using an individual's account on the website. If a user is selected here, he or she cannot be deleted from a portal until another administrator has been selected in this setting.

### Default Language

Within DNN it is possible to replace the various administrative text in your portal with text from another language. This is done through the use of *languages packs*, but it is outside the scope of this book. If you have additional language packs installed within DNN, you can choose what the default language for your portal should be. This Default Language setting is a drop-down list populated with the installed language packs for a portal. Making the selection here will make the default language change. It is possible for individual users to associate their accounts with a different language by managing their profile properties. You will learn more about profile properties in Chapter 5.

### Portal Time Zone

The Portal Time Zone setting allows you to choose the default time zone for your portal; it is recommended that you choose the time zone in which your web server is configured. This information will be used in various locations on your site that are date/time dependent. In the same manner that users can configure their own language pack, individual users can choose their own time zone in their profile properties; DNN will provide date/time information that has been changed accordingly.

## *Portal Aliases (Host Only)*

The Portal Aliases option is a host-only setting. The Portal Aliases for a DNN website control the default URL that a portal is configured to respond to. The Portal Alias is how DotNetNuke knows which portal a request is for on instances of DNN that have multiple portals running. In many cases, you will only have a single Portal Alias defined, as we do in Figure 4-7 for our book website. If you are moving your website from one domain to another or from a test environment to a production environment, it is important to configure the Portal Aliases section correctly. We discuss Portal Aliases in more detail in Chapter 8.

## *SSL Settings (Host Only)*

The SSL Settings option allows you to configure your website to run using Secure Sockets Layer (SSL), a cryptographic protocol that provides security to the information transferred between a web server and a user's web browser. The SSL functionality within DNN can be configured only by a Host/Super User account and is handled on a portal-by-portal basis. While you can change the SSL Settings here for DNN, an SSL Certificate must be procured and installed on the web server before these settings will work correctly. You can tell if a site is using SSL by looking at the browser URL. If the URL begins with `https://` instead of `http://`, it is likely using SSL.

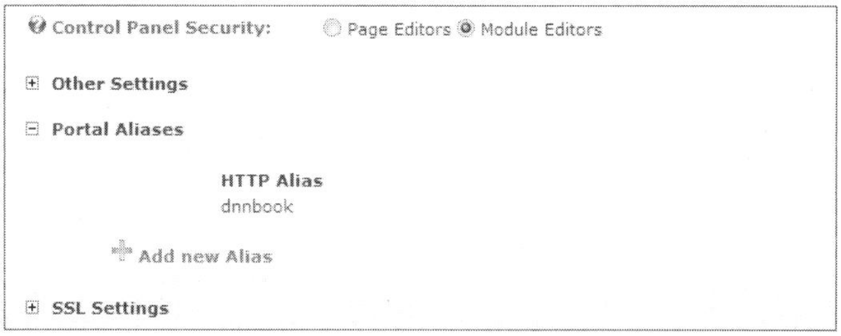

Figure 4-7

## SSL Enabled

The SSL Enabled setting allows you to turn on SSL for a particular portal. Once SSL is enabled, it is possible to require an SSL connection for each page on your site. These page-level settings don't work until SSL has been enabled by the Host.

## SSL Enforced

The SSL Enforced option will control which pages should or shouldn't be accessible based on their page setting (discussed later in this chapter). If a page is marked as secured, it won't be accessible via a nonsecure URL, and vice versa.

## SSL URL

The SSL URL option will be used only if you have an SSL certification that is different from your Portal Alias. It is common in some hosting situations to have one common secure URL. If that is the case for your hosting platform, you would place the URL provided by your host into this setting.

## Standard URL

If you have an SSL URL configured in the previous setting, in the Standard URL setting you need to provide the URL that unsecured connections to your site should use. This will likely be the same as the portal alias for the portal.

## *Host Settings (Host Only)*

The Host Setting subsection, as its name implies, is a host-only section of the Site Settings page. Most of these settings are the same as those you saw in Chapter 3 when we covered the Host Settings page. You can reference that chapter for the information about each of these settings. The difference from the Host Settings page, however, is that these settings apply only to this individual portal, whereas the similar settings on the Host Settings page apply to all new portals that are created.

## Premium Modules

The one setting that you might want to take notice of in the Host Settings section is the setting for Premium Modules. This section allows a super user to control which modules are available to a portal. As you can see in Figure 4-8 there are a number of modules that are Selected, meaning they are available for the portal to use. There are also some modules that are Available, meaning they have not been defined as available for this portal. These modules that are currently marked as Available are modules that are Host modules. You most likely don't want to give someone at the portal-level access to them, but you could. You can also, through the Extensions page, control whether a module is Premium or not, making it show up in this list of available modules. Premium modules allow you to limit certain modules from being accessible to all portals. In most cases you don't need to do this, but in some larger DNN instances, you might find this useful.

Figure 4-8

## Stylesheet Editor

The last Section of the Site Settings page is the Stylesheet Editor. The Stylesheet Editor enables you to edit a file called `Portal.css` that resides in your portal's folder. In our case, this is the `/portals/0/Portal.css` file. If you have multiple portals in your DNN instance, it might be a different number. You could just as easily modify this file through other means; DNN provides you a way to edit the file on the Site Settings page so that you can make quick CSS changes to your website through the web browser.

The `Portal.css` file is the very last CSS file that should be loaded on all DNN web pages. This means that any changes made to the CSS in this file should override any previous CSS elements from modules, containers, skins, and DNN itself. The important thing to remember with the Stylesheet Editor is that by pressing Update at the bottom of the page, you will not save any changes made to the `Portal.css` file; you will be saving the rest of the settings on the page. To save your changes to the `Portal.css` file, you must click on the Save Style Sheet option underneath the text box for the Stylesheet Editor.

A common practice for DNN 5 and greater is to remove the contents of the default `portal.css` file, as the styles that are defined there apply only to the default content on the home page of a new DNN installation. If you delete the modules or content from the home page, these styles are no longer necessary. In previous versions of DNN, the `portal.css` file contained a listing of all CSS elements for DNN, although these elements had no styles assigned to them in portal.css, it was useful information if you were looking for a listing of the common elements for DNN sites.

# Roles

DNN provides the ability to restrict the content and functionality on a website through the use of security roles. Security roles enable administrators to group users, and to provide permissions to view and edit modules and pages based on a user's role membership. We will discuss the implementation of the permissions system in DNN later in this chapter when we start to create pages and place modules on those pages. Roles can also be used for other purposes, such as sending e-mail newsletters and other types of notifications. Individual modules can also utilize roles to provide flexible functionality and the segmenting of users. Users can belong to a single role or multiple roles within a portal, and you can even configure DNN to allow users to add and remove themselves from certain roles.

Some default roles are created when a portal is created within DNN. The Administrators role is the role that all the portal administration accounts should be grouped as; this includes the Admin account that was created during the installation process. The Registered Users role is a role that all users are added to when accounts are created. This role will be useful when we look at the permissions grid for pages and modules. If someone is in the Registered Users role, it means that they are currently logged in to the website. The final default role is called Subscribers. This is another role that all users are added to when they create an account. The difference between this role and the Registered Users role is that users can remove themselves from the Subscribers role, so the role can be used to send an e-mail newsletter to the members of the role.

## Managing Roles

As an administrator, you have the ability to create and manage roles, as well as manage which users are in those roles. As you will see in Chapter 9, you can also delegate the role administration in DNN to other users within your portal. In a standard DNN configuration, the role management will occur on the Security Roles page, which can be accessed under the Admin menu or from the Roles icon in the Common Tasks section of the control panel. The Security Roles page will look like Figure 4-9. In this view, you should see the three default roles we discussed previously: Administrators, Registered Users, and Subscribers. There are a number of columns in the table listing the roles; we will talk about the data populating these columns as we look at creating a new role.

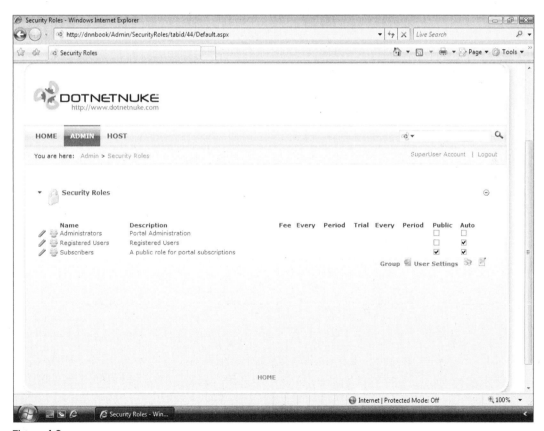

Figure 4-9

## Role Groups

You can use role groups to organize roles from an administrative standpoint. On most websites, role groups won't be necessary, but on sites that have a large number of roles, it becomes necessary to have a filtering mechanism for the Security Roles page as well as the Permissions grids you will see when modifying pages or modules. Role groups are a very simple organizational mechanism, as they do not provide any sort of a multilevel hierarchy; they are simply a grouping of roles.

To create a role group, mouse over the Actions menu next to the module title, which in this case should say Security Roles (see Figure 4-10). In this list of items, you will find the actions available to the Security Roles module. Click on the Add New Role Group link, and you will be taken to the Edit Role Group page, where you can define the information for your role group (see Figure 4-11). As you can see, creating a role group is easy; simply give it a name and a description, and then click on the Update link.

Figure 4-10

Figure 4-11

Once you've created a role group, you should see a new drop-down list available on the Security Roles page that will allow you to filter roles based on their assigned role group (see Figure 4-12).

Figure 4-12

## Creating Roles

To create a role within DNN, you should be on the Security Roles page and, as we showed in the preceding Role Groups section, you should mouse over the Actions menu for the Security Roles module. This will provide you with a link to Add New Role, as shown in Figure 4-10. Clicking on the Add New Role link will take you to the Edit Security Roles Page (see Figure 4-13).

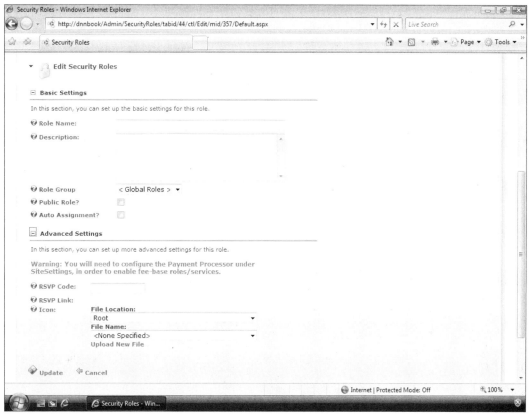

Figure 4-13

### Basic Settings

The Basic Settings are generally all you need to configure when creating a role for your DNN website. The following is an overview of each of these basic settings:

❑ **Role Name:** The Role Name is the information that will be displayed wherever you are managing permissions within your DNN site. You can't change a Role Name once it has been created, so be sure to name your roles correctly the first time; otherwise, you will have to create a new role if you want to change a role name.

❑ **Role Description:** The Role Description is used on the Security Roles page, displaying in the list of information about a role. There isn't much other use of the role description, so you can put anything in here that you need for administrative purposes. You can change the description for a role at any time.

❑ **Role Group:** As we covered previously, it is possible within DNN to group roles together with role groups. If you've created a group previously, you should be able to locate your group in the drop-down list. You don't have to define a role group upon creation; you can change the group a role belongs to at any time.

❑ **Public Role:** The Public Role setting controls whether this role is one that a user can add themselves to or remove themselves from. If a role is not marked as Public, only administrators can add/remove people from a role. A public role can be useful if you want to allow people to sign up for a newsletter subscription on your website.

❑ **Auto Assignment:** If you enable the Auto Assignment setting, this role will automatically be added to all the existing user accounts on your website, as well as any new accounts that are created on your site. You might find it useful to create a new role, make it auto-assigned, and then turn off the Auto Assignment setting. That will effectively add the role to any existing user on your website, but new users who sign up will not be added to the role.

## Advanced Settings

Although the Advanced Settings for a role are not commonly used, they provide a bit more functionality to roles that can be useful in more advanced website scenarios. If you enabled the Payment Processor information on the Admin/Site Settings page, there will be a few other options available when creating a role, although we will skip over those as they are out of the scope of this book.

❑ **RSVP Code and Link:** The RSVP Code setting allows you to define a string of characters that can be provided to users of your website to add themselves to a role. This can be extremely useful if you are sending out newsletters to your users and want to provide them with the ability to subscribe to additional newsletters. After you've created a role with an RSVP code, you can come back to the Edit role page and you will be provided with an RSVP link. This link can be e-mailed to users, and they can click on the link to be added to this role. In order for this functionality to work properly, the user must be logged in to the website prior to clicking on the link. Users can also use the Manage Services link from within their profile to add or remove roles using RSVP codes.

❑ **Icon:** The Icon setting for a role allows you to define an image to be used when referencing the role. There are not many modules that utilize the Role Icon functionality, but one in particular that can is the Forums module, which you will see more of in Chapter 6.

## *Editing Roles*

As mentioned in the "Creating Roles" section, you can edit a lot of the role information once a role has been created. However, you cannot change the name of a role once it has been created. To edit a role, go to the Admin/Security Roles page and click on the Pencil icon next to the role you would like to make changes to. This will take you to the same page that you used when creating a role.

## *Managing Users in Roles*

Another feature that the Security Roles page provides is the ability to manage which users are in a role. To do this, click on the people icon next to the name of your existing roles. This will take you to the Manage Users in Role page (see Figure 4-14). The Manage Users in Role page enables you to add users to a role, view users currently in a role, and remove users from a role.

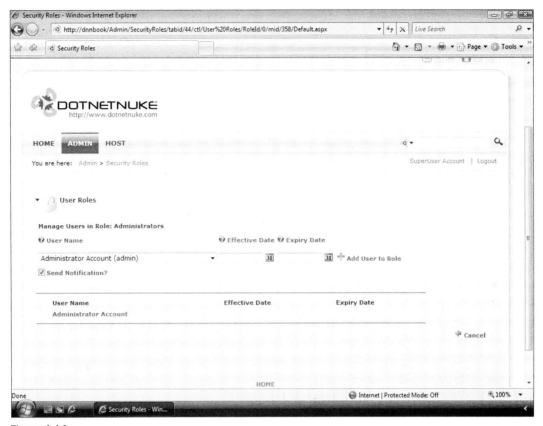

Figure 4-14

## Adding Users to a Role

At the top of the page, you will find a drop-down list that is populated with the display name property of the users on your site, as well as the username in parentheses. When adding a user to a role, you can define a date range for this role membership, making roles available for a limited time. This date restriction is handled by defining an Effective Date and an Expiry Date before you click on the Add User to Role link. One other option when adding a user to a role is to send them a notification that they have been added to a new role using the Send Notification option. This will generate an e-mail to the e-mail address defined in their profile with a message stating that they've been added to the new Role on the website along with some other basic information about the portal.

If you have a portal with a large number of users, you might want to remove the drop-down list with the existing users of your website. This drop-down list, if populated with thousands of users, can be quite large and cumbersome to find individual users in. To manage this, from the Security Roles modules, click on the User Settings option in the Actions menu. We will talk about the User Settings page in Chapter 9, but the setting on the user settings page that controls the user role drop-down list is Users Display Mode in Manage Roles.

### Removing Users from a Role

Removing a user from a role is easy. Below the section in which you can add a user to a role, you will find a list of users in the current role. Next to the names of the users is a red X graphic. Click on that image to remove the user from the current role. In Figure 4-14, you will notice that we currently only have one user in our role, the Administrator Account. We can't remove this user from the Administrators role because of a few reasons. We are currently logged in with this account, and the user is also configured as the Administrator account on the Admin/Site Settings page.

# Users

DNN provides a powerful and flexible system for managing the users on your website. You can find this functionality on the Admin/User Accounts page, or simply by clicking on the Users icon in the Common Tasks section of the control panel. From the User Accounts page, you can add new users, manage existing users, and control the custom user profile properties for your website. Figure 4-15 shows the User Accounts page for a clean installation of DNN.

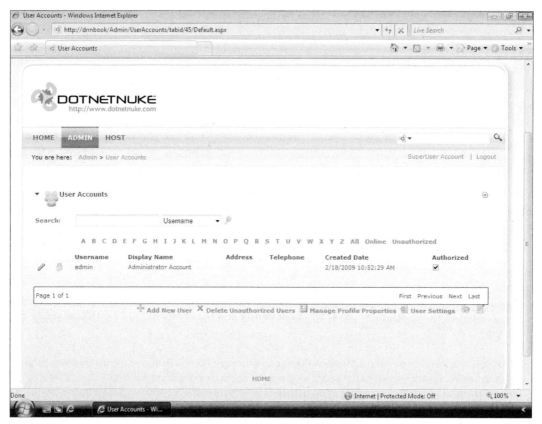

**Figure 4-15**

As we discussed when we looked at the Site Settings page, you can turn on registrations for your website so that users can create their own accounts and log in to the site, but you can also turn off registrations so that users are not able to create their own accounts. In either case, you may want to create some accounts for users yourself. This is done from the User Accounts page. The User Accounts page also allows you to delete unauthorized users, manage profile properties, and view the User Settings page. All these are available from the module's Actions menu.

## Adding Users

You can add a new user by clicking on the Add New User option in the Actions menu for the User Accounts module. This will take you to the Add New User form, as shown in Figure 4-16.

**Figure 4-16**

This form allows you to provide the necessary information to create a new account. Most of the fields are self-explanatory, but we will cover a few of them to point out features of DNN.

❑    **User Name:** This is the name of the account that a user will use to log in to the website. This cannot be changed once an account is created. The **Display Name** is a custom string that can be modified and used throughout modules for the name displayed to members of the site for a user. Users can change the Display Name on their profile at any time, unless the display name is configured by an administrator to be of a specific format. This occurs on the User Settings page, covered in Chapter 9.

❑ **Authorize:** This setting controls whether the user can immediately log in. In general, if you are creating an account for a user, you will leave them authorized. You can always edit the user and change their authorization at a later time. Earlier in this chapter we talked about the various registration options for your website. If you chose Private or Verification as your option, the users are not automatically authorized when they create an account themselves. When you edit a user you can mark them as authorized, providing them access to log in to the site.

❑ **Notify:** This option controls whether new users will get an e-mail with their account information when their account is created. If you choose not to notify users when you create an account, you will have to provide them their account information in some other fashion. If you want to create an account with a random password, you can check the **Random Password** option. This will generate a random password for the user's account. If you do this, it is recommended that you use the notification option as well; otherwise, you will be creating an account that you haven't told the user about, and when you do tell them about it, you won't know the password for their account because it was randomly generated. It is not possible for an administrator to view a user's password for the website, although you can reset it.

# Existing Users

Working with existing users is fairly straightforward. From the User Accounts page, you can search for users, and display a list of users by the first letter of their username, a list of all users, users who are currently online (assuming that users online is enabled in the host settings, although this is not recommended for performance reasons), and a list of the unauthorized users for your site. Next to the users in each of these lists you will see two images: a pencil, which provides a link to edit that user's account information, and a lock, which provides a link to a page for managing the roles a user is assigned to.

## Editing Users

If you click on the pencil icon next to one of the user accounts, you will be taken to a page to edit the information for that user. This page is similar to the Add New User page but has a bit more information about the user, such as when the user was created, logged in, and last active, and when their password was last changed. You can also see if a user has been locked out, meaning that they have attempted to log in and were unsuccessful a number of times. As an administrator, you can remove this lock, although after 10 minutes the account should be unlocked automatically.

From this Edit User Accounts page, you should see a few links above the user information, allowing you to Manage Roles for this User, Manage Password, and Manage Profile. The Manage Password page allows an administrator to reset a user's password. The Manage Profile page allows an administrator to change the various profile properties for a user's account. We discuss these profile properties later in this chapter.

## Managing User Roles

Manage Roles for this User link takes you to a page that will look very similar to the Manage Users in Role functionality available from the Security Roles page. The premise is the same but slightly reversed. Instead of managing the users who are in a role, you can manage the roles that a user is a member of. You can add a new role to a member, see the list of their current roles, and also remove any roles that you wish from a user.

## Deleting Unauthorized Users

The Delete Unauthorized users function on the User Accounts page provides a way for you to easily delete all users on your site who aren't authorized. This would be useful if you have the Verified registration setting configured, as it will remove any of those users who haven't logged in to the site with the verification code they should have received in their e-mail. The danger of using this function is that you might delete a user who has recently signed up on the site and has not yet logged in with his or her verification code.

## Profile Properties

DNN provides an extensible profile model for users within your website. You can create custom profile fields that you can allow your users, or even require those users, to fill in during registration or once they log in to the website. Controlling when users are required to update their profile, either at login or registration, is handled in the User Settings, which we cover in Chapter 9. Managing the fields, however, falls within the User Management section in this chapter.

To manage the various profile fields for your users, go to the User Accounts page and then click on the Manage Profile Properties in the Actions menu for the module on the page. This will take you to a page that lists all the available profile properties. There are a number of properties defined by default within DNN, as shown in Figure 4-17.

Figure 4-17

From this page, you can control the sort order for the profile properties using the orange and green arrows. You can control whether a profile field is required, which means that a person can't update his or her profile without having a value in that field. You can also control whether profile fields should be visible. Flagging a profile attribute as not visible means that a user can't update the field, but it might be useful to have a field that administrators can make notes in about a user.

To add a profile property, use the Add New Profile Property option underneath the Actions menu for the module. The Add New Property page provides the fields listed in the following table.

**Profile Property Attributes**

| Field | Description |
|---|---|
| Property Name | The name of the profile property you are creating. This will be used for displaying on the profile entry page, unless it is overridden with a language value, which can be defined in the next step of the property creation process. |
| Data Type | The type of information this profile property will be storing. There are a number of types of data that can be stored for the profile properties, the most common would be Text or RichText. |
| Property Category | If you are grouping multiple profile properties, perhaps for team or company information, you can define a common category for these properties to be displayed on the profile management screen. |
| Length | If there is a maximum length that this property should use, you can configure that using this length setting. This will only apply to some of the data types. |
| Default Value | If the property should have a default value, you can configure that using this setting. This might be used to provide instructions or a sample value for users to better understand what they should enter. |
| Validation Expression | If you have regex (regular expression) that you would like to use to control the data that is entered for the property, you can define that information here. Regular expressions allow for restricting the amount and type of text that is entered into a field. |
| Required | This setting controls whether this field should be required in order to update the profile or not. |
| Visible | This setting defines if users should be able to see/manage this profile property, or if it should not be visible to users and only be visible to administrators. It is highly unlikely that you would ever have a field that is required and not visible. If you do, your users will not be able to update their profile unless an administrator has put information in the invisible field. |
| View Order | You can predefine the sort order for your profile property here. You can also change it after the property has been created, by using the sorting arrows on the page listing of the profile properties. |

After filling in the attribute information for a new profile property, you can click the Next link and move on to the next step in the process, the Manage Localization section. This localization step allows you to define some of the text associated with your newly created profile property. You can choose the text for the property name and the text for the help value (the text that would appear if you click on the question mark graphic next to your new property). You can also define the text to be displayed if the field is required, and if the field fails validation. If you don't want to define any of this information, you can simply skip this step by clicking on the Return to Profile Properties List link at the bottom of the module.

# Permissions

Before we get into actually creating a page and putting content on the page through the use of modules, we will cover DNN's permissions model, as it will apply to both Pages and Modules. As we've mentioned previously, DNN provides a powerful permissions model, allowing you to create content that is visible to all visitors of your website, limited to select roles (groups of users), and even specific to individual users. Beyond the ability to limit the viewing of content, you can delegate various responsibilities for your website to roles and users as necessary.

## *Permissions Grid*

When creating or editing pages on your site, or modifying the module settings, you will be presented with a permissions grid, as shown in Figure 4-18, in which you can control the permissions for the page or module. While it is possible for modules to modify the permissions grid to provide their own extended permissions functionality, you will always find at least View and Edit columns for the permissions.

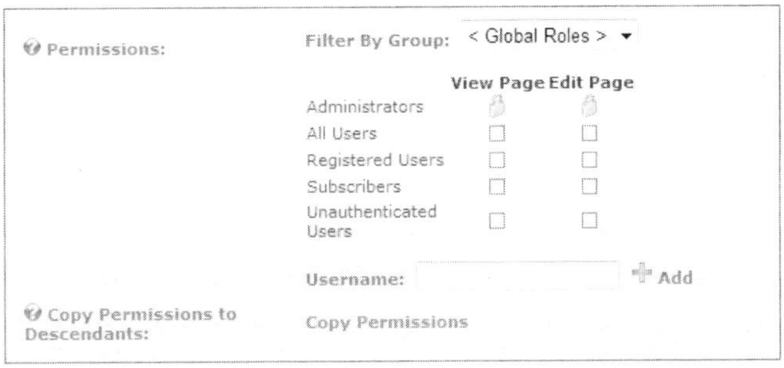

**Figure 4-18**

Using the check boxes in the permissions grid, you can provide the ability for specific roles to view or edit the item that the permission grid is for. In the first column of the grid, you will find the roles for which you can define permissions. You should see the three default roles that we looked at earlier in this chapter when we talked about roles, along with two additional options that were not on the Security Roles page. These two additional roles are All Users, and Unauthenticated users. All Users is anyone who is browsing your website, regardless of whether or not they are logged in to the website. Unauthenticated Users are anyone who is browsing the site that isn't logged in.

So with a combination of the roles available and the two permission columns, you can define if a particular role should be able to view or edit a page. This is done by checking the appropriate boxes. For example, if you wanted to configure the permissions so that All Users could view the page, and Registered Users could edit the page, your permissions grid might look like Figure 4-19.

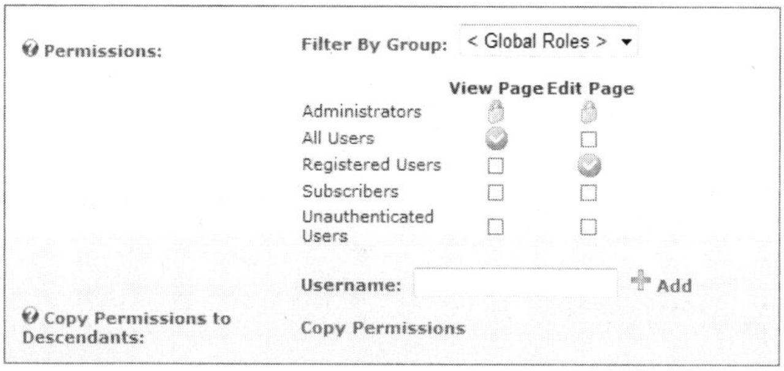

**Figure 4-19**

Beyond being able to give roles permissions, you can also provide individual permissions to a specific user through the Username text box at the bottom of the permissions grid. In this text box you can type in a specific username for a user on your website and then click on Add. This will add that user to the permissions grid. You might want to give an individual user rights to view or edit an item.

## Deny Permissions

A new feature in DotNetNuke 5 is the ability to deny access to view or edit an item either to a role or a specific user. A demonstration of the deny permissions is configuring the permissions grid to provide All Users with view rights to an item but then denying permissions to the Unauthenticated users role (see Figure 4-20). While this could easily be accomplished simply by providing the Registered Users with view rights and not all users, it does allow us to make a point. Deny permissions are superseding, meaning they override any other permissions. For example, if you set the view permission for All Users to deny, you would effectively create a module or page that wasn't visible to anyone except for the Super User/Host account. Not even the portal administrators would be able to access the item because the All Users role is denied access.

**Figure 4-20**

## Inherit View Permissions from Page

There is one difference between the permissions functionality for pages and for modules on a DNN website. Modules have the ability to inherit their view permissions from the page that they are on. This becomes useful in combination with the workflow, which is discussed in the next section. If you turn off the setting for Inherit View Permissions from Page, you can control the module's view permissions directly; otherwise, the view permissions will come from the page's view permissions. It can be useful as an administrator to make only certain modules on a page visible to normal users. You might add a module to a page and make it visible only to administrators or page editors so that you can provide instructions for the configuration of the content on the page. These instructions would be visible only to the editors, not to all visitors to the page.

## Workflow Permissions

Although DNN doesn't have a workflow model built in yet, it is possible to come up with your own workflow for adding content to your website. A common practice using the permissions grid is to first configure your content so that it is visible only to those roles that have edit rights to the content. That allows the proper users to edit the content and get it ready for displaying on the site. Once the content is correctly configured, you can go back to the permissions grid and make the content visible to those roles that should have view permissions for the content. This workflow approach can be applied to both pages and modules.

# Pages

The ability to create and manage pages easily is one of the biggest strengths of DNN. By applying permissions to these pages, you can control who can view and edit the pages, allowing site administrators to distribute some of the content management for a website to roles or individual users.

## Navigation

In DNN, pages are what control the navigation elements of your website. It is possible that some of your modules will have their own navigation structure as well but, in general, navigation is controlled by creating and organizing pages. It is possible to have a hierarchy to your navigation, and thus there's hierarchy functionality within the page system for DNN. The hierarchy is controlled by the notion of a parent page. You'll see more about the parent page option as we walk through the creation of a page, but each page can have a single parent selected. This makes the page a child, or submenu item in the navigation structure. An example of this is the Admin or Host menu in the default DNN installation. In DNN, there is a page called Admin and then there are multiple additional pages underneath the Admin page, all of which have Admin as their parent. The Admin and Host pages are unique in that, even though they are pages in the database, you can't actually click on them; they are simply placeholders in the Navigation hierarchy. You will see how to create disabled pages like these in the next section.

## Adding and Editing Pages

Creating pages in DNN is a straightforward process. You can go to the Pages item under the Admin menu in the navigation, or you can do it from the control panel. In general, we recommend creating pages from the control panel. Before we get into the process using that method, however, we will take a look at the Admin/Pages page. This page provides you with a module that lists the existing "tabs" or pages in your DNN site. Figure 4-21 shows the default pages in a clean DNN installation. From this module, you have the ability to change the order of the pages on your site using the Move Page functionality on the right side of the module. You can also choose a page from the list on the left and use the Actions options to edit (pencil), view (magnifying glass), or delete (red x) the selected page.

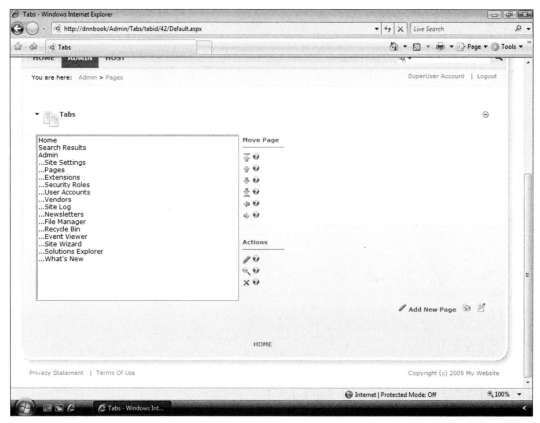

**Figure 4-21**

From the Actions menu for this Tabs module, select the Add New Page option. This will create a new page. When we start to look at the settings for this new page, you will see that the Admin page is selected as the parent, and the Pages page is selected as the Insert Page option. This causes the page to exist in the Admin menu of the site by default, which you don't want. So, rather than using the Add New Page function on the Admin/Pages option, navigate to the Home page of your website and use the control panel.

In the control panel, you will find a Page Functions section on the left. This enables you to create, edit, and delete pages, as well as copy and import/export pages from your DNN website. We won't get into the Import/Export functionality in this chapter, but we do provide some of that information in Chapter 8. The Copy page function allows you to create a new page with the modules from the existing page available as options for the new page. While this can be useful, you won't find it necessary in many cases, so we will simply walk through the Add page option.

## Page Settings

Whether you are creating a new page using the Add New Page function, or editing a page using the Edit function, you will find a common collection of Page Settings (see Figure 4-22). There are a few things in the Page Settings that will differ if you are creating or editing an existing page. We will cover those as we get to them.

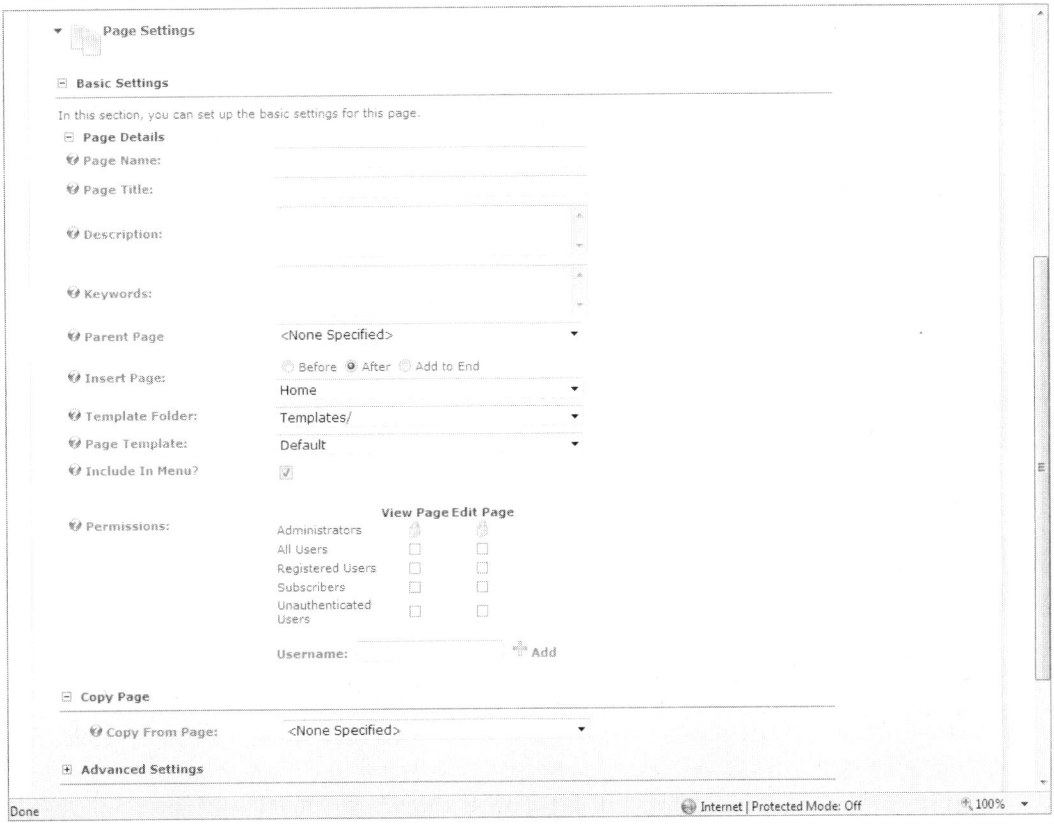

Figure 4-22

## Page Name

The Page Name setting controls what the name of the page will be. This will be used in quite a few different places. The first and most important location that the name will be used is in the navigation for your website. This is the value that will show up in the menu for your page. It will also be used in the URL for your web page. For example, if you were to create a page called BookPage, if you browse to the page, the URL would be http://dnnbook/BookPage/tabid/##/default.aspx, where ## would be the ID for the page in the database, with each page having its own unique ID. Another place the Page Name will be used is in the browser's title bar. For example, the Home page in your DNN site would show the browser title as My Website > Home, where My Website is your website name, and Home is the page name.

## Page Title

If you want to override the browser's title to make it something other than the default of Website Name > Page Name, you can provide a custom Page Title. This will simply replace all the previous text in the browser title and show only the defined Page Title. It is common to see DNN pages that have a short Page

Name for navigation purposes but a longer Page Title. The Page Title in conjunction with the next two settings is an important step in configuring your DNN pages to be better optimized for search engines.

## Description

As we discussed earlier in this chapter for the Site Settings Description, the page Description is an important aspect of search engine optimization. You can define a common description for all the pages on your DNN website in the Site Settings, and then you can override this common description with the description for individual pages. This allows you to better focus the page descriptions on the content on the page as opposed to the broader website description. A page description should be an overview of the main content on the page, using some of the main keywords that can be found in the content of the page. In some cases, a web page's description will be used as the search result description when a page is returned as a search result in one of the many popular search engines. You want to provide enough information to the user who is searching to convey what the page is about, without putting too much content into the description.

## Keywords

Like the Description and Title, Keywords are important elements whose use can improve search engine optimization for your pages. It is important to highlight some of the keywords from the content of your page here, although it is just as important not to overload the Keywords option with excess information that isn't relevant to the page. Keywords should be separated by commas to form a list for each page.

## Parent Page

The Parent Page setting, when creating a page, will be a drop-down list populated with all the pages on your website. This setting allows you to configure if the page you are creating, or editing, should be a child of another existing page. If so, you can choose that existing page from the drop-down list. It is possible to move your pages around later on to change the navigation hierarchy of your pages, so if you are unsure of where you want the page to existing, you don't have to decide immediately. The downfall of moving a page in the structure of your site is that the URL will be different, which can have a negative impact on SEO.

## Insert Page

New to DotNetNuke 5, the Insert Page option allows you to better control where a page goes within the order of pages at the same level in the hierarchy, either before, after the selected page, or if a page is not chosen at the end of the hierarchy. The before and after options allow you to choose if this page should go before or after the page selected in the drop-down list setting for the Insert Page option. Your page will go before or after whichever page is selected in the drop-down list. In previous versions of DNN, you could add pages, but they would always go to the end of the hierarchy for that level. You had to change the sort order on the Admin/Pages page.

## Template Folder (Add Page Only)

When creating a new page in DNN, you can choose a page template to base this page on. A page template is an XML file that contains information such as skin selection and which modules to use, from a previously exported DNN page. We talk more about templates in Chapter 8, but for the Template Folder option, you need to know that there is one template available out of the box in DNN. This template exists in the Templates folder, which is why that is the selection in the drop-down list for the setting. Depending on which folder you choose in this drop-down list, the next setting, Page Template, will be populated with whatever templates are available in the selected folder.

## Page Template (Add Page Only)

The Page Template setting is populated from the available templates in the folder chosen in the Template Folder setting. When creating a new page, you will likely see that the Default template is automatically chosen for you. This will install one module on your page when you are done configuring the page settings. The Default template installs a Text/HTML module on the page. If you get to the point where you are creating page templates, you will have the option of choosing whether to include the content for the modules on the page in the templates you create. The Text/HTML module in the Default template does not have any content associated with it. If you don't want to have any modules on your page upon creation, in the Page Template drop-down list you can simply choose None Specified. This will create an empty page for you.

## Include in Menu

It is very common to create pages for your DNN site that you don't want to show up in the navigation for the site. The Include in Menu setting allows you to create these pages by unchecking the option. This can be useful if you are creating a page that shouldn't be in the navigation but will be linked to from elsewhere on your website or, perhaps, linked to via an e-mail newsletter to your users. The important thing to remember when you create a page that isn't visible in the navigation is that you must somehow provide a link to it if you wish for your users to access the page. As an administrator you can view the page by finding it in the Admin/Pages listing and choosing the magnifying glass.

## Permissions

For information on the permissions grid, please review that section earlier in this chapter. One thing of note is that, by default, when you create a page, it will only be available to administrators until you configure the permissions for the page.

## Copy Permissions to Descendants (Edit Page Only)

When you are editing an existing page, you will see an additional option related to the permissions grid, the Copy Permissions to Descendants option. When you click on this link, all the permissions configured in the Permissions grid will be cascaded down to the child pages of this particular page. This will change any of the existing permissions on those pages to use the same permissions as this parent page. This function is very useful if you are changing the permissions of the parent page and want to apply these permissions to all the children, such as if you have a new hierarchy of pages that were not originally visible to the site's users because they were being configured, and now are ready for production use. The permissions can now be changed in one action, rather than having to modify the permissions for each page directly.

## Copy from Page (Add/Copy Page Only)

The Copy from Page functionality allows you to copy some or all of the modules from an existing page to your new page. This setting provides you a drop-down list populated with the existing pages in your website. Once you choose a page from this list, you will find a new setting called Specify Modules.

## Specify Modules (Only When Copy from Page Is Selected)

The Specify Modules setting allows you to select from the modules installed on an existing page, and copy those modules to your new page. You will be provided a list of modules from the page selected in the Copy From Page drop-down list, as shown in Figure 4-23. For each of the modules on the page, you can choose which of the modules you want to copy using the check box next to the name of the module. You can modify the name of the module that will populate the module's title on the new page. You can then choose from three options in the radio button list for how the content for that existing module should be handled on the new page. The following table describes what each of these options means.

### Copy Module Options

| Value | Description |
|---|---|
| New | This option will place a new module on your newly created page of the same type as the selected module. If you have a Text/HTML module that you're copying, it will place a new instance of the Text/HTML module on the page without any content defined. |
| Copy | The Copy option will place a new instance of a module on your new page but will copy the content of the module to your new page. As in our previous example, if you copy a Text/HTML module the Copy option will place a new Text/HTML module on the page, but this time it will bring over a copy of the content from the existing Text/HTML module. Any changes made to the content of the module after the page has been created will be unique to this page. |
| Reference | This option will take the existing module and place a reference to that module on the new page. This is similar to the Copy option, except in how the content of the module is handled. When copying by reference, the content on your new page is the exact same as the content on the previous page and it is also linked to that content. If you change the content on the original page, the content on the new page will change as well. The opposite is also true. If you change the content on the new page you will be changing the content on the original page. It is generally recommended *not* to use the Reference option when copying modules as it is not easy to discern copied modules after. |

### Copy Content Requires IPortable

When creating a page in DNN, you can copy the contents of an existing module to use on your page. You can choose New, Copy, or Reference for the individual modules. The Copy option will be enabled only if the module supports IPortable. IPortable is a programming interface within DNN that allows for modules to import and export content into an XML format for moving content around between modules, or even between websites. Not all modules will support IPortable.

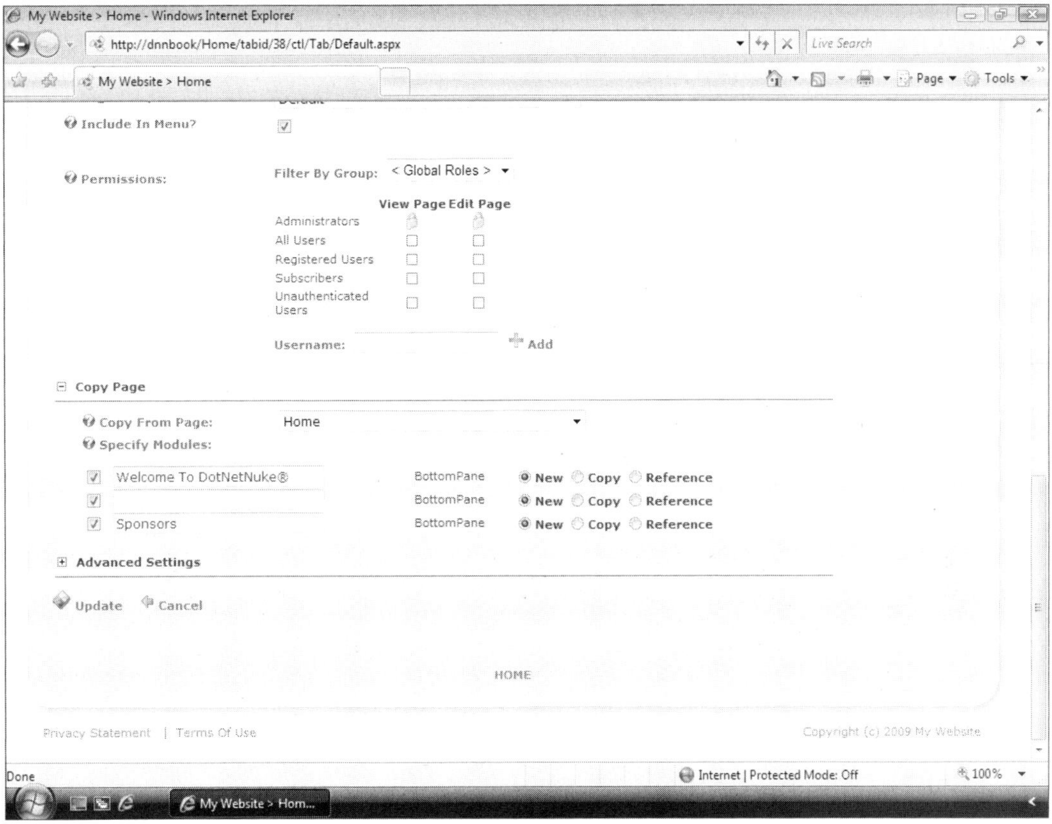

Figure 4-23

## Icon

The Icon setting for a page enables you to choose an icon for your new page that will be displayed to the left of the Page Name in the navigation menu. The best example of pages with icons can be found under the Admin or Host menu. The Icon setting, while flexible, can be a fairly dangerous setting to use, as it is very easy to choose an image for an icon that will drastically change the layout of your navigation items. DNN does not resize these images you choose as an icon, so if you choose a large image, you will get a large image displayed next to the text in the menu. It is not common to use the Icon setting for pages, unless you have a set of icons previously created by a designer fitting the dimensions of your navigation items.

The Icon setting provides you a file listing similar to that of the Logo setting on the Admin/Site Settings page, in which you can choose a folder and then from a list of files within that selected folder. New to DotNetNuke 5, there is also an option to choose a System Image. By selecting this option you will be provided with a drop-down list of images in the /Images folder, a collection of images that exist in the root of your DNN website. You aren't able to upload or delete images from this folder through the web browser, but you could access this folder from the file system if you want to modify some of these images.

## Page Skin/Container

The Page Skin and Container settings allow you to override the website's defined skin and container to apply a specific skin or container to individual pages. This functionality is extremely useful as you get into dealing with different types and layouts of content on your DNN pages. The interface for choosing a skin and container is exactly the same as it is on the Site Settings page. Refer to that section in this chapter for details.

## Disabled

The Disabled option allows you to create an item that will show up in the navigation but will not actually be a page that you or your website's visitors can browse to. The best example of this use is the Admin and Host menu items in the navigation. If you try to click on one of these pages, you will find that you can't; you can simply mouse over the modules to provide a listing of child pages underneath those pages.

Creating a page that is disabled allows you to define additional levels in your hierarchy without having to worry about creating content on these additional levels. It is extremely unlikely that you will ever create a page that you have marked as Disabled, and also not Include In Menu. This would effectively create a page that isn't in the navigation and isn't accessible at all.

## Refresh Interval (Seconds)

This option allows you to configure a predetermined amount of time, in seconds, in which the web browser should refresh the page you are creating. This can be useful in some cases, such as a page that is conveying constantly updating information, like a stock ticker, though it can be extremely annoying to users if you have a page with a large amount of content that is setup to refresh. Our recommendation is that you use this setting only in cases in which you must force a page to refresh consistently.

## Page Header Tags

The Page Header Tags setting allows you to insert HTML content in the HEAD tag of your page. This is useful if you want to include a custom stylesheet for this page or include a custom JavaScript file that is not included through other means. This setting is not something you will often use, but when you do need to add some HTML code into the HEAD tag, it is an effective and easy to use way to do so.

## Secure

The Secure setting should be enabled if you have SSL Enabled for your website and want this page to be secured. Enabling SSL for a page will force the page to be loaded via a secure connection, which can slow down load times as content must be encrypted and decrypted before the user can see it.

## Start Date / End Date

The Start Date and End Date settings are extremely useful settings that you will also see when we discuss Module Settings later in this chapter. These settings allow you to configure a timeframe that a page should be available on a DNN website. For example, if you want a page to be available on January 1st, 2010, you could configure the date for 1/1/2010. The page would then not show up on the website for normal users until then. This is useful for staging content to show up on the site without having to be online when you want to push the content live. You can also set an end date for a page. You don't have to put a start or an end date into the settings for your page.

### Link URL

The Link URL setting allows for some flexibility for the Navigation menu in DNN. Using the Link URL setting, you can create items in the navigation that don't link to new pages within DNN but link to a URL, a page, or a file. If you choose the URL option, you will be presented with a text box where you can type in an Internet address. You might type in an address to a file on your web server, or a totally separate website altogether. The Page option will provide you a list of pages in this DNN site, effectively allowing you to put an existing page in the Navigation hierarchy of your website twice, without having to duplicate the content. The File option provides you means to link to a file within your portal's file system.

### Permanently Redirect

The Permanently Redirect setting is a new feature in the latest builds of DNN that allows you to configure the Link URL options to use a 301 Redirect. This provides information to search engines about the location of pages and files, and which URL to use for those pages and files. If you are using the Link URL option with a setting other than None, it is recommended that you enable the Permanently Redirect option.

### *Page Completion*

Once you've configured all the options for your new DNN page, you can click on the Update link at the bottom of the page. This will save all the information into the database and you should be sent to your new page. If you created the page from the Add New Page function on the Admin/Pages option, you will likely be redirected back to that page, not to your new page.

Now that you have a new page created, you can start to deal with the content for your page and the modules that will reside on that page. The next section discusses the basics of modules and how to put them on a page and configure their settings.

# Modules

As we've mentioned a few times through the previous chapters, within DNN, modules provide the ability to add and maintain the content on the pages of your website. Chapter 1 provided a list of the modules that come with the packages of DNN. In this section, we will guide you with putting modules on a page and the basics of working with modules. The next three chapters actually walk you through using some of the specific modules.

# *Adding Modules to a Page*

We mentioned in the page creation process that you can copy modules from another page, but what if you want to install a module on a page that you have already created? This process is handled through the control panel (see Figure 4-24). The following tables describe each of the settings for this part of the panel, depending on whether you have selected Add New Module or Add Existing Module, respectively.

We have left out some of the duplicate settings in the table for adding an existing module, as these can be found in the table for adding a new module.

## Module Control Panel - Add New Module

| Setting | Description |
| --- | --- |
| Module | The Module drop-down list is populated with the modules available to your portal. You can choose any module in this list to place on the page. |
| Pane | The Pane drop-down list is populated with the panes that are available for your module on the current page. You can place the module in any of the available panes. As previously discussed, panes control the placement and layout of modules and can be customized by the skin that the page is using. Once a module is on the page, you can move it to another pane if you don't like the placement choice you made originally. |
| Title | The Title field is the module title. Depending on the container in use, the module title may or may not display. In general, the module title will be displayed at the top of the module above the content. This is also something that is commonly visible to users of your website, so making it relevant can be important. You can change the title at any time. |
| Insert | The Insert drop-down list is populated with two choices, Top or Bottom. Depending on if there are other modules in the pane you are adding this module to, you can choose if the module should be placed above all other modules or below the other modules in the pane. |
| Visibility | The Visibility drop-down list allows you to decide if the module should be visible only to users who have edit permissions to the page, or if the module should inherit the view permissions from the page (Same As Page). In most cases it is recommended that when you place a module on a page you choose the Page Editors Only option. This places the module on the page but makes it only visible to page editors so that you can configure the content of the module before making it visible to your website users. You can change the visibility through the permissions grid on the Module Settings, which we will cover later in this chapter. |
| Align | The Align drop-down list allows you to choose from Not Specified, Left, Center, and Right. We recommend that you leave this option as Not Specified and use the container or skin to make any alignment modifications to your modules. |

**Figure 4-24**

The Add Existing module functionality allows you to place a referenced copy of an existing module from another page in your portal onto the current page. Copying the module by reference means that if you change the content of the existing module, or the new module, both modules' content will change.

**Module Control Panel - Add Existing Module**

| Setting | Description |
| --- | --- |
| Page | This list is populated with the pages in your DNN website. You can choose one of these pages to populate the Module setting. |
| Module | This setting is populated with the modules available on the page selected in the previously described setting. |

Once you've decided how you are going to add a module to the page, either a new module, or an existing module, you can click on the Add button in the module section of the control panel. You should then see the newly added module in the pane you chose. If you have a lot of modules on the page already, you might need to scroll down to see the module. You can now configure the Module Settings for this module.

# Module Settings

You can access the Module Settings by moving your mouse over the module's Actions menu, which should be to the left of the module title, though the location of the Actions menu might be different if you are using a custom container. If you can't see the Actions menu, there are a few things to check. First, are you logged into the site with admin or editor rights? The second thing to check, and a very common problem, is that you are not in Edit mode. To check this, go back to the top of the page and look at the Mode options at the top of the control panel. Be sure to choose either the Edit or Layout modes. Once you've located the module's Actions menu, you should see a number of items listed in the menu. We are concerned with the Settings option. Clicking on this will take you to the Module Settings page (see Figure 4-25). On the Module Settings page, you will notice a number of collapsible sections to the page, Modules Settings, Page Settings, and, depending on the module you're configuring, a section specific to settings for that type of module.

## Basic Settings

The Basic Settings cover a number of the common elements of a module. Some of these are for information purposes, and others are actual settings that you can configure. You can change these settings at any time by navigating to a module's settings page.

### Module

The first option in the Basic Settings is not actually a setting, but it does provide you with the type of module that you are working with. It is not always easy to tell which type of modules are installed on a DNN page. By going to the module settings for a module, you can look here at the Module section to figure out what type a specific module is.

### Module Title

The Module Title was entered when the module was placed on the page. This information is displayed through the title portion of the container and should generally convey some message to the user about what the content within that module is providing. You can remove the module title if you don't wish to display the information, though this can cause you trouble when using the Recycle Bin or the Copy Modules from Page functionality, as you won't be able to discern which module is which if you don't have a title defined. You can also edit the Module Title inline using the inline edit capabilities of DNN. When viewing a DNN page in Edit mode, if you move your mouse over a module title, you should notice that a pencil icon appears. Click on this icon to go into the inline edit mode and make changes. You can either save those changes or cancel those changes using the toolbar that appears when in inline edit mode.

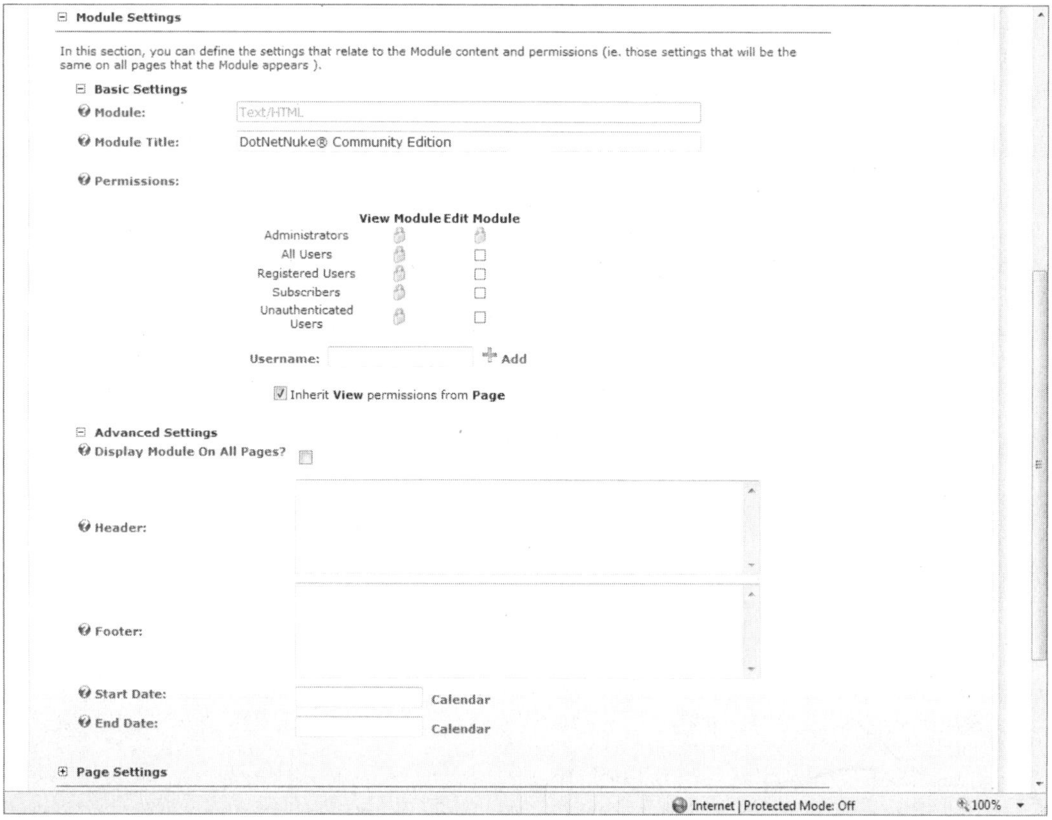

Figure 4-25

## Permissions

The permissions grid on the module settings page is similar to that of the page permissions and the permissions grid we discussed earlier in the chapter. The difference between the page permissions and the module permissions is the Inherit View Permissions From Page option available to the modules. This makes configuring the view permissions easy, as checking this option will have DNN lock down the individual view permissions in the grid and inherit whatever view permissions are at the page level.

## *Advanced Settings*

The Advanced Settings section for the module settings page allows you to configure additional functionality such as if a module should be displayed on all pages, header and footer information, as well as a start and end date for the module.

### Display Module On All Pages

The Display Module On All Pages option will do exactly what its name implies. While this might sound great at first, there are a few things to keep in mind if you want to display the same module on all pages.

- ❑    If the content is edited on one page, it will be edited on all pages.

- ❑    The module will display in the pane with the same name as the original module is placed. If that pane doesn't exist on a page, the module will be placed in the ContentPane. This might not be something you want to have happen.

- ❑    To remove the module from a single page, you can use the Delete item in the Actions menu. To remove the module from all pages, you must go to the module settings and uncheck the Display On All Pages option, and then delete the module from the current page.

### Header/Footer

The Header and Footer settings allow you to enter text that will show up before and after the content of your module. It is not very common that you will need to use these settings, but you can use these settings to wrap your module's content with custom HTML code.

### Start Date/End Date

As with the Page Settings, you can control when a module appears and ceases to appear to all users by applying Start Date and End Date settings.

## Page Settings

The Page Settings section provides some of the settings that apply design constraints to a module, such as the container, icon, and various other settings.

### Icon

The Icon setting provides similar functionality to the Icon setting for a page. The difference between a page icon and a module icon, however, is where the icon is displayed. On the module settings page, if you look just below the navigation and breadcrumb section of your page, you'll see a Module Actions Menu, an image, and then a module title of Module. The image there is the icon for the Module Settings controls. If you choose to implement an icon for your module, it will be visible in a similar location on the display portion of your module. This is assuming that the container you are using provides support for the icon, as the default containers for DNN do. Not all containers will do so.

### Alignment

The Alignment option correlates with the setting found in the control panel when adding the module to the page. It will likely be set to Left or Not Specified. We recommend that you leave the Alignment setting alone and let your container or skin control the alignment of the module.

### Color and Border

The Color and Border settings are holdovers from the early days of DNN when there were no containers to wrap around your modules. In those days you could control the background of your module with the Color setting, typing in the name of a color or the hexadecimal value of the color. For example, #FF0000 is the code for red. The border would also be defined using the Border setting. It is not recommended that you use either of these settings, as your container should define any styling for the wrapper around your module.

## Visibility

The default containers within DNN provide the ability for users to expand and collapse content on a page. This module setting provides the value for what the module should default to, expanded, collapsed, or none, meaning that the expand/collapse functionality is disabled. This is yet another setting that not all containers will support.

## Display Container

The Display Container setting is another easily confused setting within DNN. This setting will turn off the container for the module on the page. This can be useful in cases where you don't want to display a container around your module, and don't need a module title or actions to display to regular users visiting your website. The confusion comes along when a page editor turns off the container and updates the settings, but then when they view the page the container is still displayed. This occurs because when in edit or layout mode the container will always display for someone who has edit rights to a module. This is necessary because without the container you wouldn't have access to the module's Actions menu, and the Actions menu provides all the administrative functionality. To preview what the page looks like without the container being displayed, you can change to View mode.

## Allow Print

DNN provides the ability for a printer-friendly view of modules. When a user clicks on a printer-friendly link, the content from that module will be loaded in a popup window with no skin or container applied to the module. You can turn off this functionality for a module here in the module settings.

## Allow Syndicate

The Allow Syndicate setting is useful for modules that implement the ISearchable interface, meaning their content can be indexed by DNN on a scheduled basis. Part of this interface also allows for content to provide a syndicatable RSS feed. Not all modules will support this functionality. For those that do, by using this setting, you can choose if individual modules should provide RSS links for their content. In a lot of cases, modules will define and provide their own RSS links, separate from this Allow Syndicate functionality.

## Is a WebSlice

In the most recent release of Internet Explorer, IE8, Microsoft has added support for WebSlices, providing the ability for users to subscribe to portions of content on web pages. DNN has added WebSlice support at the module level, trying to get an early lead on this upcoming functionality.

## Module Container

The Module Container setting allows you to choose a specific container for this module. Containers are defined by default at the portal level. They can be overridden at the page level, and then once again at the individual module level. If you don't choose a container in the module settings, it will either use the default page container, or if not defined there either, the default portal container. Customizing a module's individual containers is common within DNN websites to differentiate a module's content from other content on a page. The interface for choosing a container is the same as we've seen previously, allowing you to choose either a host-level or site-level container from the drop-down list.

## Cache Time

DNN provides a performance enhancement to its content called *caching*. Caching is a procedure in which the content for a module is stored in memory on the server between web requests, rather than pulled from the database every time a request for a page is made. Modules have their own default cache times defined on the Extensions page for each module. You can override the cache time for modules on a page at the module settings level, though some modules will disable this altogether. This is generally not necessary and in some cases can cause problems with the functionality of specific modules.

## Set As Default Settings

If you have configured the module with settings that you would like all new modules on your site to use, you can check the Set As Default Settings option under the Advanced Settings section. This will make the settings above be the default settings for all new modules.

## Apply To All Modules

If you have configured the module with settings that you would like all modules on your site to use, you can check the Apply To All Modules option under the Advanced Settings section. This will make the settings above be the default settings for all the modules on your DNN portal. This can be useful if you are changing the overall theme of your website and want to change everything with ease. In most cases you will only use this setting when you are initially configuring a site and the number of modules and settings affected is small.

## Move to Page

If you would like to move a module from the current page to another page on your website, you can use the Move To Page option under the Advanced Settings section. This provides a list of all the pages on your website. You can simply choose the page you would like to move the module to and update the settings. The module will move to the new page in the same pane as it currently resides. If that pane doesn't exist on the skin for the other page, the module will be placed in the ContentPane.

## *Module-Specific Settings*

It is possible for each module to have its own specific settings. For some modules, but not all, these settings will be controlled via the Module Settings page after all the standard settings we just reviewed. Other modules may provide their own settings page, usually found through the Actions menu for the module. Where you have to look for the settings for a module will vary, but in general you should find most modules will use the Module Settings page for their configuration of settings. Content, on the other hand, is a totally different story! We will hit on content in the next section.

# *Managing a Module*

Once you have the Module Settings configured for a module, you can work on managing the module in other ways. This section will cover some of the basics of managing the modules, providing instruction on how to move the module to a different pane on your page, as well as how to access the edit functionality for modules.

## *Moving Modules on a Page*

Moving a module on a page is pretty easy to do. You can perform this action in either Edit or Layout mode. Switching to Layout mode makes it easier for you to see the panes available on the page and what modules are in those panes without having to see all the content. You can access a Move option in the Actions menu for the module you would like to move. You can move a module up or down within the current pane, in relation to the other modules on the pane. You can also choose a different pane on the page. You should see all the available panes listed there beneath the Move navigation item, as shown in Figure 4-26.

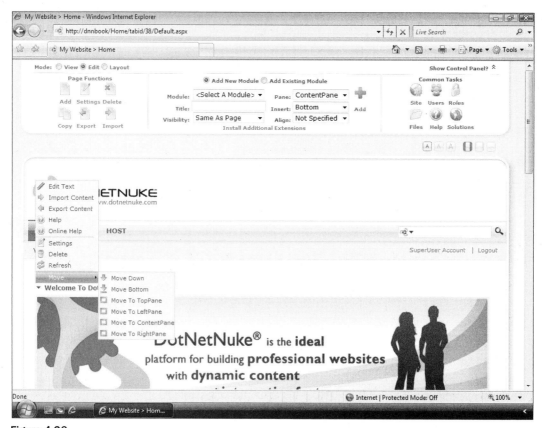

Figure 4-26

## Deleting Modules from a Page

To remove a module from a page, you can access the Delete action from the module's Actions menu. You can also go to the Module Settings for a module and use the Delete link at the end of the page. When a module or page is deleted, it is sent to the DNN Recycle Bin. We cover the Recycle Bin in more detail in Chapter 8.

## Working with Module Content

Working with module content will vary by module, but in general the administrative tools for this will be accessible from the Actions menu for the module. One of the most commonly used modules on any DNN website is the Text/HTML module, which provides basic text and HTML editing through a WYSIWYG (what you see is what you get), rich text editor. To edit the content of a Text/HTML module, you can mouse over the Actions menu for the module and choose the Edit Text link. This should take you to a page that looks similar to Figure 4-27.

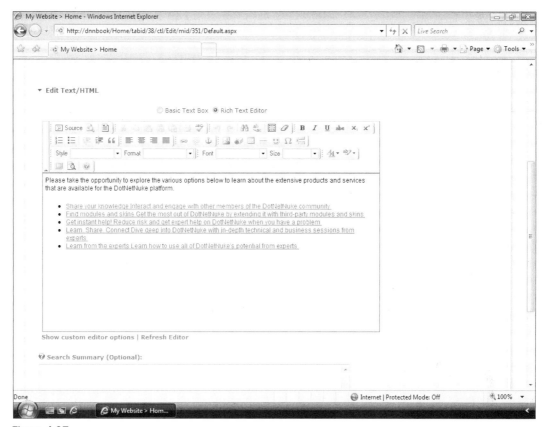

**Figure 4-27**

The Text/HTML module uses the standard Text Editor provider for DNN. We discuss providers in a bit more detail in Chapter 8, but what this means is that out of the box DNN provides you an editor using a tool called FCK Editor, a popular open source editing application. The FCK Editor provides you with a what you see is what you get interface (WYSIWYG), Microsoft Word-like appearance, allowing you to easily enter and format content. The editor allows you to add images, tables, and hyperlinks through the toolbars above the text area. You can even switch to a Source view, which will display the formatted HTML content if you want to work directly with the HTML code for the content.

When you are done editing your content, click on the Update button. DNN will store the changed content back into the database and return you to the previous page, displaying your changed content. You can edit the text as many times as you wish, though the module is limited in that each change overwrites the previous change. There is no versioning or approval workflow built into the module.

Other modules will provide similar functionality, some using the text editor, some not, some allowing you to upload images, others providing you the ability to create forms or surveys. Each module will differ in how the content is managed, but you will start to see as you work with modules they are all similar in many ways.

# Summary

This chapter described the basic administrative functionality required to configure a DNN website. After setting up the Site Settings for your website, you can create security roles and users to put in those roles. You can also now create pages and put modules on those pages. The next few chapters will walk you through some common website scenarios, configuring pages and modules to fit the needs of these scenarios.

# Creating Your Personal Site

Your reasons for creating a personal site may be just that — personal. A personal website is a place for you to write about yourself. It can be a way to tell your visitors about your thoughts, ideas, interests, hobbies, friends, family, pets, or other topics of which you're fond. It may be a way to communicate with friends and family. Your personal site may be a way for you to collaborate with others of like interests. It may be a way to publicize your personal or professional accomplishments.

Whatever your intent may be, your site should be easy to maintain and fun to keep current, and DotNetNuke (DNN) provides the tools to do just that. This chapter is an extensive guide to creating and configuring a personal site using DNN.

This chapter discusses the following topics:

- ❑ The goals and audience for your personal site
- ❑ The basic site settings to get your personal site up and running
- ❑ How to build a site map, complete with the Text/HTML, Links, News Feed (RSS), Blog, and Gallery modules
- ❑ Some of the fundamental module settings to make administering content easy

## Planning for Your Personal Site

Planning your site prior to building your content is important for websites of any size. Planning will give your website direction and focus. Well-planned websites are rarely noticed, but poorly planned websites are always noticed, for the wrong reasons. Frustrating navigation, hard to find content, broken links, and sloppy styles are all symptoms of poor planning. Although DNN enables you to make changes to your content as often as you like, a little initial planning will make administering your site simple and perhaps even fun.

When planning for a personal site, ask yourself questions such as "What are my goals for the site?" and "Who is my intended audience?" Organizing the content of your website is similar to preparing for a presentation or sending an important memo. Properly identify your purpose and audience, and the content will follow. Using the answers to these questions as the guide for your site's structure, content creation, and ongoing maintenance will help you to keep your site relevant and poignant.

## Goals for Your Personal Site

Before you start planning your personal website, it is important to establish the goals for your site. In the case of most personal websites, your site will give you a way to make your mark on the Web. As the use of the Internet increasingly occupies our daily lives, it can feel like our Web presence is uncontrollable. How many e-mail addresses have you had over the past 10 years? How many social profiles have you established and then not kept current? As personal data collection and storage via the Internet increases, and as social profiles through social networking sites rise, it can be difficult to reign in your online presence. A personal website can be a way for you to manage and control who you are on the Web. It can also give your friends and family an easy way to keep in touch with you.

Building an online presence, keeping in touch with your friends and family, and aggregating your social profiles on the web are all rooted in the goal to inform your site's visitors. Other goals for a website may include monetizing an idea or product, growing a following or online community, or instruction on a topic on which you're an expert. For the purposes for this chapter, assume that the primary goal of your personal site is to inform your visitors about who you are. In later chapters, we'll look at sites with different goals.

## Who Is Your Audience?

With the benefits of a personal site identified and a goal defined, the next consideration for your site is who will be your intended audience? The audience of your website will dictate the decisions you make, ranging from the content you create to the site settings you select.

If the goal of your site is to inform your visitors about who you are, your audience will most likely be friends and family. If you find a niche on the Web for your site, your audience might grow and the demographics might change. But to start, plan to address friends and family and hope to make more friends as your site gains popularity. With this in mind, you'll want to make your site welcoming, informal, and familiar.

# Essential DNN Setup for a Personal Site

The required setup in DNN to get any type of website live is minimal. As discussed in previous chapters, the flexibility and features for your site can be seemingly endless, but the setup to get your site workable can be fairly straightforward. In this section, we'll review the necessary setup to get your personal website live. After you've set up your site with these settings, you should be able to "run with it."

## Basic Site Settings

At site creation, the Site Administrator and Site Title were defined for your website. These two decisions were the only required elements to create your site, but there are a number of other Site Settings you should consider to start building your website with a good foundation. As with most of the settings in DNN, you can change these settings later, but this setup will help you initially lay the groundwork for your site. Figure 5-1 shows the Basic Settings available for your site. Next, we'll review some of the considerations for these settings to help you understand their importance in creating your website. You can access these settings either through the Admin menu in Site Settings or through the Control Panel using the Settings icon.

Figure 5-1

## Giving Your Site a Meaningful Title

As previously mentioned, the title for your site is required at inception. If you installed DNN yourself, you may have defined the title for your site yourself. If you had someone else create your site, the title was probably defined for you. Either way, it is important to give thought to the title of your site. The title of your site will be displayed in a number of places: in the browser's title bar, as a tooltip for your site logo, and as the default title for your site in external search engines.

Your domain name and site title are like the name you put on the welcome mat at your home. You're not going to want a welcome mat that says "Our House." Visitors to your house are going feel more welcomed and confident they have the right address if your welcome mat says, "Welcome to The Smiths." Just giving your site a title of "My Website" won't tell visitors and search engines much about your site. Pick a title that tells your visitors about the content on your site and welcomes them to it.

---

**Search Engine Result Titles**

Often, site administrators overlook the importance of explicitly defining a title for their site and pages. The title for your site will be a fallback search engine result title for all pages on your site that lack a title. To improve your search engine results, your site and page titles should be descriptive of the content on your sites and pages, and unique from page to page.

---

For a personal site, it will be important to define a title unique to you. You could include your first and last name, your city and state or country, or a unique nickname in the title of your site to specifically identify this site as yours.

## Establishing a Description and Keywords

Like the site title, the site description helps specifically define the description provided in search results in search engines. You'll want to describe your site in full sentences that explain some of the content visitors will find on your site. Again, you will want to include information about yourself to explain how your content is "uniquely you."

The keywords will reinforce the title and description provided for your site. Keywords give you the chance to highlight the words visitors might use to search for your site. More importantly the keywords will provide a reference point for the content of your site. Provide keywords that emphasize the key terms used in your title, your description, and some of the content on your site.

# Identifying Your Users in DNN

You have identified the intended audience of your site, but DNN also allows you to restrict content to users with the appropriate permissions. By utilizing user registration, you'll be able to control your site's content with permissions and also uniquely identify your visitors.

Tracking the visitors to your site can be accomplished with tracking tools like Google Analytics and Smarter Stats, and the most identifying characteristic these tools can provide to you is the visitors' IP address. This is more than enough information for understanding your site's traffic, but for some functions on your site you may wish to uniquely identify and authenticate your visitors.

For a personal site, requiring visitors to authenticate or identify themselves is more than likely overkill. There are, however, a number of reasons to give visitors the opportunity to log in and authenticate themselves with the site. Later in the chapter, as you build the content for your site, you'll see a number of configuration options that allow you to require visitors to log in to do things like post comments on your blog or respond to surveys.

In addition to the features and functionality provided by site membership, users and permissions can be used to distribute content management responsibilities. By default, DNN created an administrator and super user, or Host, account on your site. For a personal site, these two users may be the only accounts you'll need to manage the content of your site. Next, we'll review some of the specific users you'll want on your site and discuss the considerations for using these accounts to manage content and communicate with visitors to your site.

## *Who Is the Administrator?*

Since an Administrator account is required to create your site, you're assured to have at least one Administrator account on your site. This account is sufficient to perform all administrative functions on your site. As a result, a common mistake people new to DNN make is to assume that the account created with the site is their personal user account. DNN allows you to create numerous users with Administrator rights, but one user will need to be defined as the Site Administrator. This user account is tied to a number of functions within your site. As you begin to manage your site, it is important to understand these functions and decide whether you want your personal account to be the Site Administrator — the primary administrator.

If you choose to use the Administrator account as your personal account, you should change the First, Last, and Display name for the account to give the account more personality. Have you ever visited a site and seen content attributed to "admin" or "superuser?" On a personal site, more than likely you'll want to personalize and take credit for your content.

Another option is to create an additional account for yourself and assign this account Administrator rights. By doing this, you maintain a generic Administrator account and your personal account with your name and e-mail still has full administrative rights. The benefit of maintaining a generic Administrator account is that you can identify this account as the primary Administrator. DNN associates a number of responsibilities with the primary Administrator account. The site Administrator is the e-mail tied to password reminders and other system-generated e-mails.

In the Advanced Settings section of Site Settings, you should define an account as the Administrator for your site. Figure 5-2 illustrates the location of this setting. You should decide early whether you want your users to know you personally as the site administrator or whether you want to keep the administrator tasks anonymous and tied to a generic account.

## *Site Membership*

DNN allows you to manage the user membership to your site in a few different ways. Figure 5-3 shows the various options for site registration. The User Registration settings are the first option available in the Advanced Settings of your Site Settings. On a personal site, Public or Verified registration will most likely fit your needs. Public or Verified registration allows users to become members of your site, but the administrative burden is on you to manage users as they register on your site.

# *Establishing the Appearance of Your Site*

The design and layout of your site can determine the function, format, and implementation of your content, but luckily, in DNN, these decisions can be easily modified later if you change your preferences. By identifying some of the design elements of your site, you'll be able to shape the way you implement your initial content and plan for future content.

In DNN, skins determine a vast majority of the design elements on your site. Skins can control the layout of your content, generate dynamic content, and include graphic elements. Knowing the intimate details of the skin development process isn't necessary for choosing a design and layout for your content. Understanding how these elements function on a DNN site, however, will help you to manage your content and utilize fully the dynamic content provided by DNN.

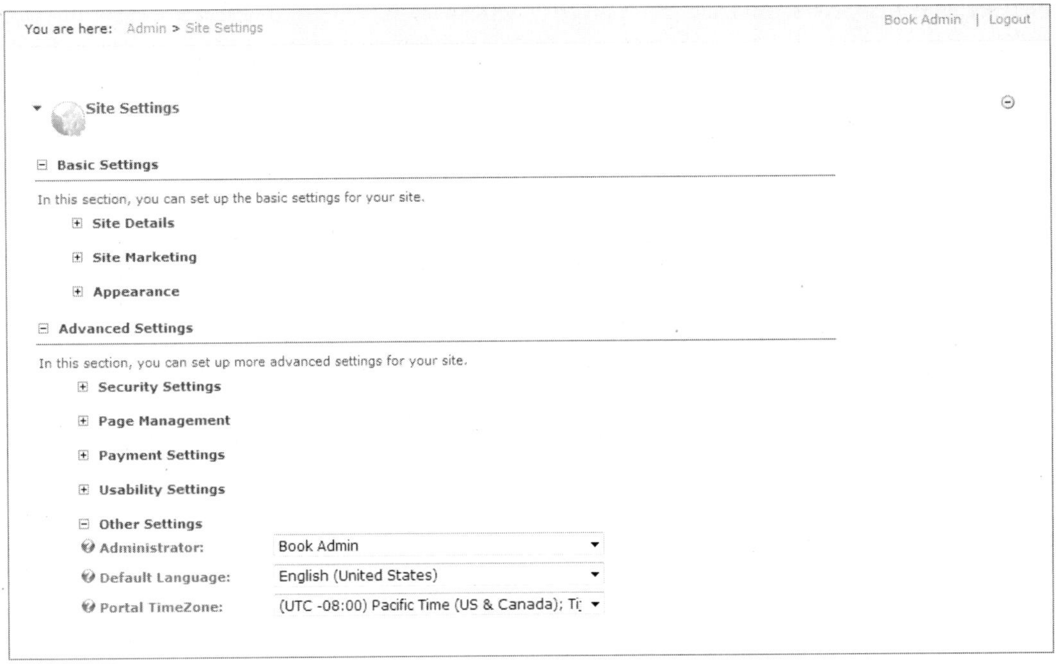

▾ 🌐 Site Settings                                                    ⊖

⊟ **Basic Settings**

In this section, you can set up the basic settings for your site.

  ⊞ **Site Details**

  ⊞ **Site Marketing**

  ⊞ **Appearance**

⊟ **Advanced Settings**

In this section, you can set up more advanced settings for your site.

  ⊞ **Security Settings**

  ⊞ **Page Management**

  ⊞ **Payment Settings**

  ⊞ **Usability Settings**

  ⊟ **Other Settings**
  ❷ Administrator:        Book Admin                          ▾
  ❷ Default Language:     English (United States)             ▾
  ❷ Portal TimeZone:      (UTC -08:00) Pacific Time (US & Canada); Ti ▾

**Figure 5-2**

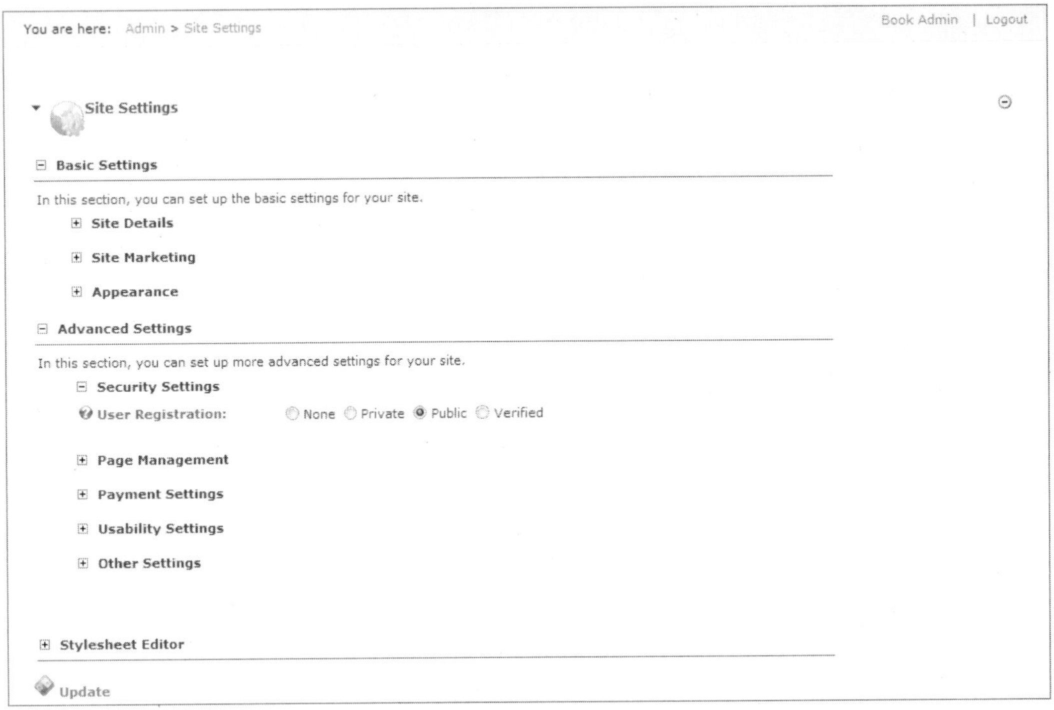

▾ 🌐 Site Settings                                                    ⊖

⊟ **Basic Settings**

In this section, you can set up the basic settings for your site.

  ⊞ **Site Details**

  ⊞ **Site Marketing**

  ⊞ **Appearance**

⊟ **Advanced Settings**

In this section, you can set up more advanced settings for your site.

  ⊟ **Security Settings**
  ❷ User Registration:    ◯ None  ◯ Private  ◉ Public  ◯ Verified

  ⊞ **Page Management**

  ⊞ **Payment Settings**

  ⊞ **Usability Settings**

  ⊞ **Other Settings**

⊞ **Stylesheet Editor**

❖ Update

**Figure 5-3**

Since DNN is installed with a default skin and container named MinimalExtropy, we'll use them for our examples going forward. By building content using the default skin, you'll get your site up and running quickly. By understanding the features included in the default skin, you'll be able to make decisions about commercial or custom skin packages, which you can implement later. The MinimalExtropy skins and containers may not be the ideal design and layout for your personal site, but understanding the basic functions in relation to the default skin will make applying a new skin a breeze.

---

### Applying New Skins After Creating Content

You can easily build your site content with MinimalExtropy as your default skin. If later you want to use another skin on your pages, all the modules on your page will default to the "ContentPane" if the new skin does not have the same pane titles.

If, and likely when, this is the case, your site is not lost. You can rearrange modules on the page easily by using the Move activity in the modules' Actions menu.

---

## Skin Design Considerations

The design considerations for a personal site will primarily include the panes in which you place your modules, the organization of your modules within a pane, the dynamically generated content your skin provides, and the page structure and navigation for your site. The MinimalExtropy skin gives you a fairly generic design that allows for a one-size-fits-all site. We'll review the default skin in terms of how it can be used in our personal site. By doing this, you should gain an understanding of the elements you'll want to look for in a commercial or custom skin.

As illustrated in Figure 5-4, some of the design elements included in MinimalExtropy are as follows:

❑ The layout is a basic three column layout with two, full-width panes above and below the three columns. In your personal site, you'll use the ContentPane for the primary content, and the Left-Pane and RightPane for supporting or related content (favorite links, blog archives).

❑ Navigation is horizontal with drop-down child menus. The horizontal navigation works well because the page structure in a personal site is typically flat (meaning that you won't have numerous levels of sub-navigation pages).

❑ The default skin uses the following tokens to create the following dynamic content: Logo, Search, User, Login, Breadcrumb, Links, Privacy, Terms, and Copyright. The use of dynamic content can help maintain consistency throughout your pages. As you evaluate MinimalExtropy, determine which of these tokens you want to use in a new skin.

*Tokens, more recently referred to as "skin objects," are placeholders used in the markup (HTML) of your skins to display dynamically generated content.*

## Container Design Considerations

The containers used on your site also determine some of the form and function of your content. Since containers wrap the content on your site, they add an additional design element to your pages. Containers can help to segregate content on a page or to call out important information. However, the use of too many different containers can create a boxy appearance on your pages.

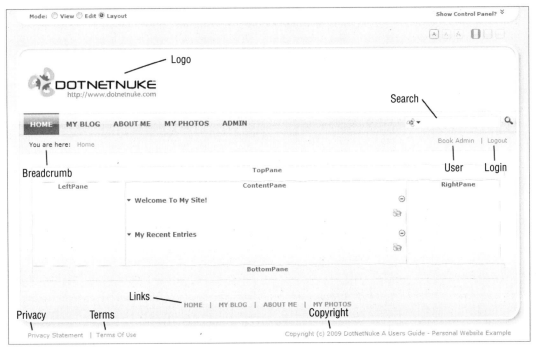

**Figure 5-4**

The containers on your page also control the function of your content in some aspects. Containers can implement activities useful for both the content administrators and the site visitors.

To demonstrate this, the MinimalExtropy containers provide the following functions and design elements (see Figure 5-5):

❑ **Title:** The container provides a title for your modules. This title is generated by the title you give the module upon adding it to the page and can be edited in the Module Settings.

---

### Module Title Appearance

The title is wrapped in a `.Head` class. If you aren't familiar with CSS, this might not mean anything to you. The good news is DNN doesn't prevent you from creating your site if you don't know what this means. What you should know is that the container title will adhere to the same styles of other modules or content using `.Head` to classify the content.

---

❑ The Actions menu is placed in the top-left corner of the container. This is the most common placement for the Actions menu.

❑ The Visibility token is used in the top-right corner of the container. This gives your visitors the ability to minimize or maximize the content placed in this container. If you prefer not to use this feature, you can override this in the Advanced Settings of the module.

❑    At the bottom of the module, the action buttons are displayed. These are some the same elements found in the action menu but made visible to the module editor when in edit mode. Additionally, your site visitors will see the Print icon. Like the Visibility function, you, as the site administrator, can override this feature and turn it off through the Advanced Settings of the module.

Figure 5-5

As you evaluate commercial skin packages, look for containers that display the elements of the Actions menu in the container. This functionality will allow you to easily administer content without using the Actions menu. Additionally, containers can offer your site visitors functionality like printing the content of the module and subscribing to syndicated content.

Another thing to note about the content provided in the container is the use of the title. The container title can act as a headline for each section of content on your site. If you're used to creating static HTML content, a common mistake is to hide the container title and use headings in your HTML to achieve titles for your content. By using the container title, you'll be able to easily refer to content from other pages when copying modules and their content to other sections of your site.

## Choosing the Default Skin and Container

Choosing the default skin and container for your site wisely can significantly ease the setup you need to do when creating pages and modules. For most sites, the default skin should be the layout and design used most frequently on your site. By choosing the most frequently used skin as your default, you'll need to only explicitly specify a skin on those pages on which you wish to override the default skin. Since the default DNN skin package comes with the single skin, "MinimalExtropy," choosing a specific skin as your default may not be as necessary as choosing the panes you'll use to administer your content. As you use other skin packages, choosing a skin as the default will become more important to you as the administrator. Figure 5-6 illustrates the settings for choosing a default skin for your portal.

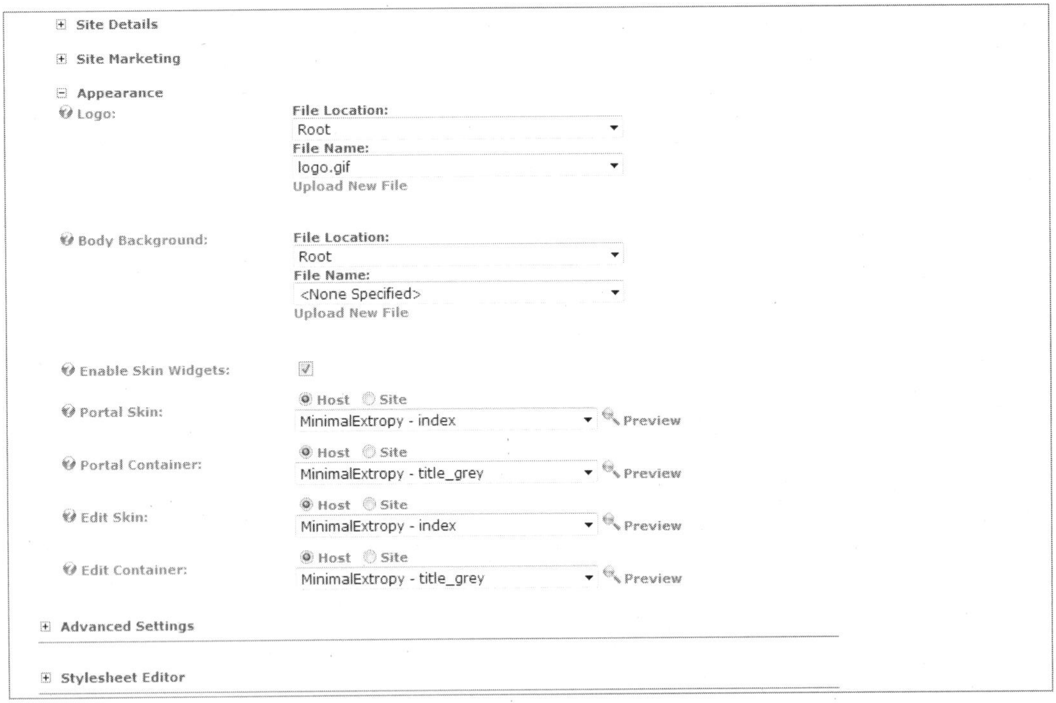

Figure 5-6

DNN also enables you to choose an admin skin and container. This feature allows you to define a skin specifically for admin functions. You'll see the admin skin when you're in site or module settings. The logical choice for the admin skin and container are the skin/container combination, which offers the most real estate for administrative actions.

## *Organizing the File System*

For a personal site, you'll have files to distribute to your visitors or to reference in your content. It's important that you organize the file system in a logical manner as you create references on your pages. Starting with an initial folder structure will help you later, because each time you restructure the organization of your files, you will need to adjust the references to these files on your site.

The most logical way to organize files is by type. Create folders for documents, images, and media. You can add more folders or subfolders later, but this will be a good start for now. As shown in Figure 5-7, we have created an initial folder structure in the File Manager to organize the files by type. Administrators can access the File Manager through the Files action in the Control Panel or through the Admin menu. In addition to the three folders we just created, there are two folders created by DNN: Cache and Templates.

These folders are used by other tools in DNN and won't affect the organization of the files you place in the File Manager.

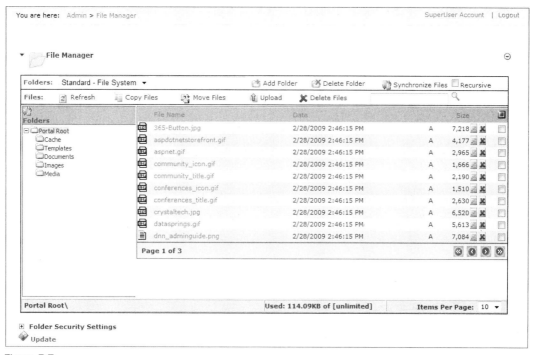

Figure 5-7

# Page Creation and Content Organization

The content of your site will drive the functionality required for your site. As a guiding rule, it is best to keep your content simple and add sophistication where you find it necessary. It is easy to be enticed by the long list of modules available with the core DNN package; it is also easy to overcomplicate your site by getting lost in "settings overload."

When planning for the content of your site, start with a set of modules you're comfortable with administering, use one or two skins, and build a few top-level pages. Once you have a strong foundation for your site, you can add sophistication and complexity.

An easy place to start in building your site is to plan the page structure, more commonly referred to as the *sitemap*. As you list the pages and the order of your pages, you can follow up and add in design, content, and advanced features to meet each page's needs. First, consider the potential sitemap shown in Figure 5-8.

As discussed earlier in the chapter, a personal site typically has a flat navigation structure. The sitemap shown in Figure 5-8 has four pages, all residing at the root, or first, level. You may find additional pages you want to create as you build out your site, but to start simply, work through each of these pages.

| **Home**<br>Welcome Message<br>Recent Blog Entries<br>Orientation to the Site | **My Blog**<br>Recent Entries<br>Full Entry Detail<br>Archive, Search, and List | **About Me**<br>Text about Me<br>Links to Friends | **My Photos**<br>Photo Galleries |
| --- | --- | --- | --- |

**Figure 5-8**

---

### Keeping Your Content Hidden Before It's Ready

All the content in this chapter's examples is "live," meaning that it is visible to all users. You may find it useful to keep your pages visible to only Administrators until you are ready to launch your site.

---

The default portal template used upon the creation of your site will start you with a Home page. Add pages for each of the pages included in Figure 5-8. The following sections will review each page individually and review some of the content management options you should consider as you build your site. At the end of the chapter, you will have a site ready to go live, with modules you should feel comfortable using on a personal website. Figure 5-8 hints at the kind of content that each page will contain. The modules used for this content and functionality will be touched on briefly in the context of creating these pages, then the settings for the suggested modules will be reviewed in more detail.

---

### Locating the Core Modules

As we build the content for the pages in our sitemap, you might notice that the modules available on your site differ from the modules used in our content creation. There are three types of core modules in DNN: installed, available, and project.

❑ Installed modules are modules that are automatically installed with your instance of DNN. To use these modules, no installation is required, but they must be available to your portal. Examples of installed modules include the Text/HTML and Links modules.

❑ Available (but not installed) modules are included with the installation package of DNN but need to be loaded in your instance. To use these modules, a host account must install the modules from the Batch Install Extensions page. Examples of available modules include the Blog, Announcements, and Events modules.

❑ Other available modules are modules developed by volunteers in the DNN community and conform to the high standards of the DotNetNuke Corporation, but they are not installed by default with your instance of DNN. To use these modules, you must download them from the DNN Development Forge and install them on your instance of DNN. Examples of other project modules include the Gallery and Chat modules.

Each of these modules was listed in Chapter 1. You can find release information and downloads for all the Core Project modules at www.dotnetnuke.com/Development/

---

Forge/tabid/824/Default.aspx. To install new modules or make modules available to your portal, you must have Superuser privileges. If you do not have Superuser privileges, it is valuable to know that these modules are available even if you don't see them on your site.

# The Home Page

The home page of your site should accomplish a number of goals. The home page acts as the information booth for the rest of your site. It should orient visitors to the content on other pages, instill trust in the visitors, and give them a place to come back to if they get lost. The menu on a home page should give users a clear idea of the navigation structure. The navigation path for visitors is very straightforward when you use MinimalExtropy, the default skin. In the site map for the personal site planned in Figure 5-8, there are four pages, including the home page. Users see the four pages to which they can navigate, and they will always be able to return to the home page by clicking on the logo or the home link on the menu.

When guests come to your home, it's only proper to welcome them and let them know they've come to the right place. Start by adding a welcome message at the top of the home page to introduce the site to the user. The Text/HTML module works well for this because it gives you an easy way to administer content, but more than likely this content will be updated infrequently. In Figure 5-9, we added a Text/HTML module titled "Welcome to My Site" to the Home page and added some content with links to other pages of your site.

Figure 5-9

Earlier, we broadly defined the goal for this site as "to inform." We can refine this goal as keeping your friends and family informed about your life. A blog can be a great tool to provide frequent updates. You could add the Blog module directly to the home page, but if you put more content on your home page in addition to the blog, the page will quickly become crowded. You will, however, want to get the most recent content on the home page to give users an easy way to see new entries.

Luckily, DNN has a tool that works perfectly for getting recent content from a blog to the home page without adding the entire Blog module. The News Feeds (RSS) module enables you to subscribe to the syndicated feed created by the Blog module but keep the clutter of the rest of the module away from your home content. Figure 5-10 shows the finished product of the Home page using the Text/HTML and News Feeds (RSS) modules.

**Figure 5-10**

Add the News Feeds (RSS) module to your home page and later we'll come back to this module and connect it with the RSS feed created by the blog module. Your home page should now have a Text/HTML module welcoming visitors to your site and a News Feeds (RSS) module awaiting the recent entries from your blog.

## The My Blog Page

Next, move on to the meat and potatoes of your site — the blog. A blog is a great way for you to add content to your site regularly without having to actively manage or organize the content.

Before diving into the setup of the Blog module, do some planning for your blog. Blog entries are typically written by one author (a person or an entity). As a result, it is important to define the voice of your blog entries. You know the intended audience of your website; give your blog a voice that will communicate with your audience. We established earlier that your personal site was going to aim to communicate with family and friends. So, the voice of your blog should be personal and informal.

You'll want to start the setup by naming your blog. Add the Blog module to the ContentPane on the My Blog page, as shown in Figure 5-11. After adding the module to the page, you can change the titles of each of the modules.

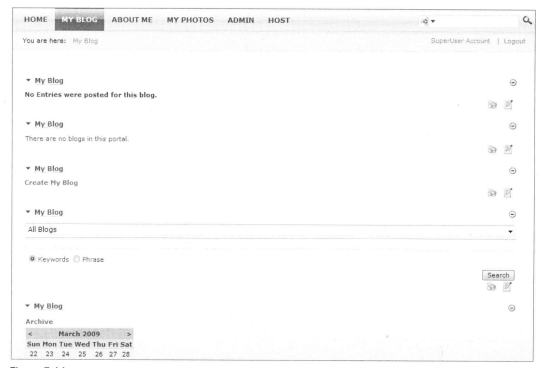

Figure 5-11

You'll notice that five modules are placed on the page. Each of these modules serves a different function for bloggers. Since all modules have the same title upon being added to the page, the following list describes the modules in the order in which they appear on the page initially.

1.   **Recent Entries:** The Recent Entries module serves a number of functions. Summaries of your entries are listed in chronological order. When visitors choose to read more, the full detail of the entry will be displayed in this module as well. From the full detail display, visitors will be able to comment on your entries. Administratively, the Recent Entries module houses the Module Options, which control the function of all the blogs on your site.

2.   **Listing:** In the case where a blog might be contributed to by multiple users, the Listing module will list the titles of each blog. This allows visitors to view the entries of just one blog. On a personal site, this may not be as relevant as on a site with numerous bloggers. The Listing module also displays the categories of your blog. In DNN, the Blog module uses Child Blogs to categorize the entries of a single blogger. As you review the setup options for the Blog module, you'll see the option to create Child Blogs.

3. **Management:** The Management module will serve as the control panel for each blogger as they administer their individual blog settings. It will be important for bloggers to have edit permissions to this module. Typically, you will make this module invisible to all users, as they have no need to see the administrative options. For a personal site, you'll most likely be the sole blogger and site administrator. For this reason, edit permissions aren't as important (they're enabled by default).

4. **Search:** The Search module allows users to search blog entries by keyword or phrases. If you have multiple bloggers on your site, visitors can refine their searches by individual blogs as well. In the case of a single, personal blog, filtering won't be necessary, but the ability for users to search is still valuable.

5. **Archive:** Because blog entries are recorded chronologically, it makes sense for entries to be referenced by date. As you create entries, the Archive module will highlight the dates on which entries were created. The current month is displayed by default, and users can scroll through months to see dates in which there were entries for past months. Additionally, each month is listed below the calendar as a hyperlink. Your site visitors will be able to review all of the entries from a specific month by using these hyperlinks.

Now that you understand the components of the Blog module individually, here's how you might want to organize the content on your page. In Figure 5-12, you'll see the five modules included in the Blog module arranged in a more usable layout.

1. Leave the Recent Entries module in the ContentPane. The entries of your blog will be the most prominent and need the most real estate on the page.

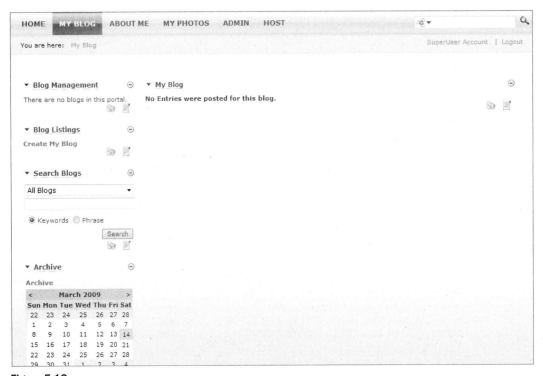

**Figure 5-12**

2. Move the Management module to a side pane. Figure 5-10 is using the LeftPane, but this is personal preference. While you're moving the module, you might as well change the permissions to take away view rights from All Users and make the module visible only to Administrators. If you have other user roles on your site, you may want to open permissions to other roles, but for your personal site, Administrators are the only users who need access to this module. By moving the Management module first, you make it the top module in the pane, and this allows you easy administration of the blog when logged in to your site.

3. Move the Listing, Search, and Archive modules to the LeftPane. There is no setup required for these modules. Again, the order in which they are stacked is personal preference.

4. As you move the modules, rename each with a title more descriptive of its function. In Figure 5-12, you can see that we named each module something more descriptive yet friendly to the site visitors. Also, the Blog Management module is visible only to Administrators.

## Creating Your Blog

With the Blog module arranged on the page, you'll next need to create your blog. Since each blog is associated with a user account, make sure that you are logged in as the user account with which you want to author your blog. To create your blog, click the Create My Blog link located in the Listing module. If the Blog module is on your page and there are no blogs established in the module, the Create My Blog action will be active in the Listing module. Once the first blog is created on your site, all subsequent users will have the Create My Blog link available in the Management module. You'll also notice in Figure 5-12 that the Management module indicates that there are no blogs in the portal. Once you have created your blog, this module will provide actions to manage your individual blog's settings.

To create your blog, only a Title and Description are required. The other Blog Options settings, as described in the following tables, allow you to control individually how your blog will function. If there were multiple bloggers on your site, each blogger could control these setting separately. In the next section, we'll discuss some of the configuration decisions important to a personal blog.

### Basic Blog Entry Options

| Setting | Description | Considerations |
| --- | --- | --- |
| Title | This names your blog and will show in the list module of the blog. | The title of your blog will be displayed in the Listing module and as the Title in your syndicated feed. |
| Description | This gives a short description for all blog entries in your blog. | When visitors click on a specific blog in the Listing module, the description of the blog will show below the title of the blog before the entries. |

*Continued*

**131**

**Basic Blog Entry Options** *(continued)*

| Setting | Description | Considerations |
|---|---|---|
| Make this blog public | If a blog is public, it will be visible to users with view rights to the blog modules. If the blog is private, only the blog's author will be able to view entries. | Keeping your blog private can be a way to pre-populate entries prior to launching your blog, but once the blog is public, you will need to mark individual entries as private to keep them hidden. |
| When Displaying Your Identity Use: | Display Name or Full Name | |
| MetaWeblog Options | This is the URL provided to integrate your individual blog with tools using the MetaWeblog API. | The Blog module allows you to post entries using the MetaWeblog API along with tools like Windows Live Writer or Mars Edit. |

**Blog Entry Comment Options**

| Setting | Description | Considerations |
|---|---|---|
| Allow users to post comments | This allows users to post comments to your blog entries. | |
| Approval for user comments required | If approval is required, comments will not post until approved. | Consider setting "send mail notification" so that you can actively manage comments as they are posted. |
| Allow anonymous users to post comments | All users can post comments without authenticating themselves with the site. | If you allow anonymous users to post comments, you may want to require your approval of the comments to prevent malicious posts. |
| Allow Trackback comments | Trackback comments can be made by other bloggers linking to your posts. | The comments made in trackbacks will post as comments in your blog entries but with links to the commenting blog. |
| Approval for Trackback Comments required | If approval is required, trackback comments will not post until approved | |
| Send mail notification after comments and trackbacks are posted | This sends the blog author an e-mail when comments are posted. | |

## Blog Entry Comment Options

| Setting | Description | Considerations |
| --- | --- | --- |
| Use CAPTCHA for comments | CAPTCHA helps to keep robot crawlers from posting comments because comments need a user interaction prior to the submission of a comment. | |
| Trackback Auto Discovery | The Recent Entries module will alert the sites to which you have linked to a trackback-enabled link. | If you link to other bloggers' posts your entries can automatically alert the blog of your reference. |

## Blog Entry Syndication

| Setting | Function | Considerations |
| --- | --- | --- |
| Syndicate this blog | Creates an RSS feed of your recent entries | There are blog module options that control the number of entries to be posted in your RSS feed. |
| Use this e-mail for the "ManagingEditor" RSS field | This allows you to set an e-mail address different from the e-mail address of the user account associated with the blog. | The ManagingEditor e-mail is included in the RSS feed and associated with each entry. |

## Blog Entry Date and Time Options

| Setting | Function | Considerations |
| --- | --- | --- |
| Time Zone | This allows the blog to have a different time zone than the time zone set for the portal. | For a personal blog, your time zone will most likely be the same as the portal's time zone. If you had multiple bloggers on your site, this setting would be more important. |
| Culture | This allows each blog to be tied to a culture. Each culture can control localized content in the blog's settings and display. | |
| Date Format | This determines the format in which the date of your entries is displayed. | |

## *Applying Blog Module Settings to Your Blog*

The Blog module has a long list of settings to meet the needs of different configurations. There are both settings that apply to all blogs on your site as well as individual settings that each blogger controls. We'll review some of the features required in this example blog implementation and then match them to the corresponding setup.

The following checklist outlines the features required in our blog:

❑    Entries should appear as authored by you.

❑    Visitors should be able to provide feedback using comments or trackback links.

❑    Posts should be syndicated automatically, allowing visitors to subscribe to the blog.

---

### What Is a Trackback Link?

When a post on another blog links to your post, it will ping, or notify, your site that your post has been referred to in an external blog. When other bloggers use the trackback link to reference your entry, a comment will be created on your blog. This way, the readers of your blog can follow other conversations that have stemmed from your initial post.

---

Next, we'll review the settings and setup that will allow for these requirements. As you review the Blog module, you'll find a number of other settings that may be of use to you. Feel free to try them out and see how you like the way your blog functions. These settings are found in the Management module of your blog. You may have renamed this module, but for the sake of referencing a familiar term, access the Blog Setting through the actions links in the Management module, as shown in Figure 5-13.

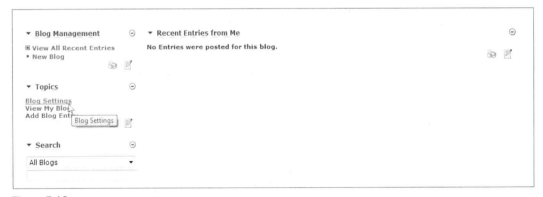

Figure 5-13

First, you want credit for your posts. There are two things to do to make sure that you are listed by name. In your individual blog settings, display the identity of the blog author as Full Name. When you select "Full Name," the first and last name you provided in your user record will be displayed as the author of your posts. If you prefer to use a moniker, select User Name. Figure 5-14 illustrates the option for choosing the way that your identity is displayed. When we defined the Site Administrator for your site, we mentioned that using a personalized user account would be necessary. If you are administering your site with a generic administrator account, it might make sense now to go back and update the profile information for your user.

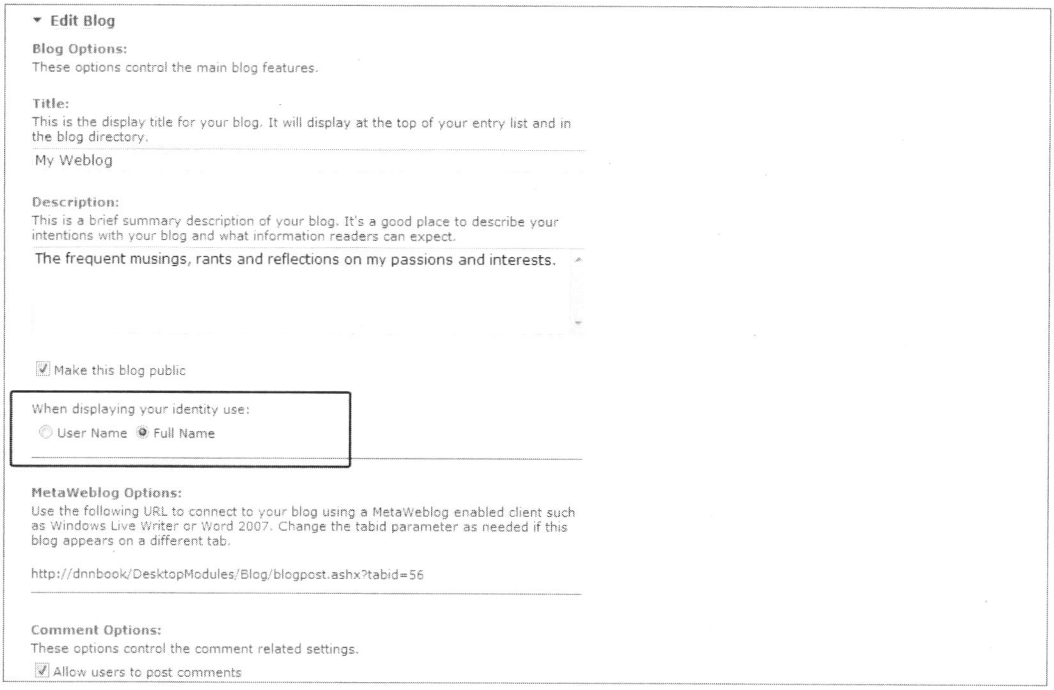

**Figure 5-14**

The next requirement is that your visitors be able to provide feedback on the posts using comments or trackback comments. The Blog module allows you to allow or restrict comment and trackback posting. Additionally, you can moderate the posting of these comments. Figure 5-15 shows the options for handling user comments and trackbacks. If you require notification after comments and trackbacks are posted, you will receive an e-mail for each posted comment.

In the Recent Entries module, you can configure the settings that control how comments and entries look and feel across all blogs. From the Actions menu in Recent Entries, select Blog Options. These options set the defaults for all blogs on your site. For a personal blog, the choices you make for the settings here may not be relevant because your blog is the only blog on the site. However, it is valuable to review the options here to understand the full set of features in the Blog module. For example, in Blog Options, you can allow the use of avatar images for authenticated users leaving comments on your site. Using an avatar is a good way to incorporate personality to your comments. If the commenting user has an avatar associated with his or her e-mail account, the image will be used alongside the comment. In the Blog Options, you can set a default image for users who do not have an avatar selected. There are a number of other settings you may want to apply to your blog, such as enabling social bookmarks. When you enable social bookmarks, users can easily create links to your blog entries in external social networking sites like Facebook.

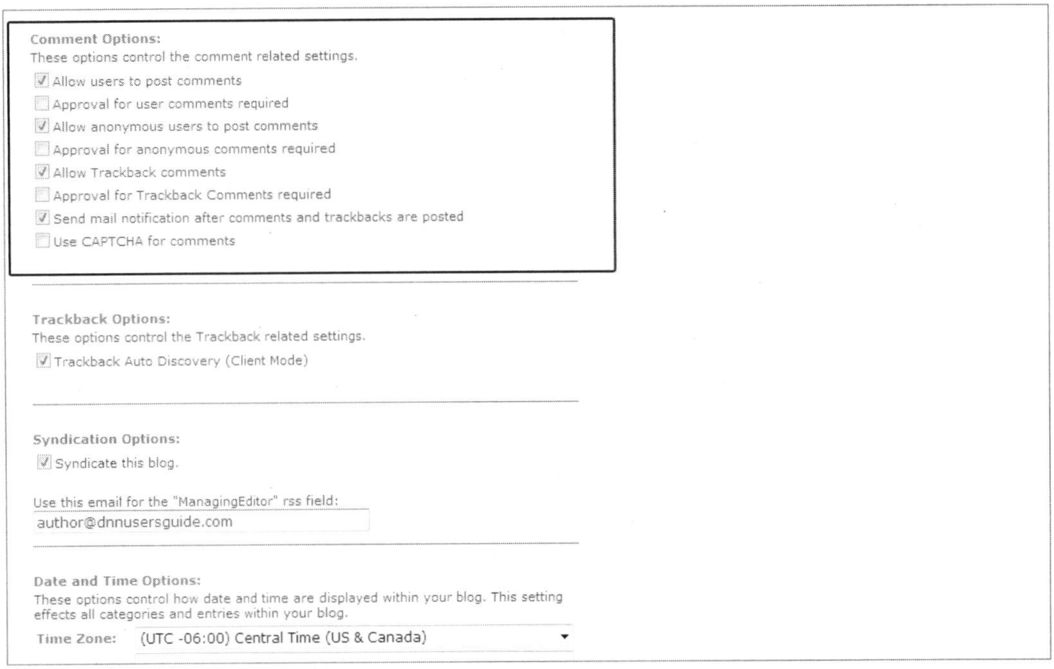

**Comment Options:**
These options control the comment related settings.
☑ Allow users to post comments
☐ Approval for user comments required
☑ Allow anonymous users to post comments
☐ Approval for anonymous comments required
☑ Allow Trackback comments
☐ Approval for Trackback Comments required
☑ Send mail notification after comments and trackbacks are posted
☐ Use CAPTCHA for comments

**Trackback Options:**
These options control the Trackback related settings.
☑ Trackback Auto Discovery (Client Mode)

**Syndication Options:**
☑ Syndicate this blog.

Use this email for the "ManagingEditor" rss field:
author@dnnusersguide.com

**Date and Time Options:**
These options control how date and time are displayed within your blog. This setting
effects all categories and entries within your blog.
Time Zone:     (UTC -06:00) Central Time (US & Canada)          ▼

**Figure 5-15**

The last requirement for the blog is the ability to syndicate entries using RSS. To accomplish this, there are a few settings scattered across Blog Options and Blog Settings that you'll need to review. In the Blog Settings for your individual blog, there is simply a checkbox to enable syndication of your entries. In addition to this option, you'll want to define the e-mail address defined as the ManagingEditor. Figure 5-16 illustrates these two settings in Blog Settings.

In Blog Options, you can determine the number of entries to display in your RSS feed. The default entries syndicated in your feed is 10 entries. Using the default setting will most likely satisfy your needs. If you find a reason to restrict or expand the number of recent entries, you can revisit this setting.

---

### Real Simple Syndication (RSS)

Real Simple Syndication, or RSS, is technically a standardized file format. The standardized format includes similar data elements like title, link, author, publishing dates. To the common website visitor, an RSS feed means that they can subscribe to your feed in a RSS reader or feed reader. These tools aggregate RSS feeds and allow the visitors to automatically receive updates when new content is published.

---

With syndication turned on and the settings reviewed, the Blog module automatically creates an RSS feed for your entries and adds to your feed with each new blog entry. Also, the feed is provided to your site visitors through a number of clues. First, next to the blog title in the Listing module, there is an RSS icon (see Figure 5-17). If you click on this icon, the feed URL will launch in your browser. Additionally, each entry will display the RSS icon next to the entry title when you're viewing the entire entry.

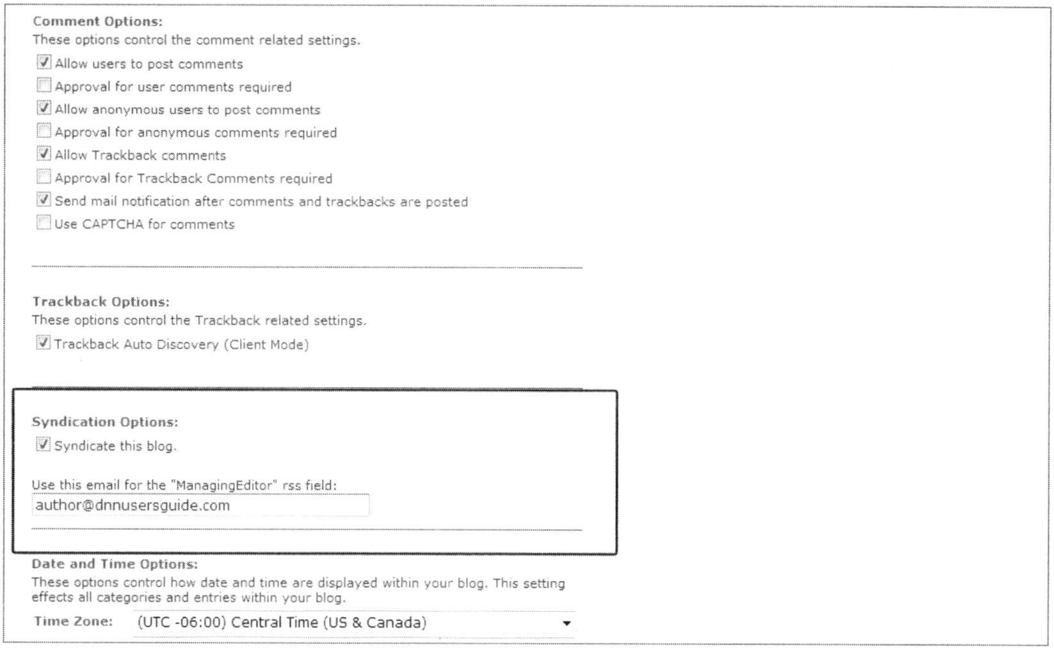

**Comment Options:**
These options control the comment related settings.
☑ Allow users to post comments
☐ Approval for user comments required
☑ Allow anonymous users to post comments
☐ Approval for anonymous comments required
☑ Allow Trackback comments
☐ Approval for Trackback Comments required
☑ Send mail notification after comments and trackbacks are posted
☐ Use CAPTCHA for comments

**Trackback Options:**
These options control the Trackback related settings.
☑ Trackback Auto Discovery (Client Mode)

**Syndication Options:**
☑ Syndicate this blog.

Use this email for the "ManagingEditor" rss field:
author@dnnusersguide.com

**Date and Time Options:**
These options control how date and time are displayed within your blog. This setting
effects all categories and entries within your blog.
Time Zone:    (UTC -06:00) Central Time (US & Canada)          ▼

Figure 5-16

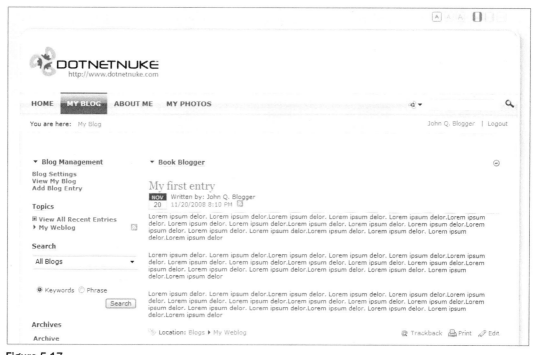

Figure 5-17

The other benefit to syndicating your blog entries is that you can subscribe to your own feed and publish content from your blog to the home page of your site. Now that you know the URL to your feed, go back to the home page and add this feed to your News Feeds (RSS) module. There are two steps to using the News Feeds (RSS) module with the syndicated feed from your Blog module. First, add the RSS to the module. In Figure 5-18, we have added the URL of the feed generated by our blog to the News Feeds (RSS) module that we placed earlier on the Home page.

**Figure 5-18**

Next, review the module settings for the News Feeds (RSS) module to define the display and function of your feed. In Figure 5-19 we've set the My Recent Entries settings. We've kept the first three settings as the default for the module. The Default Cache Time, Retry Times, and Retry Timeout settings all dictate how frequently your News Feeds (RSS) module will attempt to communicate with the feed's URL. The next settings dictate the look of the content coming from the syndicated feed. We've applied the `Default.xsl` file to translate the feed and we're only going to show the three most recent entries. The XSL Transformation file used will determine how your RSS feed displays on the page.

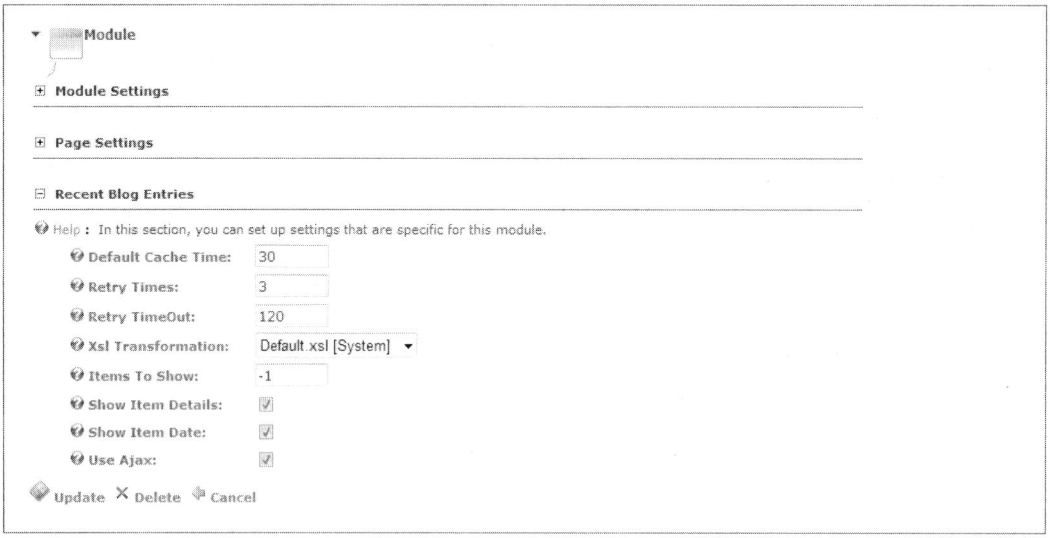

**Figure 5-19**

---

**What Is an XSL Transformation File?**

An Extensible Stylesheet Language Transformation file (XSLT) is a style sheet applied to Extensible Markup Language files (XML). You're applying an XSLT file to an RSS feed because RSS files use XML. That's a lot of initials for something that happens so simply in DNN. Simply, the XSL transformation file you select in the module settings takes the XML produced by the Blog module and translates the RSS markup into something more friendly to your web browser (HTML). It maps out the elements from the RSS feed, such as Title and Author Name, and tells the browser what they should be like in the browser.

---

# The About Me Page

You didn't want to clutter the home page with text-heavy content, so the About Me page can be a place for you to give more information about yourself. Since you are more than just a narrative or short biography, you will want to add other hints about you who you are by listing your favorite links or links to friends' sites.

An About Me page may give more specific information about you personally or professionally. The About Me page might explain your reasons for creating your site and give your visitors information on what to expect from the site. Since most of the content on an About Me page is going to be static or infrequently updated, you can use the core Text/HTML module to create most of the content on this page. When you first created the About Me page with other pages in the sitemap, a Text/HTML module is automatically added to the page using the default page template.

With the Text/HTML module on your About Me page, let's spice up the content by adding an image and text using the FCK Editor. Chapter 4 introduces the FCK Editor as the standard WYSIWYG, rich text, HTML editor. Without any knowledge of HTML, you can add an image and text to your page using the FCK Editor. To add an image to your content, click the image icon in the FCK Editor's toolbar. This will prompt you to locate the image on your file system. Once you have located the file from your file system, you can add some simple formatting to the image. Using the Image Properties activity, as shown in Figure 5-20, the image is left-aligned, with a 2-pixel border, and 2 pixels of horizontal spacing.

Continue adding content to the About Me page by including a list of friends' sites to the RightPane (see Figure 5-21). This list could be a list of favorite sites or blogs you follow. For this content, use the Links module. You can also create links using the Text/HTML module, but the Links module enables you to track visitors' clicks and assign an icon to the links easily. The following section discusses the settings of the Links module; for now, just add the content and bask in your content editing prowess. With a few more additions of the Links module, your About Me page is quickly filling up.

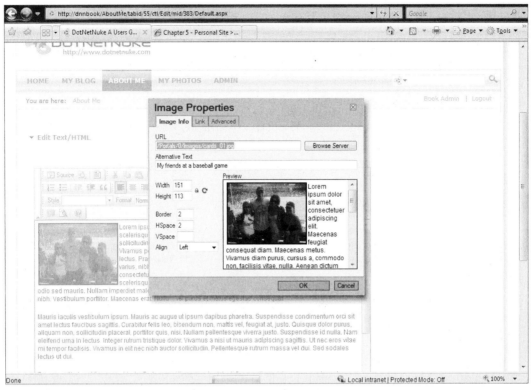

Figure 5-20

Figure 5-21

## Links Module Setup

The Links module is appropriate for creating lists or groups of links. Additionally, you can give your links descriptions, icons, and some different format options. However, if you want to embed a link in a block of copy, the Text/HTML module may be more appropriate. The Text/HTML module also provides the ability to create hyperlinks on your page, but it does not provide the click tracking and listing functions that the Links module provides.

As shown in Figure 5-22, the Links module offers a number of different configuration settings to control the look of your list and a few additional features to include with your links, such as an icon and a description.

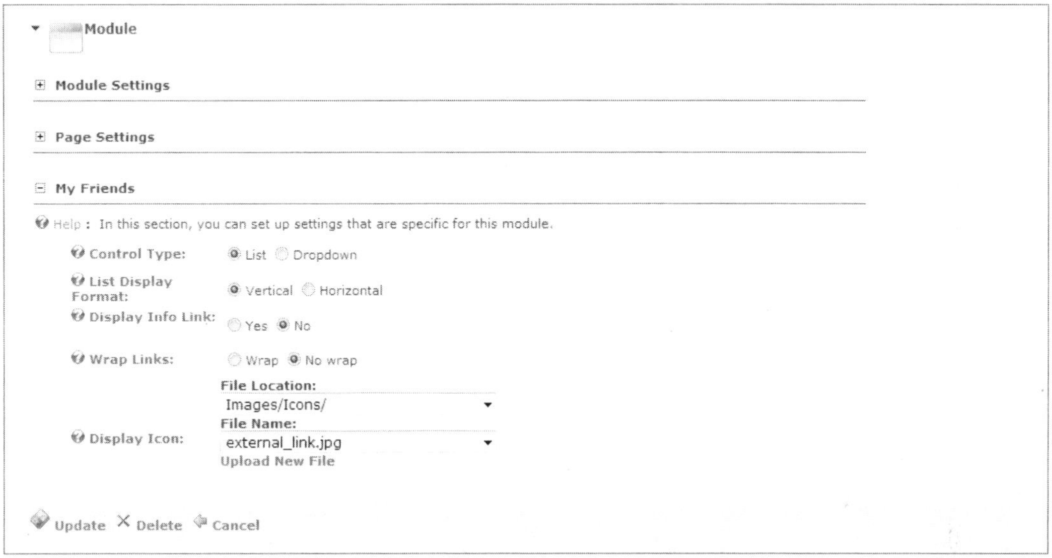

**Figure 5-22**

You should ask the following questions when setting up your Links module:

❑   Do you want your links to be displayed vertically or horizontally? If you choose to display them vertically, you can choose whether the links appear as a list or as a drop-down menu.

❑   Do you want to include a description with your link? The link will pull from the description of the link you provide. An ellipsis will appear next to the link, and when clicked, it will display the description of the link.

❑   Do you want links to have a fixed width or should the content area grow with the length of the link? If you choose for your links to wrap, the ContentPane will maintain its width. If you choose for your links not to wrap, the ContentPane will grow with the title of the links.

❑   Do you want to include an icon next to your links? In the example, an icon image stored on the file system is attached to each link. The icon will display to the left of the link title.

The task of creating links to include in the Links module is very simple. There is one action in the Actions menu of the Links module: Add Link. As you start to add links to your About Me page, two elements are required: the title and the destination (Link Type). Depending on the type of link you're creating, the destination will vary, but in all cases you'll need to specify where you want the link to point. Links can be to external resources (what you typically think of as a hyperlink), other pages on your site, a file on your site, or the profile of a user account on your site. Figure 5-23 shows a link to the home page of the DotNetNuke Corporation.

**Figure 5-23**

You can also choose to track the number of times a link is clicked, as well as the user, date, and time of each click. This tracking information will be displayed to you as the administrator when you edit the link after saving it for the first time.

The last setting to cover is View Order. If you do not specify a view order for your link, the links will be displayed alphabetically by the title of your links. If you want control over the order in which your links appear, give them a numeric ranking, with one being the highest or topmost link. Any links that have the same numeric value will be sorted alphabetically within their ranking.

---

### Setting the View Order for Your Links

If you want to control the order in which your links are listed, give each of your links a numeric View Order value. When you set a value for your links' View Order, it is best practice to use broad increments to your numbering. For example, if you have five links listed, avoid numbering the links 1–5. Using increments of 5 or 10 in your numbering, will allow you to easily add new links in the View Order without having the renumber each link.

---

# The My Photos Page

As the cliché goes, a picture is worth a thousand words. In a website, this holds especially true. You can use the Text/HTML module to generate static content that can include images, but it's more likely you'll want some sophisticated functionality to organize your pictures into albums by date, location, or category. To accomplish this, use the Gallery module to manage the pictures on your site.

The Gallery module enables you to create albums for your photos, provide details about your albums, and give your visitors the ability to sort through your pictures. Of course, the Gallery module has a number of settings to make the implementation more sophisticated, but to make it easy, start by adding albums and photos and then go back later to add features to your gallery. This chapter's sample website uses Gallery module v.4.3.0. This version is not supported in production environments, but the core modules are updated regularly and your version may be different or enhanced. Additionally, there are other commercially available modules that provide photo gallery functionality.

The content for the My Photo's page is going to be simply the photos stored in the Gallery module. In Figure 5-24 we have placed the Gallery Module on our page.

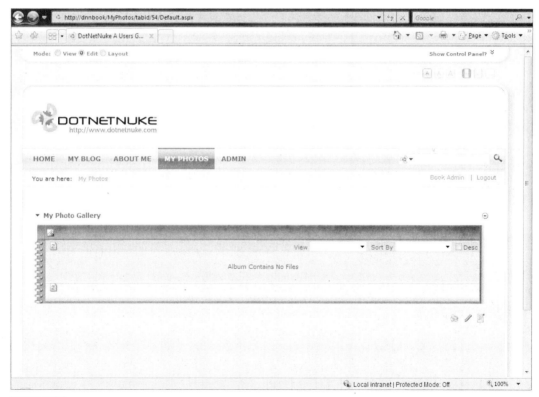

Figure 5-24

Before starting to add albums and photos to the Gallery module, let's review the settings available in the Gallery module. By reviewing the settings available through the Configuration action, we will establish configuration choices like file location, file size limitations, and display options. Figure 5-25 illustrates the Gallery Configuration. To view the Gallery Configuration action, locate the Configuration action through the Gallery module's Actions menu.

The other settings in the Admin Settings section are important for you as the administrator to know about, but for this chapter's site the defaults will work. There are three other sections to the Gallery Configuration options. In Display Settings, you can define a Title and Description for your gallery. Additionally, you can determine the fields to display and the fields used in sorting your photos. In Features Settings, you can determine how your photos display in a slideshow and specify which user roles can download the photos from your site. Last, in the Private Gallery settings, you can restrict the entire gallery to only users in specific roles.

---

### File Size Limits

The default file size limit for your images is 1000 KB. If you have larger images you want to add, you'll either need to reduce the file size or increase this limit. Many digital cameras store images with higher file sizes than 1000 KB, so you may run into issues with this setting until you adjust it. Keep it at the default for now because it will help your gallery load quickly.

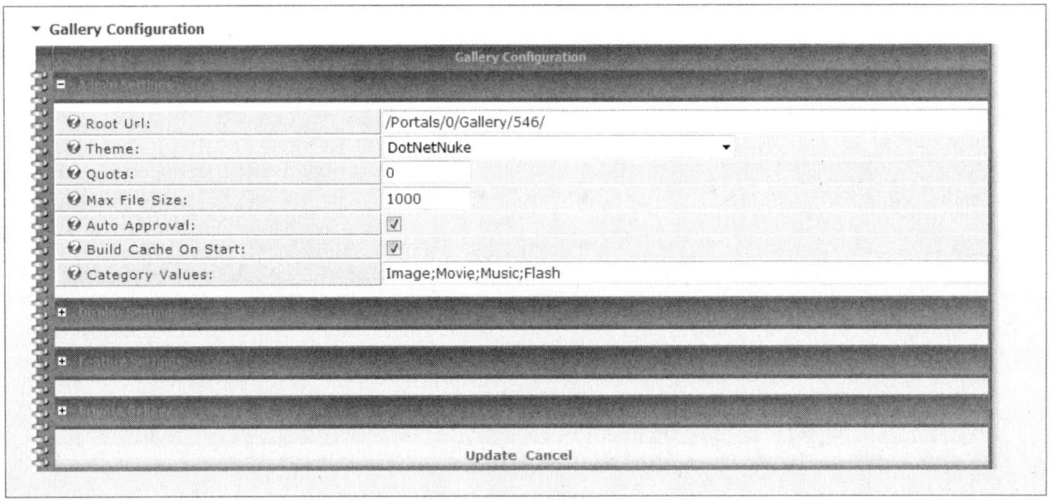

---

Figure 5-25

In our personal site example, the pictures are organized by occasion. Each occasion will be an album in the gallery. With this simple setup complete, start adding albums and photos to your albums. In the example, I've created three albums as a start to store my recently taken pictures: Vacation in Colorado, Andy's Wedding, and Cardinal's Game. The icon in the top left of the module gives you the action options.

The addition of albums is straightforward. From the Actions menu, select Add Album, and then provide details for your album, as shown in Figure 5-26. The more information you provide for your albums and photos, the more functionality you'll be able to use in sorting and the more detail you'll have available to display for your photos.

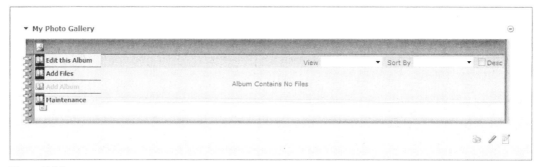

**Figure 5-26**

With your album created, you can begin to add photos to it. To add photos to the album, hover the mouse over an album to which you want to add photos. With your mouse hovering over the album, an Actions menu will appear. Select the Add Files action. Once you're in the Add File activity, saving photos to your album is a three-step process (see Figure 5-27). First, click the Browse button and select the photo from your computer and provide details for the image. Next, click the Add File button, which will add the photo to your the Pending Files queue. Once you've added all the images, click the Upload link to upload the queue to the album.

**▼ Edit Album**

Gallery    Trip to Colorado

Add File

File Upload Extensions:

| | |
|---|---|
| **Add File:** | C:\Users\prenner.ETG [Browse...] Add File |
| **Title:** | Great Sunset |
| **Author:** | Book Author |
| **Client:** | |
| **Location:** | Grand Junction, CO |
| **Description:** | A great sunset from the first day of vacation |
| **Categories:** | ☑ Image  ☐ Movie  ☐ Music  ☐ Flash |

| | Name | Title | Description | Categories | |
|---|---|---|---|---|---|
| **Pending Files:** | family_photos.JPG | Family Picture | A family photo from vacation | Image | ✕ |

Upload

| | Name | Title | Categories | Size | Approved Date | | |
|---|---|---|---|---|---|---|---|
| | BlackStallion.JPG | Two Beautiful Horses | | 51765 | 12/13/2008 | ✎ | ✕ |
| | CoalCreekHike.jpg | Wild Mustangs | | 27309 | 12/13/2008 | ✎ | ✕ |
| | cutecouple.jpg | Taking a Break | | 32267 | 12/13/2008 | ✎ | ✕ |

**Figure 5-27**

Adding photos to your album is the final step to creating a photo gallery on your personal site. Figure 5-28 illustrates the completed Gallery module with three albums.

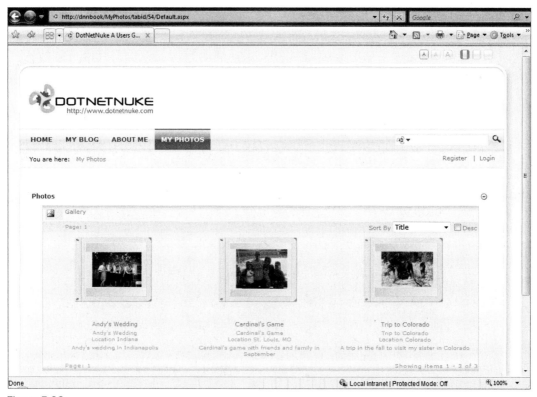

Figure 5-28

# Summary

This chapter reviewed a number of the important considerations you should make when using DNN to create a personal website. Through careful planning, you have developed a website that will be easy to maintain and provide your site's visitors with a wealth of information. Using the core functionality of DNN, you implemented the Blog and News Feeds (RSS) modules to post personal and timely entries. Additionally, you used the Text/HTML module to easily manage static content on your pages. Finally, you created a photo gallery to give your personal site even more personality. With an understanding of the Site Settings and configuration options available to you, you should feel confident about creating a personal site of your own.

# Creating a League Website

Small organizations and groups increasingly are finding a home on the Web. For some organizations, the Web may be their only home. For local organizations such as theater groups or recreational sports leagues, a website can easily replace phone trees and bulky information packets as a way to distribute information to members. For organizations fitting a niche, a website is an easy way to pull together people with like interests from across the map. In all cases, the organization's website serves as a meeting ground for members to share ideas, information, and resources.

This chapter will review a typical use case for a content management system like DotNetNuke (DNN) by creating a website for a sports league. There are a number of tools built into DNN that suit the needs of a small organization well. The membership tools allow a DNN website to collect information from its users. Additionally, the permissions-based content can allow information to be tailored directly to the interests of the site's members. Through the use of page and module permissions, this chapter's website will provide content specifically to targeted members and restrict content from access by unintended visitors.

Chapter 5 built a personal site page by page; because a personal site has limited scope in terms of functionality requirements, content administration, and site membership, reviewing each page individually was possible to fully explain the site. This chapter will again build a website in DNN but will review the implementation in three sections. First, by reviewing the site settings, configuration options, and administrative setup for a softball league, you'll gain an increased understanding of more configuration options available in DNN. Next, this chapter will outline the navigation structure, site map, and page permissions for a sample league site. With settings and site structure determined, you'll be able to easily manage the content of your site — pages, modules, and permissions. The third section of this chapter will review the modules you might use in creating a site for a small organization.

This chapter discusses the following topics:

❑ Reasons for a sports league's site

❑ Features and functionality you might want for your league's site

❑ Ways you might organize and manage your content

❑    Using the Announcements module to easily post messages to your league

❑    Using the Forum module to foster discussion and feedback within your league

❑    Setting up the Events module to post schedules and reminders

# Reasons for a Sport League Site

A website can help foster communication between the members of your organization. Additionally, DNN can ease the burden of facilitating this communication by distributing the administrative responsibilities to multiple people. Gone are the days when a league organizer had to initiate a phone tree or stuff and stamp dozens of letters. A website can streamline these types of tasks for organizers and give members a single place to access information. Additionally, a website can help grow ideas and increase communication by offering tools like forums to stimulate conversation within a small organization. In this chapter, you'll see a number of features, functions, and settings to make administering a website for a small organization easy and powerful.

Regardless of your organization's charter, small organizations share some similar needs and goals for a website. All organizations seeking a presence on the Web want a place to communicate with non-members and facilitate communication with and among members.

We'll use a small softball league's website as a case study to demonstrate the ways that DNN can help establish your organization's website. Like your organization, this softball league will have a variety of audiences. Each type of visitor may be looking for something different. The sample softball league's website will utilize a number of user roles to segment its visitors as well as its content. Additionally, you'll share the responsibilities of managing the content on your site with the coaches of the teams. Using core DNN modules, the administration of this content will be easy and highly functional.

# Setting Up Your Site

Regardless of your hosting situation, once you have DotNetNuke installed, there will be some setup necessary to make your site unique to your organization. This section reviews some of the site settings and configuration options relevant to a small organization's website. Some of this setup is done in DNN; some of the setup will be done outside of DNN and is simply good practice for any website administrator. Although the settings used will be focused on a softball league, the concepts should easily translate for any small organization.

In Chapter 5, you defined a site title, keywords, and descriptions for your personal site. These same tasks and concepts also apply to a small organization. In a website for a small organization, there are additional settings that will make your job as web administrator easy. The following sections will cover setting up the site administrator account, webmaster tools, and user registration.

## Identifying the Site Administrator

Regardless of how "techie" you would like to think of yourself, somehow you have found yourself responsible for administering your organization's website. Along with these responsibilities come tasks that might make you wince, such as defining meta tags, submitting a site map to search engines, and setting up website permissions. Fortunately, DNN makes performing these tasks quite easy.

The first task is determining who will serve as the Administrator in the eyes of DNN. Multiple users can have administrator rights, but only one can serve as the site administrator as this role relates to some of the administrator functions DNN completes for you. This setup can be completed at any time, and you can change the primary administrator at any time, but it will help if you determine this prior to making your site available to league members because registration e-mails, password reminders, and a number of other functions are tied to this setting.

For your website, you'll want to create a generic user to serve as the site administrator. As you create your site, a default administrator account is created. On a personal site, making this account a specific person works because there is no question as to who runs and operates a personal site. However, for an organization's website, it makes more sense to keep this user generic.

## Creating a Generic Administrator E-mail Account

In most organizations, the webmaster has a generic e-mail address. This allows the webmaster to send and receive e-mails from an anonymous e-mail account. It also allows the webmaster e-mail to be shared, delegated, or detached from a specific person. On a small organization's website, using a generic e-mail account for the primary administrator's user account can provide the same benefits.

The company you have registered your domain with or the hosting provider will most likely offer some type of e-mail plan. At the very least you should be able to create an e-mail-forwarding account. E-mail forwarding enables you to have e-mail messages redirected to a specific e-mail account. For example, you can set up the e-mail account admin@yourdomain.com to forward all messages to any e-mail account, for example you@yahoo.com. You don't have to create a generic administrator e-mail account to complete your website, but if you decide to do so, check with your hosting provider for available options.

## Changing the Administrator Account's E-Mail

Once you have an e-mail account for the administrator of your organization's site, associate this e-mail account with the administrator user account. The administrator account for your portal is just like any other user account on your site. To access the User Accounts, you can either click on Users from the Common Tasks in the Control Panel or locate the User Accounts page in the Admin menu. After you have located the account, you can edit the e-mail address by clicking on the Edit icon next to the account's username. Figure 6-1 demonstrates changing the e-mail account for the default administrator user. While you're in the User Account activity, you'll want to create a user account for yourself to completely separate your activity on the site from the action of the site administrator.

Figure 6-1

Once you are dissociated from the administrator user in the eyes of DNN, the administrative functions of DNN will use the e-mail account you created. By default, the administrator account created with your portal will be identified as the site administrator. Later, if you wanted to assign these functions to a specific user, you could change the setting in the Site Settings, as shown in Figure 6-2. To access this setting, navigate to the Site Settings through the Admin menu. The Administrator associated with the portal is located in Advanced Settings ⇨ Other Settings.

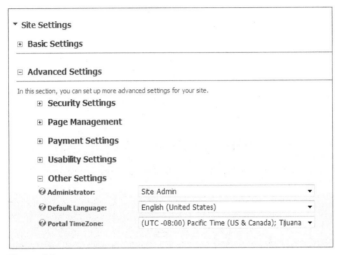

Figure 6-2

# Setting Up External Webmaster Tools

There are a number of tools available to you as a website administrator (commonly referred to as a *webmaster*), to help with the more technical tasks of establishing and maintaining your website. DNN allows you to leverage these tools easily by incorporating settings into your site that "play nicely" with these external tools.

First, to ensure that search engines index your website accurately, you'll want to submit a site map to some of the major search engines. The submission of your site map should be saved until you have completed building your publicly available pages, but reviewing the settings initially will help you to come back later to complete the task. In its simplest terms, a *site map* is a list of the pages on your website. Creating and submitting a site map helps make sure that search engines know about all the pages on your site.

## Creating a Site Map for Search Engines

DNN automatically creates and maintains an XML file that search engines easily understand — Sitemap.aspx. There is nothing you will need to do to manage your site map file. Many webmasters manually create XML site maps to submit to search engines. DNN completes this task for you. As you add pages to your site, the file will recognize the pages and add them to its list. Figure 6-3 shows an example of the `Sitemap.aspx` file generated for this chapter's softball league's site.

```
<?xml version="1.0" encoding="UTF-8" ?>
- <urlset xmlns="http://www.sitemaps.org/schemas/sitemap/0.9" xmlns:xsi="http://www.w3.org/2001/XMLSchema-instance"
    xsi:schemaLocation="http://www.sitemaps.org/schemas/sitemap/0.9
    http://www.sitemaps.org/schemas/sitemap/0.9/sitemap.xsd">
  - <url>
      <loc>http://www.yourdomain.com/Home/tabid/36/Default.aspx</loc>
      <lastmod>2009-01-19</lastmod>
      <changefreq>daily</changefreq>
      <priority>0.8</priority>
    </url>
  - <url>
```

**Figure 6-3**

If the output of this file looks foreign to you, don't worry because it's easily interpreted by the search engines. To see your own site's `Sitemap.aspx` file, append `/Sitemap.aspx` to your URL (www.yourdomain.com/Sitemap.aspx).

## Managing Your Site Information with Search Engines

In addition to creating a site map for you, DNN provides an administrative tool for you to submit your site map to a number of the major search engines. By submitting your site map to a search engine, you're telling the search engine, "Hey, here's my site and this is the place to look for our site's links and content." In the Basic Settings ➪ Site Marketing section of your Site Settings, you can select the option to submit your site for indexing to Google, Yahoo!, and Microsoft. To submit your site, simply select the search engine to which you wish to submit your site and click Submit. You can submit it to all three search engines, using this tool, by repeating the submission process for each search engine.

Outside of DNN, there are a number of other tools available to you, as the site administrator, to monitor how your site is indexed. For example, Google provides a toolset called Google Webmaster Central. Although other tools are available, the Google tools are free and easy to understand.

To use these tools, you'll need to create an account with Google and sign up for Webmaster tools (visit www.google.com/webmasters). Once you have signed up for the Webmaster tools, Google requires you to verify you are the owner of the site you wish to monitor. Google offers two ways to verify your site: either add a meta tag to your code or upload an HTML file to your site. Figure 6-4 illustrates the verification options available in Google's Webmaster tools. DNN will assist in creating the HTML file. All you need is the unique filename Google provides (something like `google55e555555555d5e5.html`).

When you copy the filename from Google (as illustrated in Figure 6-4) and paste it into the Site Marketing section of your Site Settings, DNN will create the HTML file for your site. Figure 6-5 illustrates pasting this code into your site settings.

Paste the verification code provided by Google into the Verification field in Site Settings, and click Create. The file will automatically be placed on your file server, and Google will be able to verify your site.

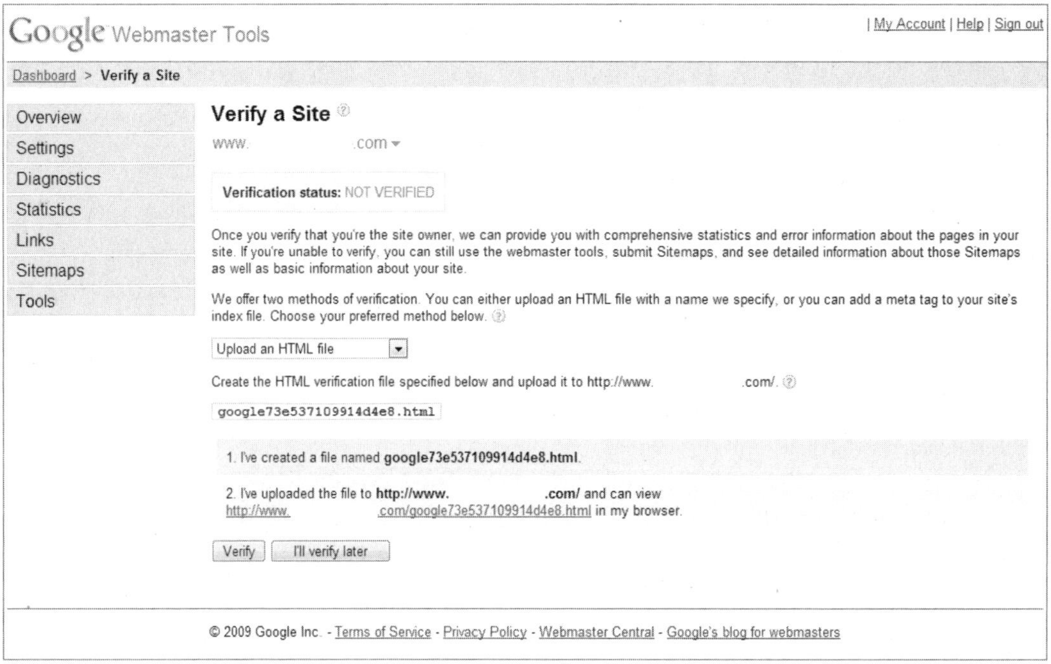

Figure 6-4

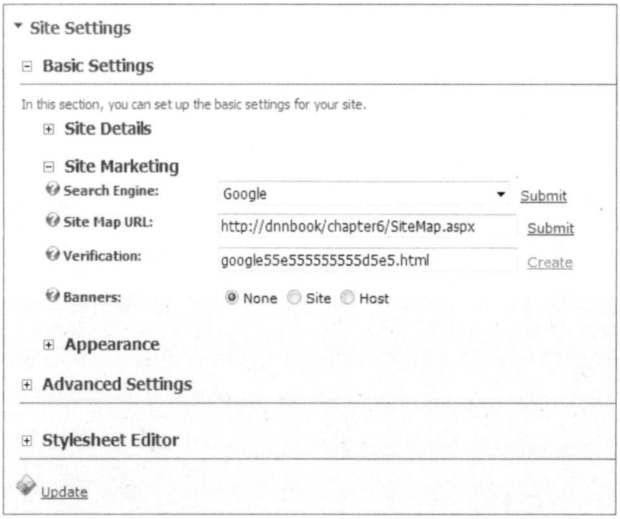

Figure 6-5

## *Organizing the File System*

An organization's website will most likely have files that are time relevant. More than likely, documents like team rosters, team schedules, and directions to the league picnic all are specific to the season of the softball league. For this reason, adding folders in your file manager to organize documents by date will help you to maintain your files from year to year.

In addition to organizing documents by season or year, you'll still want to create folders for content that does not change from year to year, as well as create folders by file type. This way content specific to a given timeframe (in this case, season) will be grouped together and content that is general to any season in the league (the league logo or graphics used on your site, for example) will be organized by file type. As you plan your website, it is important to understand the organization of the file system. See Chapter 8 for the full administrative features and functionality of the File Manager.

# Establishing Membership Online

For a social group, being able to capture and maintain membership information may be the single most valuable feature of your DNN website. For a small organization, a membership database can be tedious and difficult to maintain. DNN enables you to use the membership features to control content permissions and also collect additional information from your users in the form of user profiles. Using your website and the membership tools available in DNN, you can place the burden of maintaining member information back on the members of your organization.

For the softball league website, we'll perform the following three steps to collect and maintain accurate membership data:

❑ First, you'll ensure the validity of your members by requiring them to verify their registration. In doing this, you won't be completely sure that users registered on your site are members of your league, but you also don't have to manage each user manually, and you can be sure that the registration information provided belongs to the registered user.

❑ Second, you'll require a complete profile from your users after they register to collect additional information.

❑ Last, you'll allow users to add themselves to the appropriate roles on the site by using RSVP codes to enable users to manage their services (roles) on the site. By creating additional roles and identifying members of your league with these roles rather than the roles DNN automatically assigns, you can be confident the content restricted to our members is available only to your league members.

## Verifying User Registration

In Chapter 5, you allowed an open registration without filters or restrictions as to who registered or what registration data they provided. Since your league site has a defined group of members, you're going to want to authorize a more accurate group of users. The first way to help ensure that the users on your site are the members of your organization is to have users verify their registration. This will prevent visitors to your site from creating phony user accounts.

As shown in Figure 6-6, the User Registration for your site is set to Verified. The User Registration settings are located in the Security Setting section of Advanced Site Settings.

User accounts created by site visitors won't be authorized until the users have confirmed their registration. A verification e-mail is sent to your users upon registration, and they will be authorized upon verifying that the e-mail they provided is their e-mail account. Verified user registration won't guarantee the users on your site are all members of your organization, but it doesn't require the site administrator to authorize each registration as users register. Additionally, you can at least be assured that the e-mail address provided at registration is an active e-mail account for your members.

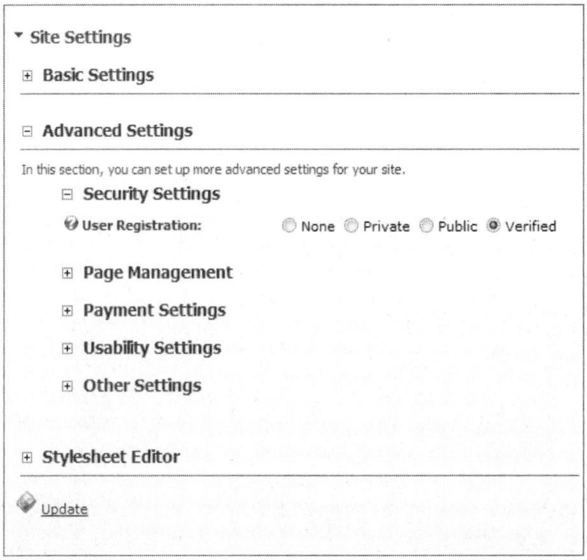

Figure 6-6

On the User Accounts page, DotNetNuke allows you to manage the user accounts for your site. As visitors register for your site, user records will be created but the account will not be authorized until the user completes the verification process. To maintain your user records, you will want to delete unauthorized accounts regularly. To view all unauthorized users accounts, navigate to the User Accounts page, using either the Admin menu or the Users icon in the Control Panel. Unauthorized user accounts are indicated by a blank check box in the Authorized column. Additionally, you can sort by just unauthorized users by clicking the Unauthorized link. Figure 6-7 illustrates the list of unauthorized users on the league's website.

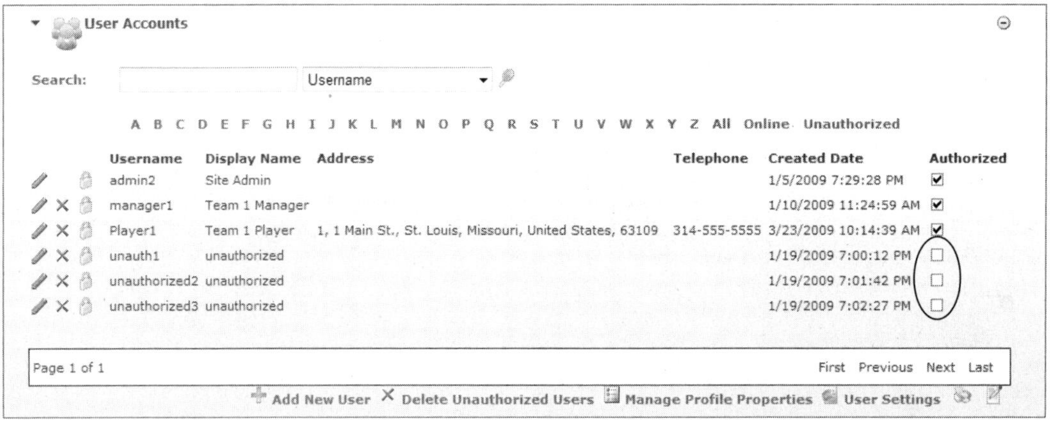

Figure 6-7

DNN gives you the option to delete all unauthorized users, but since your site keeps users unauthorized until they have explicitly verified their registration, you run the risk of deleting users who haven't checked their e-mail yet. Instead, you should frequently check unauthorized users and delete unfamiliar records as needed. Once the league registration time period has ended, you can batch delete unauthorized users as needed.

## Collecting Information from Your Users

Once our members have registered for the site, we'll collect additional information from them. In our softball league, we'll want to collect their mailing addresses, phone numbers, emergency contact names and numbers, and shirt size.

DNN enables you to collect profile information from your users, but to do this there are a few settings we'll need to review and configure. First, review the standard profile fields available by default in DNN and determine which of these fields we're going to use and which are going to be required. You can access the list of profile properties through Manage Profile Properties link on the User Accounts page.

### Standard Profile Fields

| Profile Property | Visible to Users? | Required? |
|---|---|---|
| Prefix | No | N/A |
| FirstName | Yes | Yes |
| MiddleName | Yes | Yes |
| LastName | Yes | Yes |
| Suffix | No | N/A |
| Unit | Yes | Yes |
| Street | Yes | Yes |
| City | Yes | Yes |
| Region | Yes | Yes |
| Country | Yes | Yes |
| PostalCode | Yes | Yes |
| Telephone | Yes | Yes |
| Cell | Yes | No |
| Fax | No | N/A |
| Website | No | N/A |
| IM | No | N/A |
| Biography | No | N/A |
| TimeZone | No | N/A |
| PreferredLocale | No | N/A |

In addition to the standard profile fields provided by DNN, there are three fields we want to collect from our players and coaches. Since these additions are custom profile properties, we've listed the new field with the type of data we wish to collect as well. When you create new profile properties, you'll need to determine the format of the data you wish to collect. Next, we'll step through the process of creating custom profile properties.

### Custom Profile Fields

| Profile Property | Type of Data | Visible to Users? | Required? |
| --- | --- | --- | --- |
| Emergency Contact Name | Text | Yes | Yes |
| Emergency Contact Number | Text | Yes | Yes |
| Shirt Size | List | Yes | Yes |

To create custom profile properties, click on the Manage Profile Properties link in the User Accounts page. In the Manage Profile Properties activity, you can add additional properties by clicking Add New Profile Property in the Actions menu. There are either two or three steps to creating a custom profile property, depending on the type of data you're going to collect. For the shirt size, since we're going to provide a list of the shirt sizes for our members to pick from, we'll need to create the field and the list.

First, specify the details for your new property. There are four required traits you'll need to define for new properties. You'll need to give the property a name, specify its data type, assign a category, and determine the view order. The name of your new property cannot contain spaces because it is the name of the column in the database. The next step in this process will allow you to define a user friendly name for the property. The data type can determine how the data is collected for the property. When we create our property for the emergency contact number, we'll use a Text property. To collect our member's shirt size, we'll use a List property. Your category for your property can help you to classify the properties you collect. The view order of your property will determine where in your list of properties the new property will display. It will be important to place your properties in a logical order to make the registration process logical for your users. For our softball league we've only made the fields we want to collect visible to reduce the number of fields our members need to complete. Figure 6-8 demonstrates the creation of our new property for emergency contact name.

Once you have defined the details for your new property, you can manage the localized text. Because you could have different users speaking different languages, DNN allows you to localize this text and create different names for the field in different languages. Since your softball league is local, your users are from the same locale, so you won't have additional languages on your site. However, if your organization is global, you might need to use this feature more fully. In addition to localizing your property for other languages, Localization allows you to specify a more user-friendly name for your property. To Manage Localization, click Next on Edit Profile Property Definition. The Property Name is displayed to users as they review their profile. The standard DNN properties include a colon in the Localized Property Name. You may want to continue this naming convention to keep your properties consistent. The Property Help will be displayed in the blue question mark icon next to your property and can provide the users more information about the information you are collecting. If you require the new property, as we do for Shirt Size and Emergency Contact Number, specify the Required Error Message. Figure 6-9 demonstrates the Localization for the emergency contact phone name.

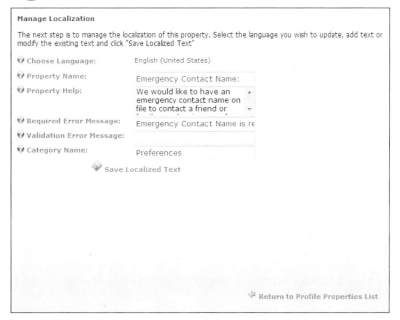

▼ Edit Profile Property Definition

**Add New Property Details**

The first step in setting up a Profile Property Definition is to define the property's details. Enter the details in this page and click "Next" to create the Property Definition. **Note:** All fields marked with a red arrow are required.

Property Name:            EmergencyContactNar
Data Type:                Text
Property Category:        Preferences
Length:                   0
Default Value:
Validation Expression:
Required:                 ☑
Visible:                  ☑
View Order:               16

➡ Next    ⬅ Return to Profile Properties List

Figure 6-8

▼ Edit Profile Property Definition

**Manage Localization**

The next step is to manage the localization of this property. Select the language you wish to update, add text or modify the existing text and click "Save Localized Text"

Choose Language:          English (United States)
Property Name:            Emergency Contact Name:
Property Help:            We would like to have an
                          emergency contact name on
                          file to contact a friend or
Required Error Message:   Emergency Contact Name is re
Validation Error Message:
Category Name:            Preferences

◆ Save Localized Text

⬆ Return to Profile Properties List

Figure 6-9

As mentioned earlier, list properties will require a third step in the creation process. When we created the Shirt Size property, we also specified the list of sizes available to our members to keep them from ordering a size you didn't offer. Figure 6-10 demonstrates the shirt sizes we're offering the members of our softball league.

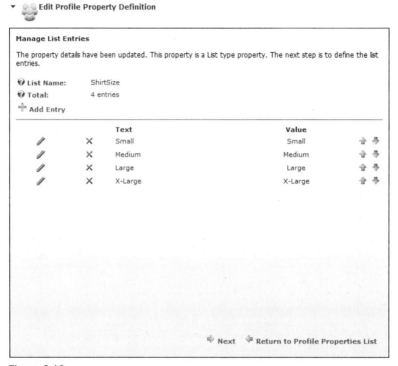

**Figure 6-10**

For a list property, you will need to add list entries in the Manage List Entries activity. Once you have defined the details for your new list property, click Next to Add Entries to your list. In Figure 6-11, you can see the process of adding a new entry to your list.

## Requiring a Profile from Your Users

With our profile properties defined, we can now require your users to complete their profile the next time they log in to the site. Since we have required profile properties, DNN allows us to require your users complete their profile at login or at registration. Since your registration already requires verification, it doesn't make sense for you to require a full profile of users who are not verified. You are going to require a valid profile at user login. If you define your required properties prior to your member's initial login, they will only need to complete their profile the first time they log in to your site. If you add required properties, your site members will need to complete the additional fields each time a required property is added. For this reason, you can see the importance of keeping the changes to required profile properties infrequent.

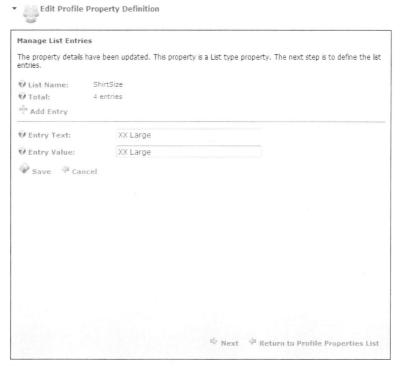

Figure 6-11

Requiring a valid profile at login is a setting you can configure in the User Accounts Settings page. To require a valid profile from your users, navigate to User Accounts Settings from the User Accounts page (see Figure 6-12). Chapter 9 reviews all the User Settings in detail.

## Specifying Specific Registration and Login Pages

Using the set up described for our softball site, you can image the registration and login process for our site's visitors is becoming a little complicated. We're requiring visitors to verify their registration prior to authentication and collecting profile information from your users at their first login. For many of our visitors, this will be their first encounter with the league's website. Considering the user's experience as you establish your user's online membership will be important in collecting accurate and thorough user information. Next, we'll describe a configuration option that will allow you to provide more information to your users as they register and log in to your site.

DNN's default behavior for user registration and login is efficient but not always the most user-friendly. DNN loads the Registration and Login controls on the page from which visitors access these actions. The users don't actually leave the page they were on, but DNN will load the controls using the skin you have specified as the Admin Skin (specified in Site Settings). Figure 6-13 demonstrates DNN's default behavior. As you can see, the User Log In control loaded on the Fundraising page but the content from the Fundraising page has disappeared.

You're going to want to provide more information for your team members as they register or login. This way you can let your visitors know why you're collecting their registration information, provide them instructions on logging in, or thank them for their membership. To create this more robust registration and login experience, you'll need to first create pages specifically for login and registration. On these pages, you gain more control of the look and feel of the login and registration activities. After these pages are created, you can incorporate them into the standard DNN registration and login behavior in two steps.

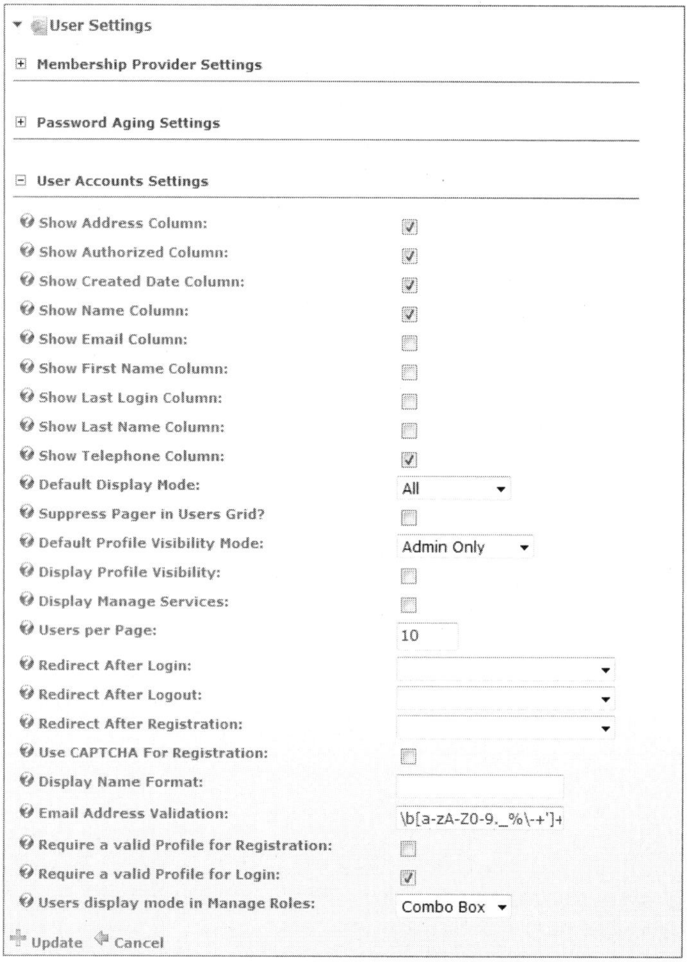

Figure 6-12

First, you'll need place the Account Login module on the Login page and the Users and Roles module on the Registration page. With these modules placed on the page, the functionality exists on the page; however, DNN doesn't know the pages should be used for Login or Registration.

Next, to make sure these pages are used when a user clicks on the Register and Login links in your skin, you need to specify to DNN that these are the pages to use for the Login and Registration activities.

Figure 6-14 shows the Site Settings that allow you to specifically identify your own Login and Registration pages. To access these settings, navigate to Site Settings ⇨ Advanced Settings ⇨ Page Management. The Login Page will determine where users are directed when they click Login from your page, and the User Page will determine where users are directed when they click Register or attempt to edit their profile information once they have logged in.

Figure 6-13

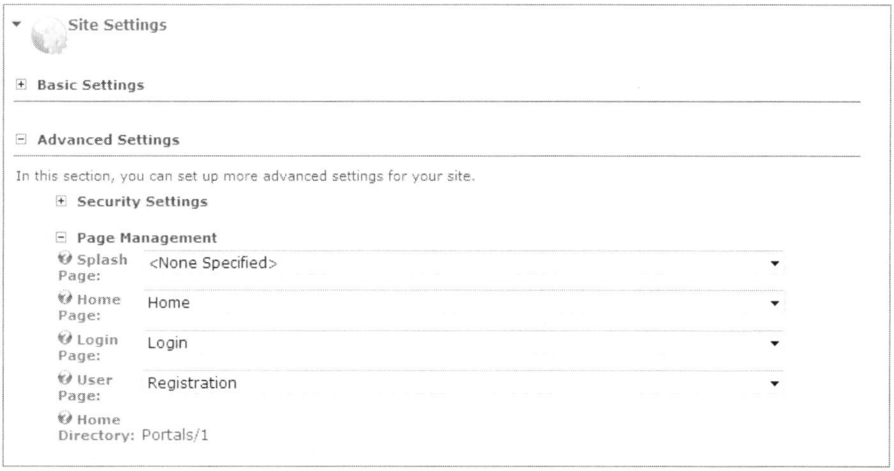

Figure 6-14

## *Adding Users to Roles*

As discussed earlier, the user roles in DNN allow you to segment your users and specify permissions to your content using these roles. For the sample softball league's website, we'll use roles to differentiate our members from outside visitors. Additionally, we'll group our users into two roles: coaches and players. Within these groups, we'll also group users by team. By segmenting our users by team, each team can view team-only content. The coaches will have additional editing capabilities, as well as content specifically for their eyes only. The following table lists the required roles for the softball league's website.

### League Roles

| Role | Who | Access |
| --- | --- | --- |
| Administrator | League manager | View and edit for all pages and content |
| All Users | Any Internet user | View publicly available pages |
| League Members | Players and coaches in the league | View publicly available pages View league-only pages<br>View team pages, but only some modules on the team pages |
| Coaches | Coaches | View events on the schedule for them, forums for only coaches |
| Team 1 | Team 1 coaches and players | View team 1 only information on team 1 page |
| Team 2 | Team 2 coaches and players | View team 2 only information on team 2 page |
| Team 3 | Team 3 coaches and players | View team 3 only information on team 3 page |
| Team 4 | Team 4 coaches and players | View team 4 only information on team 4 page |

Chapter 4 reviewed the process of creating roles, applying the roles to users, and using roles to restrict content (pages or modules or both). For our softball league's website, we'll use roles to allow players on specific teams to see content intended for only their team, but all players in the league will be able to see the content available to league members. In DNN the pages visible to only league members will have View permissions available to only the users in the League Members role, as shown in Figure 6-15.

Each team will have their own page. These pages will be visible to all league members. Additionally, each team page will have content visible to only the team members. For example, we'll use module-level permissions to give Team 1 players access to announcements on their team's page. When a member of Team 1 logs in, they will see more content on the Team 1 page. When other members of the league (belonging to League Members role) view Team 1's page, they won't see the announcements.

As you can gather from the numerous roles listed previously, assigning roles to the correct users could become a tedious task. Wouldn't it be nice to assign a role in batch to a group of users? You're in luck. DNN has a great feature called RSVP code that allows you to create a login code and even a link to allow users to automatically join a role by either entering the code or following the link.

As you create a role, you can create an RSVP code for the role in the Advanced Settings for the role. Once you have given the role a code, a link will be generated. When users click this link while logged on to your site, the corresponding role will be added to their account. As a refresher, you can access the

Security Roles page through the Roles icon in the Common Tasks of your Control Panel or through the Admin menu. You can add an RSVP code to a role as you create it or after the fact by editing a role. To add an RSVP code to a role, expand the Advanced Settings and give the role an RSVP code, as shown in Figure 6-16.

Figure 6-15

We'll use this feature to give players the ability to add themselves to the League Members role and their team's role. Then we can provide the team manager the code with the link included.

## User Registration — Putting It All Together

The preceding sections covered a number of features to use when creating a registration process for our users. Each feature required some type of configuration and as you went through this setup, the user experience can get lost. Before moving on, it will be valuable to review the user experience in total.

1. A league member visits your site and sees the same information as any visitor.

2. The member clicks Register to register on your site.

3. DNN will collect the member's first name, last name, username, display name, e-mail, and password.

4. The member is unauthorized until he or she verifies the registration by clicking the verification link in the e-mail generated by DNN and sent by the site administrator.

5.      After verifying his or her registration, the member can now log in. The member is prompted to provide optional and required information to complete his or her profile.

6.      As the site administrator, you send an e-mail that includes a link to an RSVP code to all league members.

7.      The member logs in to the site and clicks the RSVP code in the e-mail. By clicking this link included in the e-mail the member is assigned to the League Member role.

8.      The next time the league member logs in to the site, he or she will see pages visible only to league members.

9.      As the site administrator, you can log in and view all users in the League Member role and validate it against league rosters.

Figure 6-16

# Organizing, Creating, and Managing Content

Putting thought into the site map for your league's site will help to make building your pages easy and straightforward. In the process of setting up the login and registration processes, you've already created a few pages for your softball league's website (Login and Registration, respectively). Additionally, with the roles created, we've implied some site map structure because some of your roles will have different access to different areas of the site. To achieve this segmentation, you'll use page permissions to present the pages most relevant to our visitors and to avoid cluttering our page structure.

Using roles to segment users and the content available to them also enables you to distribute the responsibilities of content management by giving roles edit permissions on all pages or on specific pages.

## Planning Your Site Map

The softball league's website will have four types of content: content available to all users, content available to anyone in the league, content for coaches only, and content specific to individual team players. To achieve this segmentation, use page permissions to present users with the content most pertinent to them.

With the segmentation of the types of content in mind, start to map the architecture of the pages. Figure 6-17 shows the site map for the softball league's website with the user segmentation designated to groups of pages.

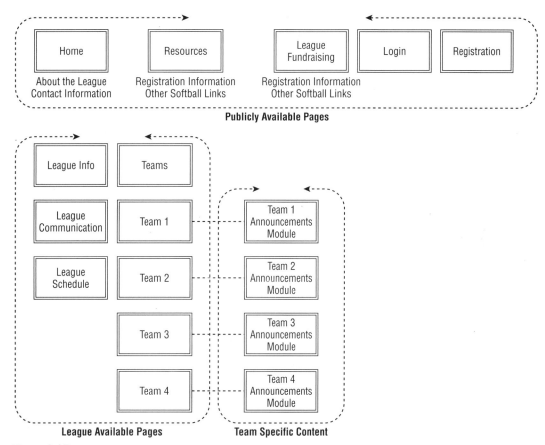

Figure 6-17

The next step is to apply the appropriate permissions to the pages to achieve this segmentation.

> ### Keeping Pages Visible to Administrators Only
>
> As you build your pages and apply permissions, it is assumed that your site is not live. If your site is already publicly available and you're adding pages to your site, you can apply permissions once the content is ready. As you build the content on your pages, you may want to keep the pages hidden and visible only to administrators.

## Applying Permissions

Earlier in the chapter, you defined the roles for your users. Using these roles, there are three levels of permission you can control across your DNN site. As you apply permissions to the content on your site, we'll demonstrate applying permissions at a page level and at a module level, and later as you create content you'll see that some modules provide additional levels of granularity for content.

The broadest level of permission is at a page level. As you create pages, you can define the roles or even specific users who will have permission to either View or Edit the page. By default, the pages you add to the site will be visible (and editable) only by site administrators. Using the site map defined previously, we're going to build the pages listed as Publically Available and give View permissions to All Users.

As you continue to build the site map for your softball league, you'll use page permissions to segregate your content. Using the roles you created for your league, you'll create pages only visible to League Members. You've created a role for League Members, and your league members should have this role applied to their accounts by applying the RSVP code provided. As we previously demonstrated in Figure 6-15, you can grant View permissions to a specific role (League Members). You'll use this setup to grant View permissions to the other pages visible to only the members of your league. When the members of your league log in, they will see additional pages in the menu.

Next, you can use Edit permissions to distribute the content management responsibilities of your site. Users with Edit rights will have the ability to edit page settings, add modules to the page, and create child pages. To demonstrate this, we'll grant the coaches edit rights to their specific team's page. The sample softball league has only four teams, so instead of creating a role specifically for the coach of Team 1, for instance, grant edit permissions to Team 1's page specifically to an individual user account (manager1). Below the permissions grid in Team 1's Page Settings, you can specifically grant permissions to a user by typing in their username and clicking the Add icon. Figure 6-18 illustrates granting permissions to an individual user.

To demonstrate the use of module-level permissions, you'll override the page permissions for the announcements content placed on each team's page. As you can see from Figure 6-17, each team will have announcements specific to that team. Later in this chapter we'll review the setup of the Announcements module to provide the content for these pages, but for now we'll focus on the module-level permissions. As you add modules to your page, understanding that module permissions can override the page permissions can help you to avoid building redundant pages just to provide slight variations in content.

Continuing with the example of Team 1's page, we'll override the page permissions on the Announcements module. This will allow all league members to see Team 1's page and a team bio or coaches' contact information, but only the team members will be able to see announcements by their coach. Also, since the coach of Team 1 was explicitly granted permission to edit this page, the site administrator won't have to manage all the content on this page. In Figure 6-19, we edited the module settings to override page permissions and grant View permissions to only members of Team 1. Since you are overriding View permissions, you have to uncheck Inherit View Permissions from Page and explicitly set View permissions for the module. If you were just overriding the Edit permissions for the module, you could keep the View permissions from the page and override only the Edit permissions.

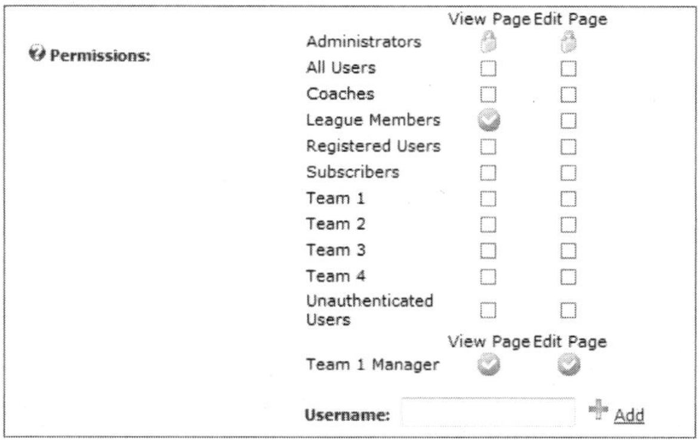

Figure 6-18

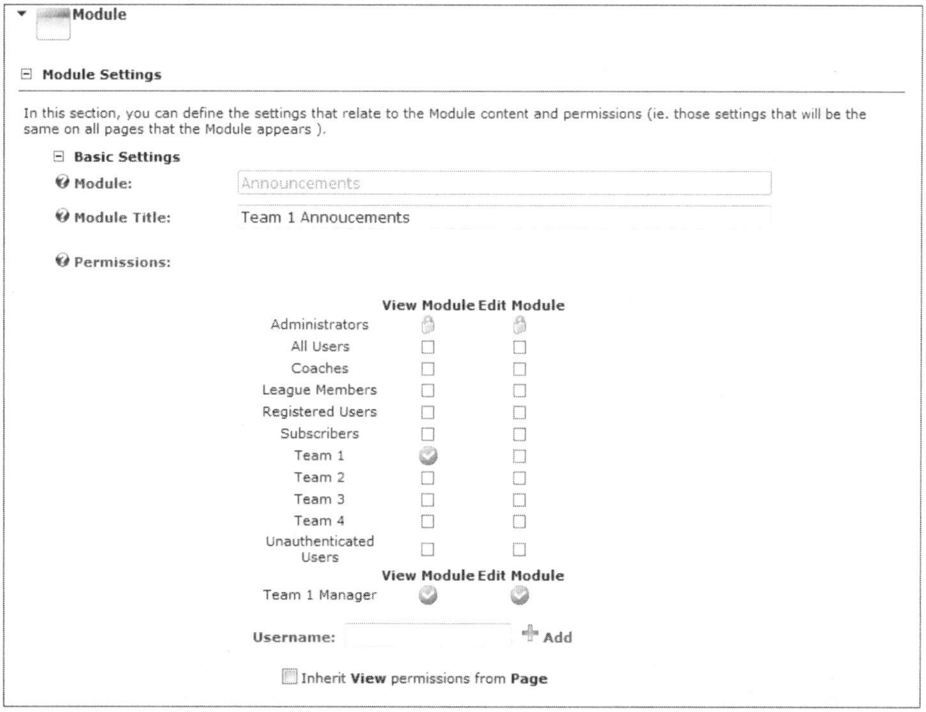

Figure 6-19

As you add and configure additional modules for your pages, you'll see that some modules have additional configuration options to grant or restrict permissions to the modules. For example, as you build the Events module later in the chapter, you'll be able to post events on your league schedule to which only coaches will be able to register. This is done through a distinct setting in the Events module that is more granular than the permissions found in the Basic Settings for the module.

# Administering Content with Modules

The content for this site has already been implied a number of times throughout the course of explaining the setup for your league's site. In Chapter 5, you learned the details of how to set up the Text/HTML, Blog, and Gallery modules. You can apply this knowledge to a league's site just as easily, and these modules can be just as valuable on a league's website as they were on your personal site.

In this chapter, you'll add to your DNN arsenal by setting up the Announcements, Events, and Forum modules. Each of these modules has specific functionality to give you a more powerful and easily maintainable site than a static web page or a DNN site using only Text/HTML modules. As we review these modules, we'll step through the basic setup necessary to make these modules useful on a league website. Once you're familiar with this setup, you can tailor the modules to your specific needs and get creative with the numerous options available.

## *Announcements Module*

The Announcement module allows you to post time-sensitive information to your site. The Announcements module also gives you the ability to attach images, link the post to a number of sources, track clicks, sort entries, and set publish/expiration dates. Additionally, as an administrator, you can set a template for the posts to allow multiple users to post announcements and still maintain a consistent format for the announcement entries.

This chapter's example league's website uses the Announcements module in two ways. One instance of the Announcements module is placed on the League Messages page. You'll use this instance of the Announcements module to post league-wide announcements, such as registration cutoffs, schedule postings, or general reminders to all league members. A second use for the Announcements module will be on each team's page for the coaches of the team to post announcements to their team members. The module settings for both of these use cases are the same, but, as discussed earlier, the module permissions will give different roles access to the module.

The Announcements module can be used as soon as you add it to a page. The default settings for the module will allow you to start adding announcements without additional setup. There are two configuration options and, depending on how savvy you are with HTML, you can have complete control of the look and layout of the announcements, using the template tool built into the module. The two configuration options are History and Description Length. The History option will determine how many days to display your announcements. The Description Length option will determine the number of characters to display in the search results of DNN's core search and the Syndicated feed created by the Announcements module.

The third configuration element in the Announcements module is the template display of your announcements. By default, the module will provide a display template using some of the most common tokens. The tokens are used as a placeholder to display the content input by the creator of each announcement. If you feel comfortable with HTML, you can create a unique layout for the displaying of your announcements using the template fields and the tokens available with the module. If you're not comfortable with creating your own display layout, the markup provided by default will display any of the information you provide for your announcements.

---

**Buried Treasures in the Help Link**

The Announcements module includes very well-documented help text. In the Announcements Settings section of the module settings, there is a link titled "Help" that will take you to full documentation to each setting in the module.

---

In addition to module settings, it is important to understand the inputs that make up your announcement posts and how each piece will affect the displaying of your announcements. Each announcement must have a title and a description. Optionally, you can attribute an image and a link to your announcements. If you choose to create a link with your post, the [READMORE] token will generate a link to the destination you specified. In Figure 6-20, we have created an announcement to the softball league. Next, we'll explain some of the fields used for this announcement.

The Announcements module can track the number of times the link is clicked and even document the user, date, and time of each click. This feature can be especially useful if you want to track the effectiveness of your announcements for particularly crucial news.

One of the most significant features for the Announcements module is the ability to set publish and expiration dates for your posts. By default, the announcements will be sorted by publishing date in ascending order. If you want to specify the order of your posts manually, use View Order to specify the order in which the announcements should appear. The lower the number, the higher up the announcement will appear in your list of posts.

We're often asked what benefits the Announcements module has over a standard Text/HTML module. Since the Text/HTML module (and all modules for that matter) can have a start and end date specified, it could act as a way to post time-sensitive announcements on your site. However, the main benefit of using the Announcements module is that it enables you to post multiple announcements in the same module, track the clicks if you're using a link to more information, and to create a template for your posts. This last benefit is especially useful in your softball league's website as you open up the permissions to allow team managers to post announcements.

## Forum Module

A forum is a way for users on your site to create conversation threads. Forums encourage an online community to converse with each other and use your site as a reference point for topics relating to your site. In the case of a softball league, forums can be places to have players discuss topics like the rules of the league or the results of games. Unlike a blog, where the blogger is the discussion leader and the user community can chime in with comments and trackbacks, the forums on a site can be a way to generate user interaction organically.

The Forum module can be as complex or simple as your requirements dictate. In this section, we'll review some of the core concepts to forums in general and apply these concepts to the Forum module. By understanding these core concepts, you'll be able to expand on the basics and flex the module to your needs.

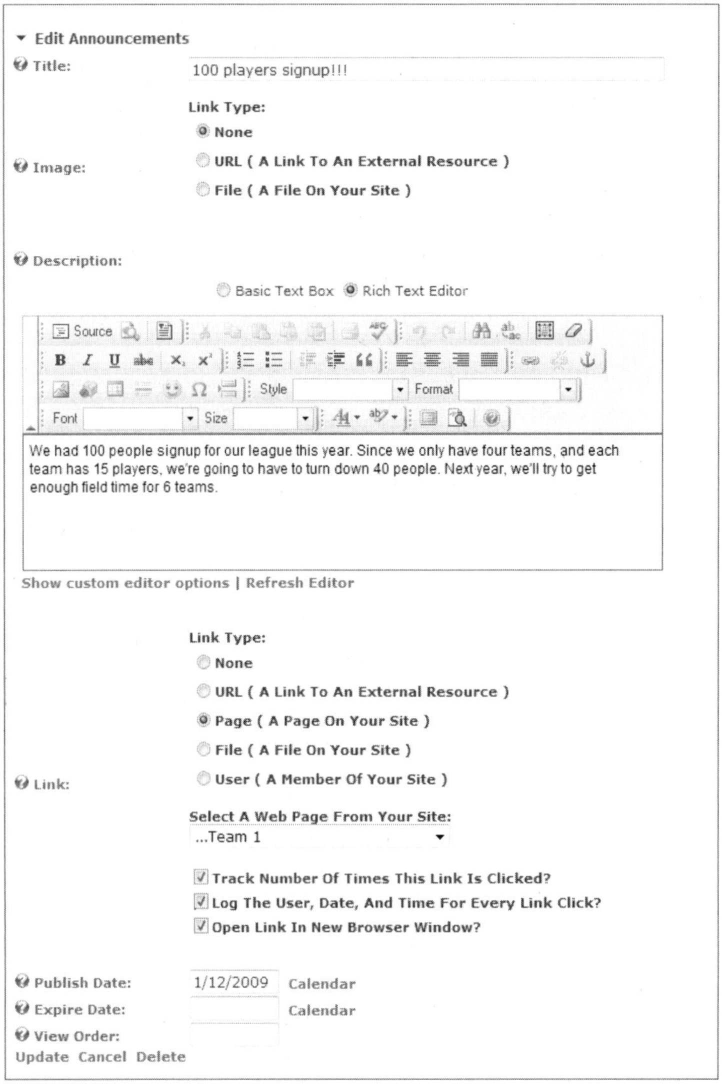

▾ Edit Announcements

⊘ Title:

100 players signup!!!

Link Type:
◉ None
○ URL ( A Link To An External Resource )
○ File ( A File On Your Site )

⊘ Image:

⊘ Description:

○ Basic Text Box  ◉ Rich Text Editor

We had 100 people signup for our league this year. Since we only have four teams, and each team has 15 players, we're going to have to turn down 40 people. Next year, we'll try to get enough field time for 6 teams.

Show custom editor options | Refresh Editor

Link Type:
○ None
○ URL ( A Link To An External Resource )
◉ Page ( A Page On Your Site )
○ File ( A File On Your Site )
○ User ( A Member Of Your Site )

⊘ Link:

Select A Web Page From Your Site:
...Team 1

☑ Track Number Of Times This Link Is Clicked?
☑ Log The User, Date, And Time For Every Link Click?
☑ Open Link In New Browser Window?

⊘ Publish Date:      1/12/2009     Calendar
⊘ Expire Date:                     Calendar
⊘ View Order:
Update  Cancel  Delete

**Figure 6-20**

The first concept of a forum to understand is the organization of conversations. In a forum, each conversation is called a *thread*. Forums are groups of like threads, and like forums can be bundled as forum groups. The Forum module in DNN uses this same organizational structure to manage conversations. Additionally, the Forum module allows you to apply permissions and behaviors to each forum to dictate the manner in which threads can be posted, replied to, and managed. The forum administrators are responsible for creating forums and groups of forums. The threads within a forum are created by anyone with access to the forum. Figure 6-21 illustrates how threads are grouped into forums and forums are grouped into forum groups.

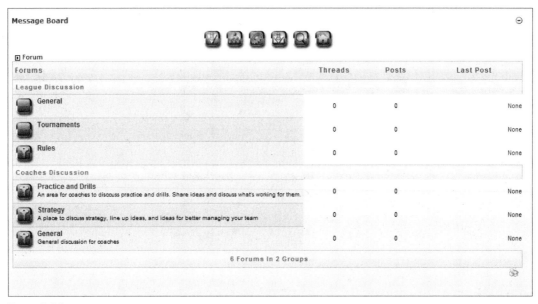

Figure 6-21

As a forum administrator, you can organize the forums within the module by clicking on the Admin icon. The Admin action is located through either the Actions menu (see Figure 6-22) or the Actions icon in the main page of the Forum module.

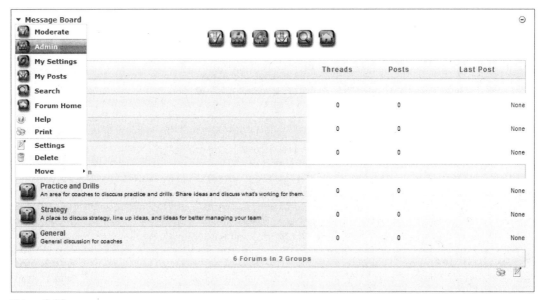

Figure 6-22

Once you are in the Forum Administration action, you can click Manage Forums/Groups to begin creating and organizing your forums. Figure 6-23 shows the Forum Administration options.

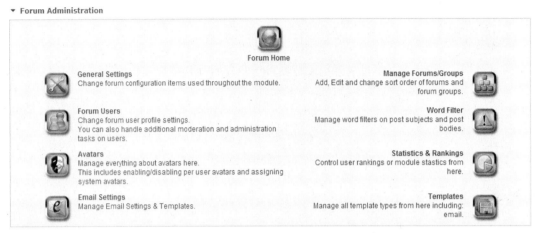

Figure 6-23

The next core concept of a forum is the behavior of posts within your forum. As you begin to add forums to the Forum module, you will have to determine the behavior of the forums. Figure 6-24 illustrates how we have determined the forum behavior for the General forum by editing the General Settings. Next, we will describe how forum behavior settings will determine how users interact with your forums.

There are three decisions you will need to make as you determine the behavior of your forums:

❑ **Will your forum be public or private?** This is an additional layer of permissions that allows the forum administrators to create forums visible only to specific users. Public forums are visible to anyone with View permissions to the module. All threads within the forum will be visible. Private forums are only visible to users with View Permissions to the forum. In Figure 6-25 you can see the forums in the Coaches Discussion forum group have a key icon to indicate they are private forums. We have set these forums as private and granted permissions to only users in the Coaches role. Figure 6-25 illustrates the Forum Behavior set for Practice and Drills forum.

❑ **Will posts in your forum require moderation?** As users post threads or reply to threads, the posts can be moderated by users granted Moderation permissions. There are additional intricacies to post moderation because the Forum module allows you to define even greater configurability for moderation. If a forum is moderated, all posts must be approved unless the user is a page or module administrator, granted Forum Administrator rights, identified as a moderator, or identified by a moderator as Trusted. As you can see in Figure 6-26, when a forum is moderated, you will have to determine which roles will moderate the posts.

❑ **Will posts in your forum be restricted?** As an administrator, you can determine which roles will be able to Start Thread or Reply Thread. If users have rights to Start Thread, they can start new threads and reply to existing threads. If users have rights to Reply Thread, they will only be allowed to reply to existing threads. Figure 6-27 demonstrates a forum with Post Restrictions. When a forum has post restrictions, you will need to determine which roles have Start Thread and Reply Thread permissions.

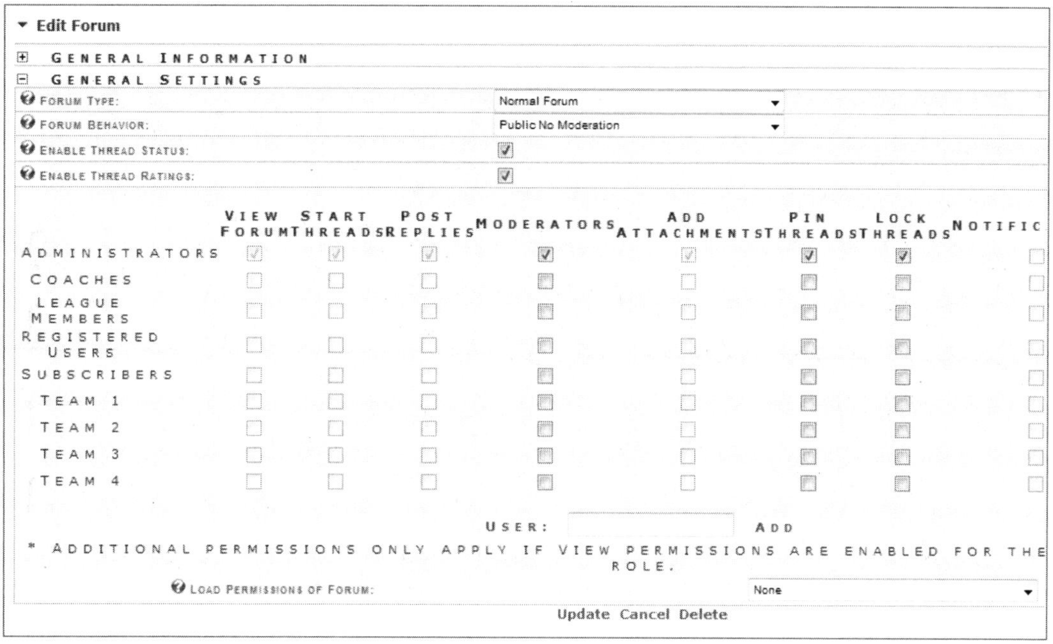

Figure 6-24

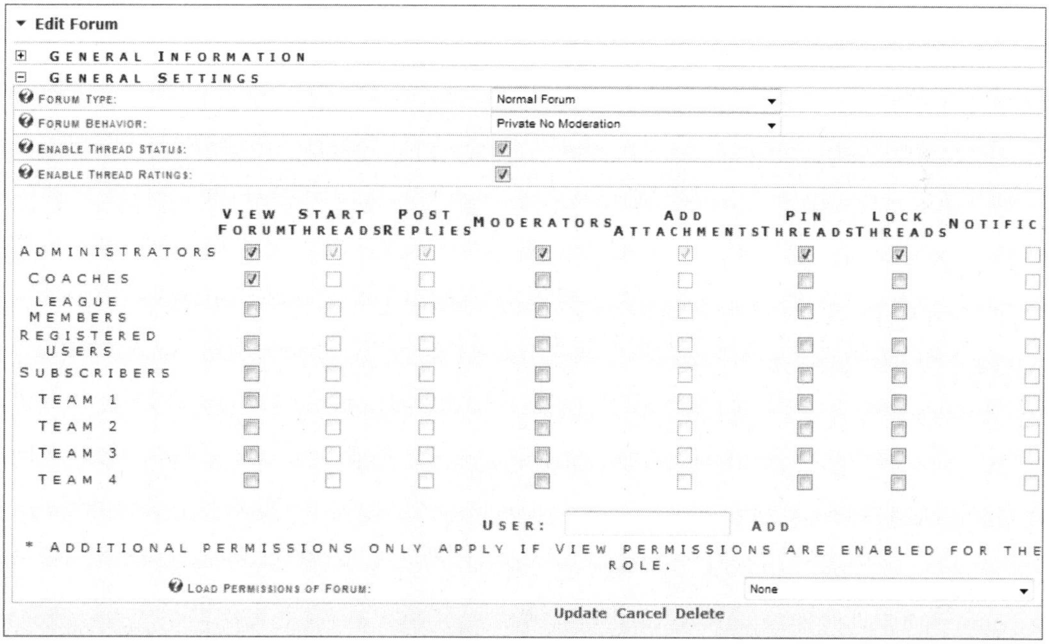

Figure 6-25

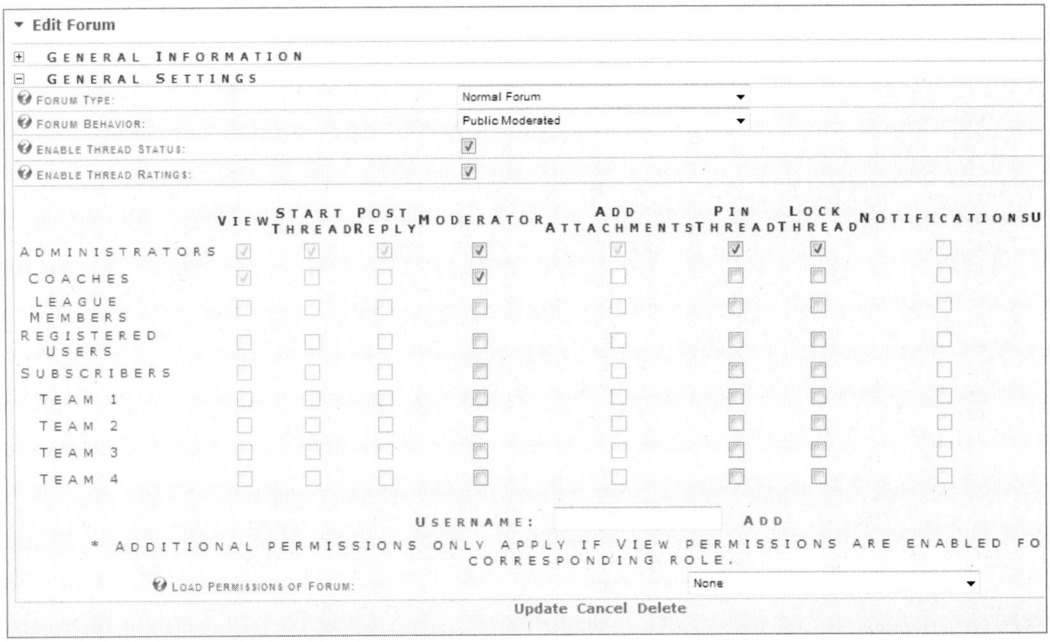

▼ **Edit Forum**

⊞  GENERAL INFORMATION
⊟  GENERAL SETTINGS

| ❷ FORUM TYPE: | Normal Forum ▼ |
| ❷ FORUM BEHAVIOR: | Public Moderated ▼ |
| ❷ ENABLE THREAD STATUS: | ☑ |
| ❷ ENABLE THREAD RATINGS: | ☑ |

| | VIEW | START THREAD | POST REPLY | MODERATOR | ADD ATTACHMENTS | PIN THREAD | LOCK THREAD | NOTIFICATIONS | U |
|---|---|---|---|---|---|---|---|---|---|
| ADMINISTRATORS | ☑ | ☑ | ☑ | ☑ | ☑ | ☑ | ☑ | ☐ | |
| COACHES | ☑ | ☐ | ☐ | ☑ | ☐ | ☐ | ☐ | ☐ | |
| LEAGUE MEMBERS | ☐ | ☐ | ☐ | ☐ | ☐ | ☐ | ☐ | ☐ | |
| REGISTERED USERS | ☐ | ☐ | ☐ | ☐ | ☐ | ☐ | ☐ | ☐ | |
| SUBSCRIBERS | ☐ | ☐ | ☐ | ☐ | ☐ | ☐ | ☐ | ☐ | |
| TEAM 1 | ☐ | ☐ | ☐ | ☐ | ☐ | ☐ | ☐ | ☐ | |
| TEAM 2 | ☐ | ☐ | ☐ | ☐ | ☐ | ☐ | ☐ | ☐ | |
| TEAM 3 | ☐ | ☐ | ☐ | ☐ | ☐ | ☐ | ☐ | ☐ | |
| TEAM 4 | ☐ | ☐ | ☐ | ☐ | ☐ | ☐ | ☐ | ☐ | |

USERNAME: [_____]  ADD

\* ADDITIONAL PERMISSIONS ONLY APPLY IF VIEW PERMISSIONS ARE ENABLED FO
CORRESPONDING ROLE.

❷ LOAD PERMISSIONS OF FORUM:  None ▼

Update  Cancel  Delete

Figure 6-26

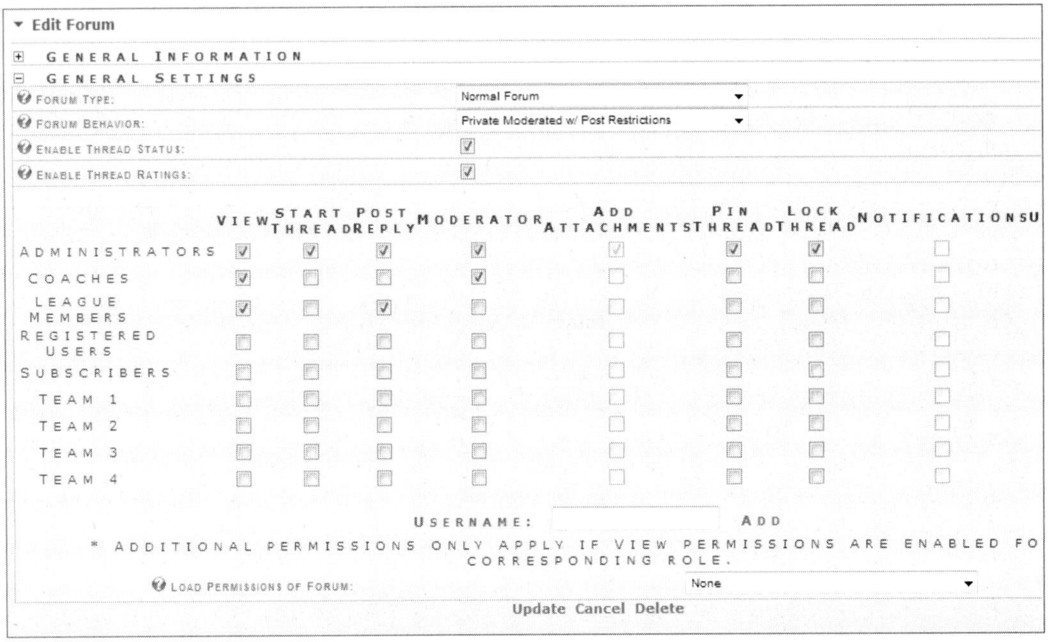

▼ **Edit Forum**

⊞  GENERAL INFORMATION
⊟  GENERAL SETTINGS

| ❷ FORUM TYPE: | Normal Forum ▼ |
| ❷ FORUM BEHAVIOR: | Private Moderated w/ Post Restrictions ▼ |
| ❷ ENABLE THREAD STATUS: | ☑ |
| ❷ ENABLE THREAD RATINGS: | ☑ |

| | VIEW | START THREAD | POST REPLY | MODERATOR | ADD ATTACHMENTS | PIN THREAD | LOCK THREAD | NOTIFICATIONS | U |
|---|---|---|---|---|---|---|---|---|---|
| ADMINISTRATORS | ☑ | ☑ | ☑ | ☑ | ☑ | ☑ | ☑ | ☐ | |
| COACHES | ☑ | ☐ | ☐ | ☑ | ☐ | ☐ | ☐ | ☐ | |
| LEAGUE MEMBERS | ☑ | ☐ | ☑ | ☐ | ☐ | ☐ | ☐ | ☐ | |
| REGISTERED USERS | ☐ | ☐ | ☐ | ☐ | ☐ | ☐ | ☐ | ☐ | |
| SUBSCRIBERS | ☐ | ☐ | ☐ | ☐ | ☐ | ☐ | ☐ | ☐ | |
| TEAM 1 | ☐ | ☐ | ☐ | ☐ | ☐ | ☐ | ☐ | ☐ | |
| TEAM 2 | ☐ | ☐ | ☐ | ☐ | ☐ | ☐ | ☐ | ☐ | |
| TEAM 3 | ☐ | ☐ | ☐ | ☐ | ☐ | ☐ | ☐ | ☐ | |
| TEAM 4 | ☐ | ☐ | ☐ | ☐ | ☐ | ☐ | ☐ | ☐ | |

USERNAME: [_____]  ADD

\* ADDITIONAL PERMISSIONS ONLY APPLY IF VIEW PERMISSIONS ARE ENABLED FO
CORRESPONDING ROLE.

❷ LOAD PERMISSIONS OF FORUM:  None ▼

Update  Cancel  Delete

Figure 6-27

These three decisions can be mixed and matched to give you the eight options available for Forum Behavior, as shown in Figure 6-28.

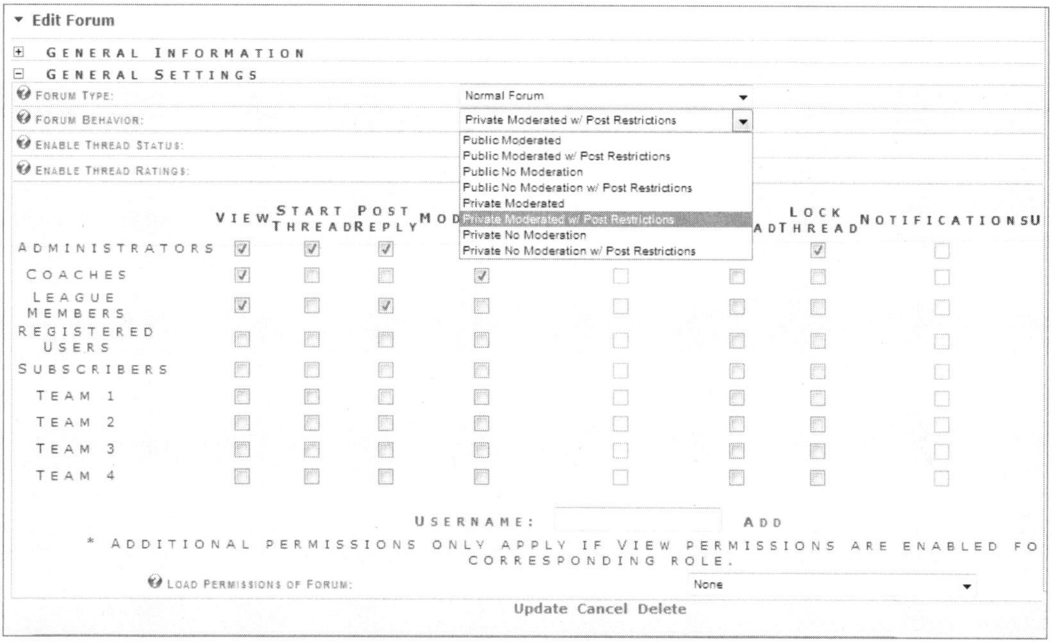

Figure 6-28

Forums with moderation or post restrictions are most apt for forums in which discussions need to be topically correct or if users of the forum cannot be trusted to provide accurate or appropriate content.

The Forum module has a very robust set of features, configuration options, and activities for the forum administrators and forum users. Next, you'll apply the concepts of a forum to the implementation of the Forum module on the League Communication page of our softball league's website. This page is visible only to league members, so inherently your forums are restricted to a trusted group of users. Therefore, our forums will be public, without moderation, and unrestricted.

We'll create two groups of forums: one for all league members and one for coaches only. To create forums and group forums, you need to access the Forum Administration action through the Actions menu, and then click on the Manage Forums/Groups icon to start adding groups or forums to existing groups. You'll create two groups for your softball league: League Discussions and Coaches Discussions. In the League Discussions group, you'll create forums organized by common topics — Rules, Tournaments, and General. In the Coaches group, there will be the following forums: Practice and Drills, Strategy, and General. In Figure 6-29, we have created the League Discussion Forum Group.

In the Coaches Discussions group, all forums will be private and accessible to only users in the Coaches role. When coaches visit the League Communication page, they will see an additional set of forums in which they can participate.

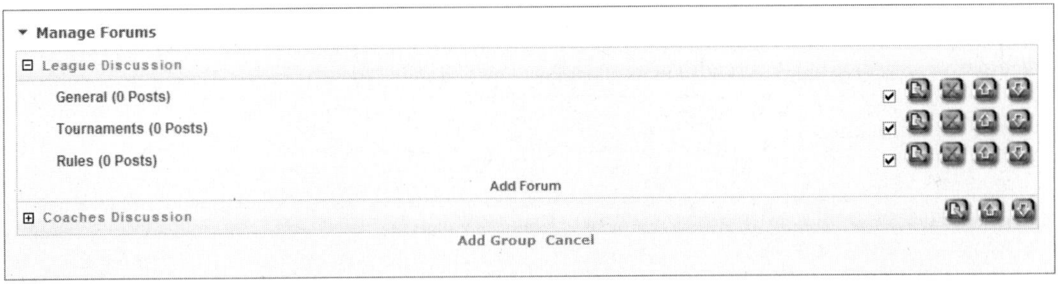

**Figure 6-29**

An additional setup option for each forum is the Forum Type. To configure the Forum Type, navigate to the General Settings upon creating or editing a forum. There are three types of forums — Normal, Notification, and Link. Our softball league will exclusively use Normal forums. This type of forum allows your threads to function best for conversations and dialogue. Notification forums function similarly to Normal forums, but you can specify roles for which you want to force the users to receive a notification for each new post. If we had forums for each team, we could create a Link forum to serve as a link to each team's forum.

## Events Module

An event calendar is a great tool for any organization. For a softball league, an events calendar can be used to list game schedules, registration deadlines, coaching clinics, or team parties. The core Events module in DNN offers a wide range of features and configuration options to allow for flexibility in the way you display your events as well as great features for advanced setup or unique use cases. In the softball league example, we'll focus on a few of these features to meet your specific needs.

In the page structure for our softball league, we created a page for League Schedule. This page is only visible to league members. There isn't anything extremely private that you need to post to the calendar, but since there is a section of the site specifically geared toward our league members, we'll continue to group content under the League Members section of the site. Also, it gives your league members a benefit to registering and logging in to the site. The first step toward setting up a calendar is to place the Events module on the page.

After adding the module to the page, you could immediately begin to add events to your calendar. However, before you begin adding events, review the Event module settings to determine which settings make sense for your calendar. For the softball league's calendar, you'll change a few of the settings to tailor the module to your needs.

In the General Settings section of the Event module's settings, there are a number of configuration options you want to set for your league's schedule. First, you want to validate that the time zone is correct. By default, the time zone should match the time zone set for your portal in Site Settings, but since the accuracy of your schedule is important, confirm that it is correct in the module as well. Next, review the skins for the calendar to pick a look for the events. On the sample site, we have set the Calendar view as the default and only view. Figure 6-30 illustrates the General Settings we have chosen for the League Schedule.

**Figure 6-30**

Since we are exclusively using a Calendar view for our events, the Month View settings are important to review as well. We recommend that on the Month View you enable "Show Events on Next Month (or Prev Month)" and "Show Event Start Time in Title." In Figure 6-31, you can see the Month View Settings for our League Schedule. If you allowed other views, you should also review the settings for Event List and Week View.

Next, we'll review some of the other settings available in the Events module. Later in this section you'll apply a number of these setting by adding a variety of different events to our schedule. In the Reminder Settings for the module, the Events module allows users to subscribe to events for reminders. If your calendar is publicly available, you can also allow unauthenticated users (visitors not logged in to the site) to subscribe to reminders. Figure 6-32 shows the Reminder Settings set for your League Schedule. Since only authenticated users will be viewing the Events module, you can ignore the Remind Anonymous setting.

In addition to reminders, you can allow events to be created with enrollment. If an event has enrollment enabled, the users can indicate their attendance to the event. The enrollment details are established when the event is added to the calendar, but if you wish to collect payment for user enrollment, the payment processor needs to be established in the module settings, as illustrated in Figure 6-33.

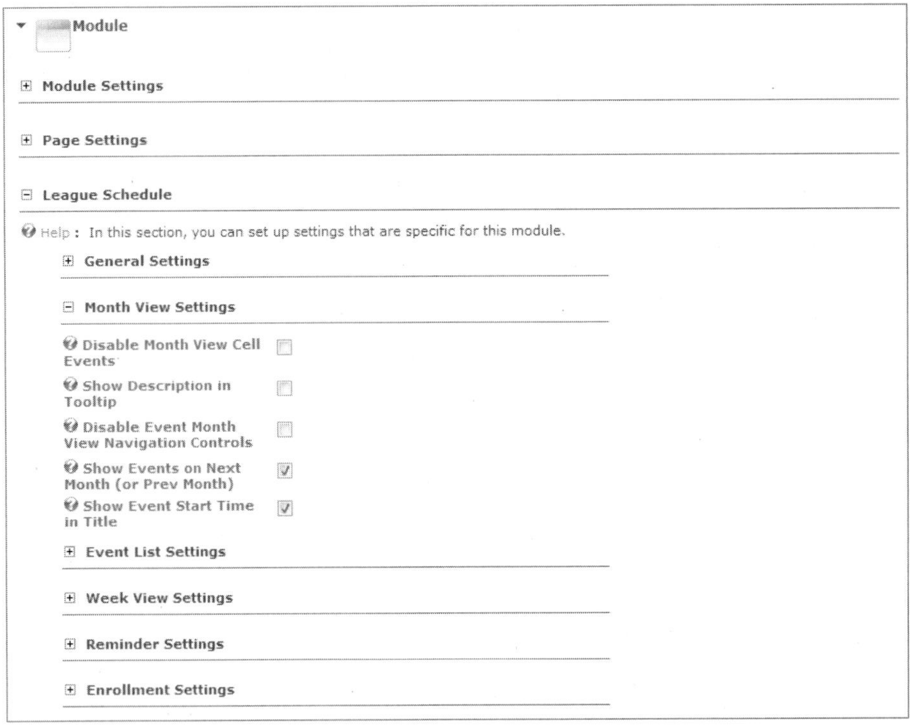

Figure 6-31

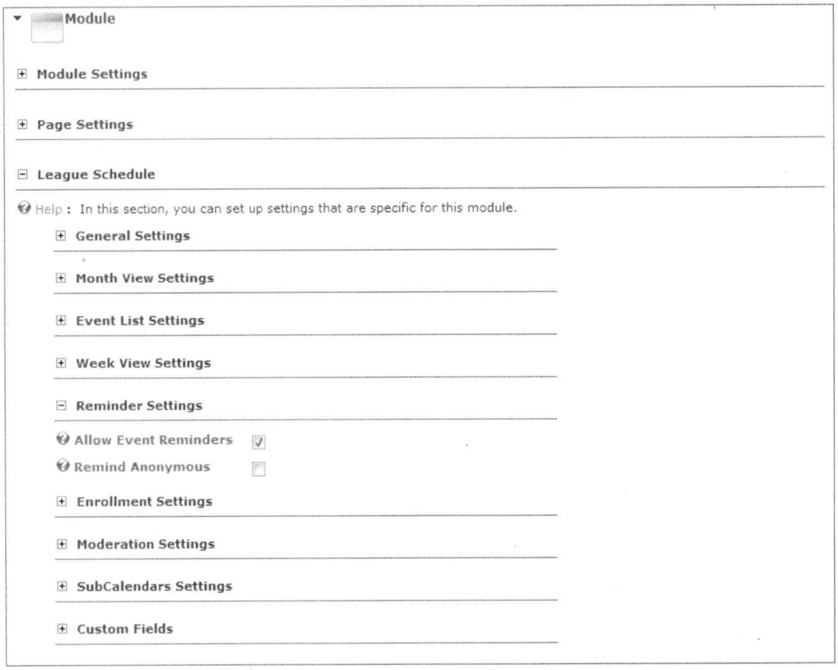

Figure 6-32

**Figure 6-33**

As the module administrator, you can choose to moderate the submission of Events. This setup only makes sense if you are granting other users Edit rights to the Events module. The users with Edit rights to the module will be able to add events, but the event will not be published until a user with Moderator rights approves the event. In Figure 6-34, you can see the Events module has an additional level of permissions available to the module administrator.

If you build multiple calendars on your site, you can create a master calendar to aggregate the events for each of the subcalendars. To enable the aggregation of calendars, you must specify that the calendar should Include Other Site Event Modules. Additionally, if you chose the Add SubModule Name option, the module's title will be added to the Event on your master calendar. To add subcalendars to your master calendar, select them from the list of Event modules on your site and click Add. These settings are shown in Figure 6-35.

The final settings for the module are the custom fields. By default, each event collects a title, start and end dates, importance level, category, location, notes, and the ability to define two custom fields. We'll use Custom Fields for your League Schedule to give your members more information about the events in a consistent manner. These custom fields will be very helpful for the game and scrimmage schedules because we will want to define a Home and Away team for each game. These custom fields can be named Home and Away, using the Language Editor.

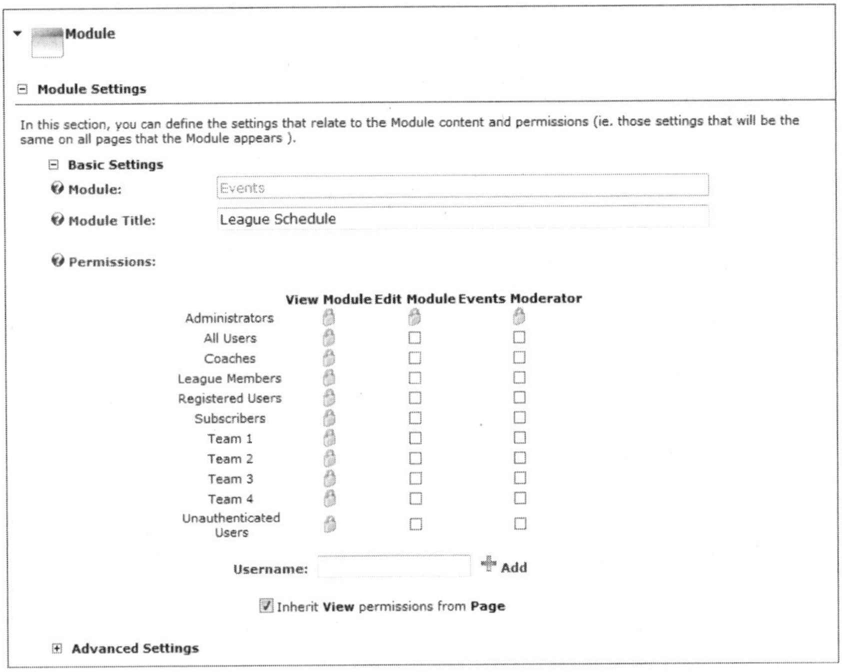

Figure 6-34

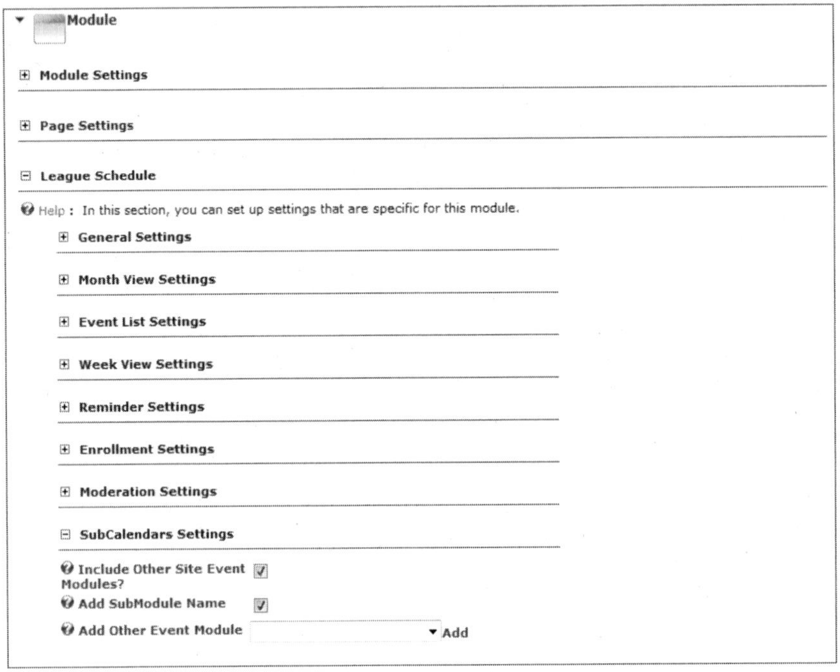

Figure 6-35

**Modifying the Custom Fields Using the Language Editor**

The Events module uses the Language Editor to allow administrators to customize the names of their custom fields. To rename your custom fields to Home and Away, complete the following steps:

1. Go to the Admin menu and select Extensions.

2. In the list of Extensions, edit the Default Language extension.

3. Within the Default Language extension, edit the Language Files.

4. In the tree menu on the left, expand Local Resources and then expand `DesktopModules`.

5. Within the `DesktopModules` node, expand Events and then `App_LocalResources`. This will give you a list of resource (`.resx`) files. These files include the fields with which you can customize the module for your use.

There are three resource files you should update to make sure that you maintain consistency throughout the module. Figure 6-36 illustrates the navigation of the Language Editor to locate the resource files used to customize the custom fields.

❑ Update the fields for Custom Field 1 and Custom Field 2 in `EditEvents.ascx.resx`. For your softball league, you are updating Custom Field 1 to specify the Home Team and Custom Field 2 to specify the Visiting Team. You'll need to update these fields in each place the field appears.

❑ Update the fields for Custom Field 1 and Custom Field 2 in `EventDetails.ascx.resx`.

❑ Update the fields for Custom Field 1 and Custom Field 2 in `Settings.ascx.resx`.

With the initial module settings determined for your League Schedule, next you'll complete the organizational tasks available in the Events module. The Events module allows you to define locations and categories for your calendar. The locations and categories for your module will be available for each Event as you begin to add Events. To add locations and categories, navigate to Edit Categories and Edit Locations in the Actions menu. With an initial list of locations and categories defined, you'll be able to associate our events to these fields as soon as you start to add events. As more categories and locations are needed, you can add them to your lists, but for now you'll set up the initial list.

There are four types of events we'll post to our calendar: games and scrimmages, league parties, monthly coaches meetings, and coaching clinics. We'll use these four types of events as the categories for your calendar. Additionally, we'll want site visitors to be able to filter the events using categories. By default, the Events module allows categories to act as filters. If you want to disable this feature, you can locate the setting in the General Settings for the module. Figure 6-37 illustrates the creation of the categories for the league's events. To add or edit categories for your Events module, navigate to Edit Categories in the Actions menu.

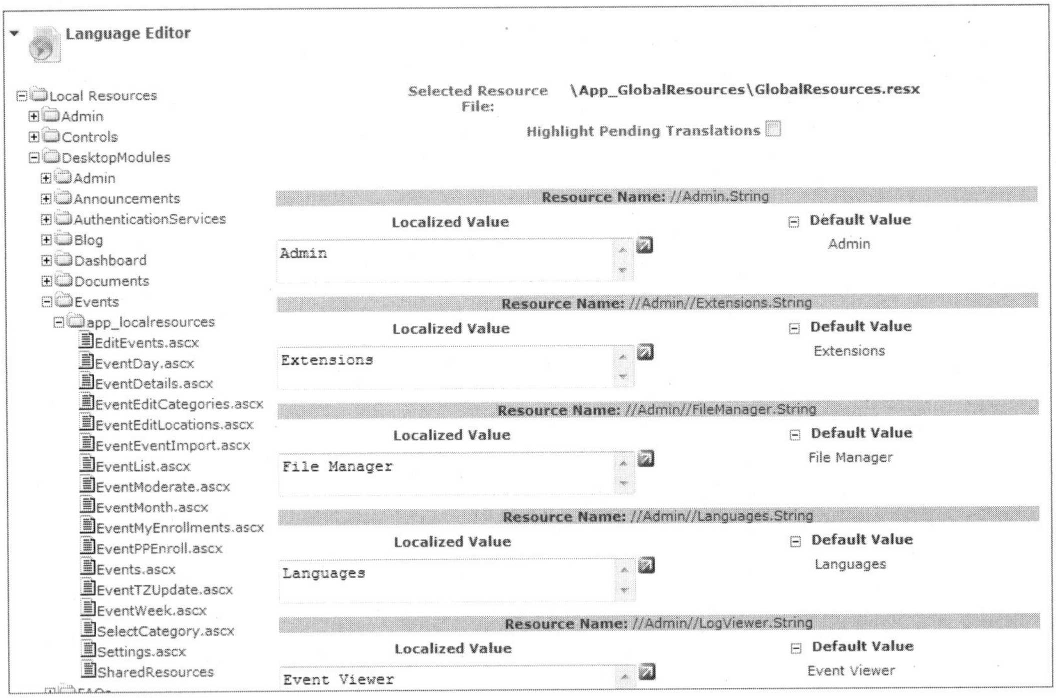

**Figure 6-36**

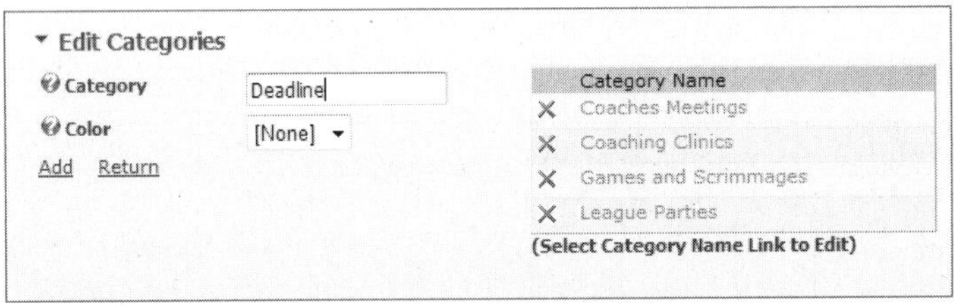

**Figure 6-37**

Our league has two fields at which games are played. In addition to the softball fields, there's a league office. The two fields and the league office will be the three locations for the events to start. Each location can have a location link attached. This is a great tool to link to an external map provider. Most map providers will allow you to plot your locations and create a link with the coordinates populated in the link. To edit the locations for your Events module, navigate to the Edit Locations action in the Actions menu. Figure 6-38 lists the three locations with links to maps in Google Maps.

With your module settings configured and your categories and locations defined, you're ready to start adding events. There are three examples of events we'll add to your calendar to demonstrate some of the functionality in the Events module.

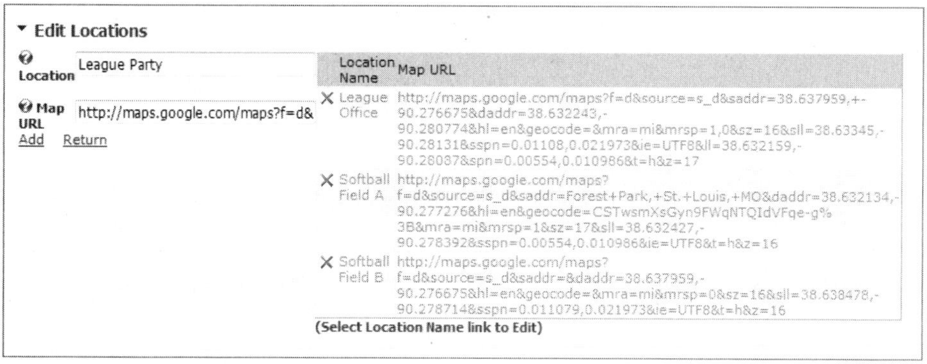

**Figure 6-38**

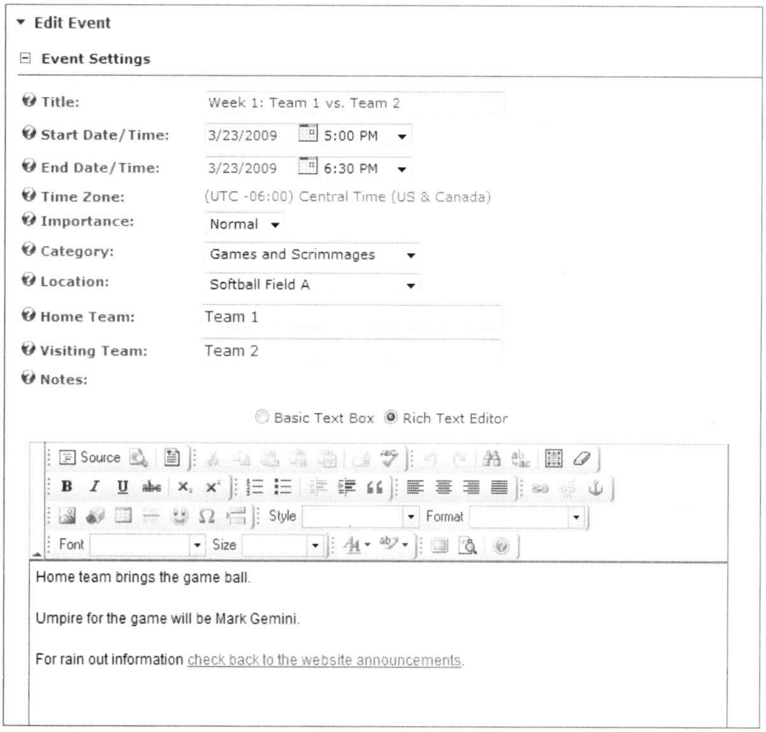

**Figure 6-39**

First, we'll add a basic event to our calendar. To add events to the calendar, select Add Event from the Actions menu. The game schedule will be a good exercise in adding basic events to the league calendar. Figure 6-39 illustrates the addition of a game between Team 1 and Team 2. For each game, we'll fill out the following fields:

❑ **Title**: Title of the game played (Week 1: Team 1 vs. Team 2).

❑ **Start and End dates**: You'll use the Start and End dates for each event to specify the date and time of each game.

❑   **Category**: Games and Scrimmages.

❑   **Location**: The field in which the game is played.

❑   **Notes**: Instructions to the coaches, possibly the umpire for the game, and instructions for rain-outs.

❑   **Reminder Settings**: Send a reminder to anyone who requests notification.

Next, we'll want to add the monthly coaches' meetings as recurring events. Adding these events will be the same as adding a basic event, except that we'll set recurring settings to avoid having to add each event individually. The coaches' meetings take place on the first Monday of the month and end in October. Figure 6-40 illustrates the setup for a monthly recurring event. To specify an event as recurring, expand the Recurring Settings when you are adding or editing an Event.

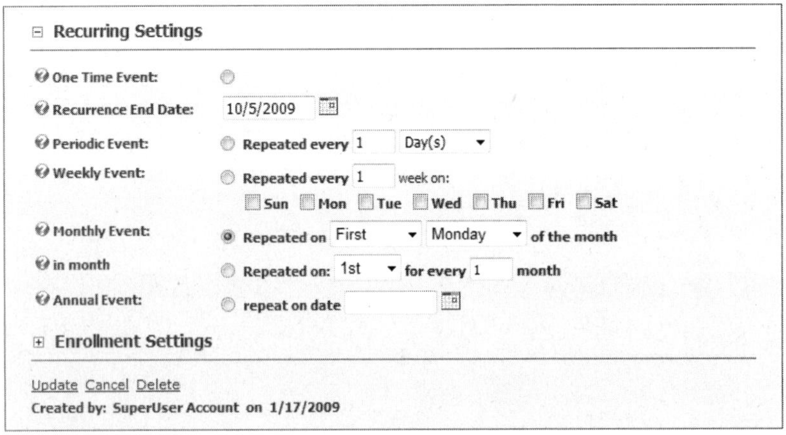

Figure 6-40

The third type of event we'll want to add is for coaches' clinics. The coaches' clinics require registration and payment for the registration. Again, we'll complete the Event settings, but additionally we'll configure the Enrollment Settings. Like the Recurring Settings, Enrollment Settings are collapsed by default below the Event Settings. Expand the Enrollment Settings to enable enrollment for your events. The coaches' clinics cost money. You'll collect payment ($10) at registration by using PayPal. Figure 6-41 illustrates the setup required to allow enrollment and collect registration payment. As you can see, we have restricted enrollment to only coaches by specifying an enrollment role. The event will be visible to all other roles, but the link to enroll in the event will not be shown.

Later, you can check back on your event registration by accessing the event through the Edit Event activity. By expanding the Enrollment Settings for your event, you can review the enrollment options and view Enrolled Users. In Figure 6-42, you can see we have one team manager enrolled in our coaching clinic. From here, you can send an e-mail to all enrolled participants or delete users from the enrollment.

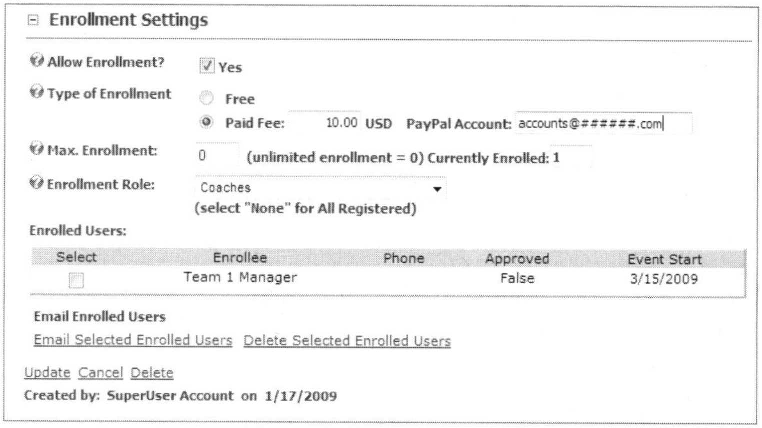

Figure 6-41

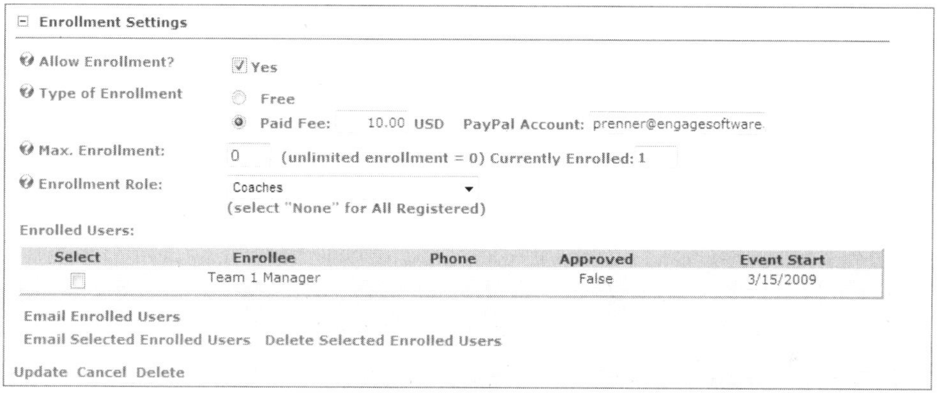

Figure 6-42

# Summary

Using DNN's core functionality, this chapter implemented a robust website tailored to a small social organization. With some thoughtful decisions and carefully planned setup, you can use DNN to make administering and maintaining a website for your organization easy.

Your softball league now has a rich database of league members. The content is maintained by your members and the user accounts are easily used to tailor your content to your users. Using page and module permissions, you were able to give various user groups access to a wealth of information while making sure that the content is relevant to their visit to your site.

By implementing the Announcements module, you have a manageable way to provide current updates to your league members as well as a way for your coaches to post announcements for solely their team members. Using the Forum module, your league members can facilitate conversations organically. Additionally, you can have private forums for your coaches to discuss strategy and coaching ideas. The Events module allows you to eliminate printed schedules and rainout hotlines by keeping your schedule and league events in one place.

# 7

# Creating a Small Business Website

Whether or not your small business should have a website is no longer the pressing question for most small business owners. The more pertinent question is which technology you'll implement to create, manage, and grow your small business. A content management system (CMS) is an ideal tool for small businesses to use, and DNN is the perfect solution as a CMS.

It is likely DotNetNuke (DNN) already has piqued your interest or maybe you've already committed to using DNN for your small business. Good for you; you've chosen a very powerful tool that will allow you to grow your site as you grow your business. And even better yet, DNN is easy to use and offers a long list of features to give your site a professional look without a full-time web administrator.

In this chapter, we'll review the features of DNN that will enable you to build out a powerful, flexible site while keeping it easy to manage and maintain. This chapter differs from previous chapters in that we'll discuss some of the considerations important for you to understand to start extending the core technology that DNN provides.

By reviewing the Store, FAQ, and Feedback modules, you'll have three great tools to provide your customers value as they visit your website. We'll also review some of the essential features to consider in the site administration and setting up of your DNN installation.

This chapter discusses the following topics:

❑   Why a content management system like DNN can benefit your small business

❑   The administrative considerations for your small business website

❑   The use of SSL to secure pages in an e-commerce site

❑   The design considerations important to understand before you purchase a custom or commercial skin package

❑   Administering content for your small business website using the Store, FAQ, and Feedback modules

# Why Use DotNetNuke for Your Small Business Website?

Before we dive into the detailed setup and implementation of a small business site, it is important to emphasize the value that a CMS provides to you as a small business owner. Complicated website design and implementations can be hard to justify for a small business. Hiring a web designer and developer or employing a full-time webmaster can be costly. A CMS such as DNN will make sure that you keep these expenses to a minimum.

A CMS enables you to manage your site's content separately from the design of your web pages. In a traditional, static website implementation, a site's content is ingrained in the design and layout of the web pages. In DNN, content is managed in modules that store the content in a database server. The content is separate from the design and layout of your website. When your site needs a new design, the content will continue to live within the modules, and your skin can easily be swapped out for an updated design. Additionally, you have control over a number of other elements on your site, such as the image for your logo, through administrative functions.

Being able to manage your content without knowing HTML or more complex web development languages means that you can own the content on your site and make frequent updates as needed. As search engine rankings become more refined, the importance of up-to-date, relevant content is a critical factor in keeping your site high in the rankings. Using tools like announcements, blogs, or other modules we've already reviewed, you'll be able to create new content often and easily.

## Goals for Your Website

Reviewing the goals for your website is the first step for any type of site. For a small business or e-commerce site, this task is absolutely crucial. A website can be a valuable asset to a business when done right and implemented with a goal in mind. Your site can generate revenue, decrease support calls and questions, provide customers with resources, and even build loyalty or a customer community.

Often a website lacks focus as the result of attempting to accomplish all things for all people. How many times have you visited a website and become frustrated because you can't find what you need? Or have you ever visited an e-commerce site intending to buy something but gave up because the checkout process was confusing or you didn't feel right about completing the purchase? These experiences are examples of a website lacking focus and clearly defined goals. Additionally, these types of experiences highlight the importance for your website of providing not only a place to purchase products but also a place to reinforce trust with your customers.

In this chapter, we'll set up a website for a small business selling artisan soaps, Smelly Soaps, Inc. The website will provide users with an easy way to view products, purchase soaps, find answers to their questions, and contact us if they need assistance. Each of these goals can be satisfied with core modules included with DNN.

# Site Administration Considerations

In terms of site administration tasks, no settings or configuration options differ significantly from the configuration options reviewed in previous chapters. Again, evaluating the security settings you apply to membership registration, determining how you want to handle the default administrator, and explicitly determining the Login Page and User Page are all relevant settings to consider for your small business website. How you choose to set up your site's settings will be determined by your specific business and personal preferences.

## Site Settings

We have stepped through a number of the Site Settings in Chapter 4 and applied these settings in Chapters 5 and 6. In contrast to previous chapters, this section will focus more on the considerations for the site settings relevant to a small business site and less on the setting up of these configuration options. We will, however, use our soap company's website to demonstrate how easy it is to apply these decisions in practice. For our small business website, we'll use Public site membership to grant visitors authentication immediately upon registration. Using Public membership may cause our user records to become less reliable; however, since we're going to set up e-commerce pages on our site, we don't want to add additional steps to the purchase process. Keeping visitors engaged in our site and actively guiding them toward purchase will be important to our business.

As we discussed in Chapter 6, it can be valuable to provide visitors more information and direction at the login process. To accomplish this, we'll create specific pages for user login and registration and associate these pages with the Login and User Account activities, respectively. Figure 7-1 shows the setting to associate the Login page with the Login activity and the Account Info page to the User Page. These settings are found in the Advanced Settings section of Site Settings.

**Figure 7-1**

In addition to creating specific pages for the Login and User activities generated by the tokens used in our skin, we'll add content to these pages to provide information. These pages could even provide an opportunity to create custom skins to really tailor your visitors' experience on your site. The design and skin considerations for a small business are discussed in more detail in the upcoming section "Custom Design Considerations."

## Allowing Users to Manage Services

Allow Users to Manage Services is a single setting in the User Setting found in the User Accounts page, but the impact of this setting can be very powerful for you as a site administrator. "Manage Services" simply means manage the roles assigned to their account. Allowing users to manage their services is a way DNN give users control over their own permissions to your site. As discussed previously, roles in DNN can be used to grant or deny permissions, as well as to segment your users. As you segment your users with roles, you can also give them the ability to identify themselves with a segment by assigning or unassigning roles to their user account. It's likely you're not going to want to offer users the ability to manage their own roles for all of the roles on your site. DNN allows you to explicitly determine whether users should be able to opt in or out of a role by marking it as Public. Marking a role as Public means that the role will be available to users to either Subscribe or Unsubscribe to through the Manage Services activity. Figure 7-2 illustrates how you can set a role to be Public. To mark a role as Public, access the Security Roles page through the Common Tasks in the control panel. As you create or edit a role, you can mark the role as Public. In Chapter 4, we review all of the settings available to creating roles.

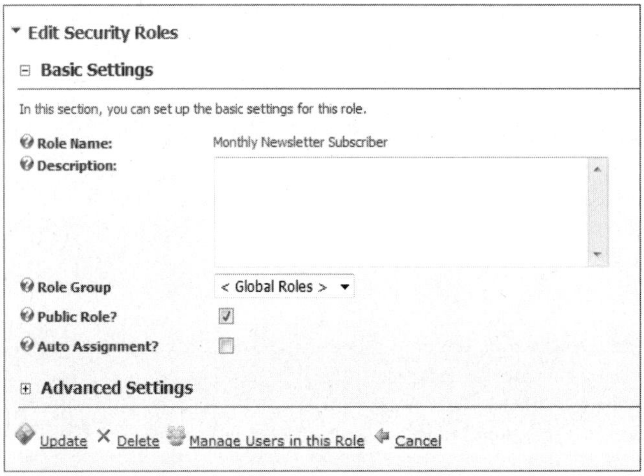

Figure 7-2

Once you have Public roles created, you'll want to give users the ability to subscribe or unsubscribe from these roles. To do this, you need to allow users to manage their services. By default, Manage Services is enabled for your site. To confirm this setting, access the User Setting through the User Accounts page. Figure 7-3 illustrates what users will see when Manage Services is available. The Manage Services activity is available to users in Manage Profile. For users to access this activity, they can click on their Display name while logged in to your site. For the user's Display Name to appear on your site, the skin must be using the USER skin object. MinimalExtropy utilizes the USER skin object in the top-right corner of the skin, directly below the search box.

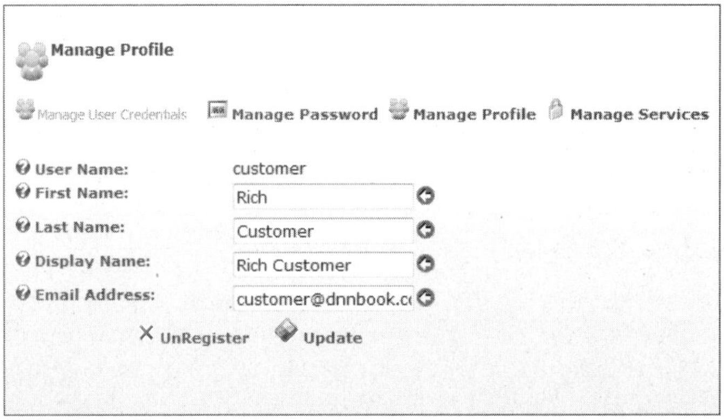

Figure 7-3

For this chapter's website, we're going to send a monthly newsletter and a quarterly newsletter. We also want to allow users to subscribe or unsubscribe to these newsletters. You can use Public roles to accomplish this functionality. Figure 7-4 shows the Manage Services activity located in Manage Profile used by users of your site to manage their Public roles.

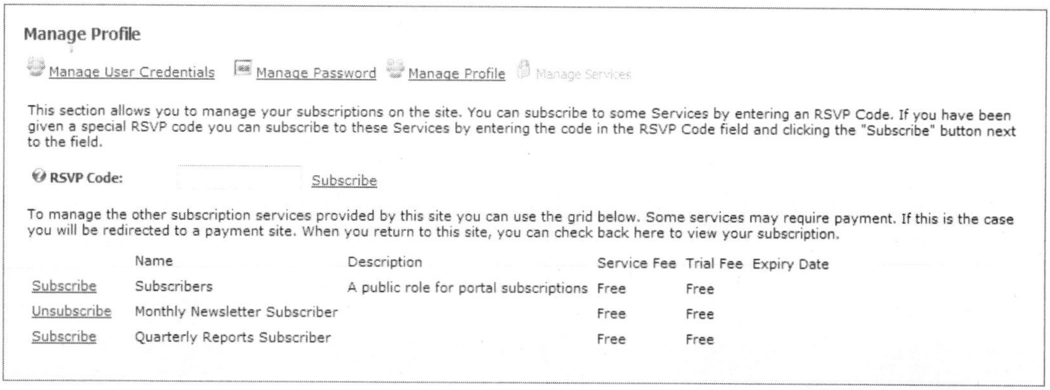

**Manage Profile**

Manage User Credentials    Manage Password    Manage Profile    Manage Services

This section allows you to manage your subscriptions on the site. You can subscribe to some Services by entering an RSVP Code. If you have been given a special RSVP code you can subscribe to these Services by entering the code in the RSVP Code field and clicking the "Subscribe" button next to the field.

RSVP Code: [          ]    Subscribe

To manage the other subscription services provided by this site you can use the grid below. Some services may require payment. If this is the case you will be redirected to a payment site. When you return to this site, you can check back here to view your subscription.

| | Name | Description | Service Fee | Trial Fee | Expiry Date |
|---|---|---|---|---|---|
| Subscribe | Subscribers | A public role for portal subscriptions | Free | Free | |
| Unsubscribe | Monthly Newsletter Subscriber | | Free | Free | |
| Subscribe | Quarterly Reports Subscriber | | Free | Free | |

Figure 7-4

DNN automatically has one Public role available, Subscribers. We used this role as an example for the roles we want on our site, but afterward we'll delete it since we have two more specific subscription roles for our newsletters. This role might work for your site if you require only a single Public role titled Subscribers.

# Creating Secure Pages

Because the Smelly Soaps website will contain e-commerce pages, the security of our customer's content is crucial. The actual security, encryption, and protection of your customer's sensitive data are also closely tied to the trust and reassurance you provide your users in their purchase decision. To provide an additional level of security and peace of mind for our customers, we'll use the Secure Sockets Layer (SSL) protocol to encrypt the content transmitted on specific pages.

To encrypt the content of your pages, you will need to work closely with your hosting provider to establish a certificate. The implementation of SSL on your site will take coordination between you, the site administrator, and the Host account, or super user. Later in this section we'll describe the configuration required to implement SSL on your site.

## What Is Secure Sockets Layer?

Before we continue too much further with the setup of our secure pages, it is important to briefly review some of the basic concepts of attaining a SSL certificate and creating a secure page. First, from a technical standpoint, what is Secure Sockets Layer? The SSL protocol is a form of data encryption. It's like a lockbox for the data sent to and from your server to the end user's browser. The data is packed up and encrypted between the browser and server. An SSL key or certificate is passed from the server to the browser to validate the online entity's (your website's) credentials.

What does this mean to you as someone trying to set up a website? To validate your credentials, you need to apply for a certificate with a third-party certificate authority. This third-party authority will verify that you (and your website) are who you claim to be. There are various levels of verification. The level of encryption of the Secure Sockets Layer is the same regardless of the verification level you choose to attain. The variety in SSL certificates you'll find primarily differ by the complexity of the verification process. Once you've applied for and purchased a certificate and the certificate is granted, it will be stored on your website's server. As you create pages using SSL, the certificate will be passed as the key. Most likely, you'll need to work with your hosting provider or their systems administrator to establish the SSL certificate for your site.

Next, what does a Secure Sockets Layer mean to the end user? Figure 7-5 illustrates the change to a browser's address bar when entering a secure page.

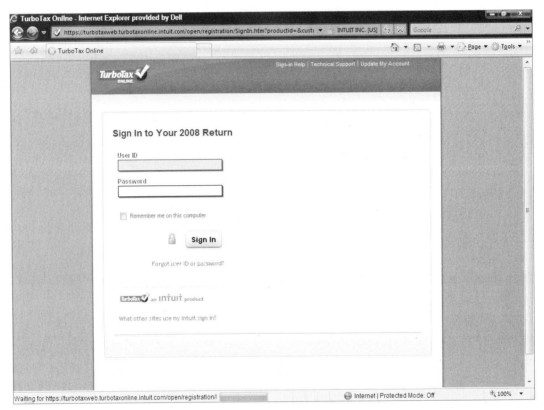

**Figure 7-5**

Different levels of verification will present different visual indicators to your site's visitors. Additionally, different browsers will indicate encryption differently. The important take-away is that your visitors should be and will be looking for encryption when they input sensitive information.

When you send information to the website, it is encrypted at your computer and decrypted at the website. Under normal circumstances, the information cannot be read or tampered with while it is being sent, but it's possible that someone might find a way to crack the encryption.

## Secure Sockets Layer Settings in DotNetNuke

DNN allows you to explicitly secure specific pages using the settings for individual pages. As the site administrator, there is only a single setting for you to configure to mark a page as secure. Figure 7-6 shows the setting in the Advanced Settings located in Page Settings. To mark a page as Secure, access Page Settings through the Page Functions section of the control panel.

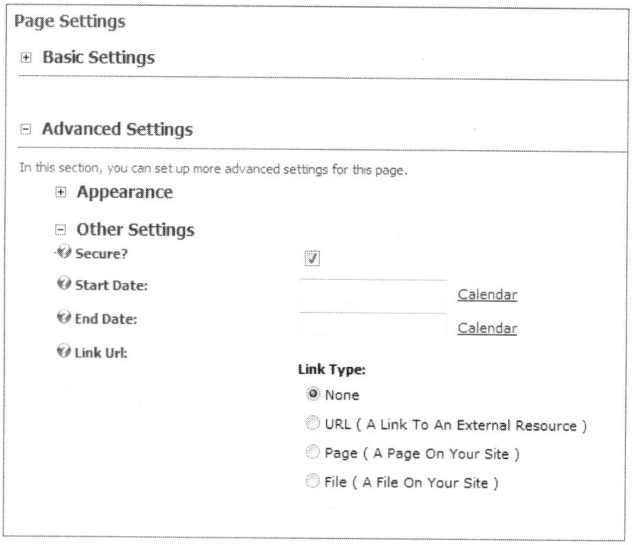

Figure 7-6

This setting is only one part of the set up of your secure pages. Prior to marking a page as Secure, the site must be enabled to use SSL. The Host account, or super user, has additional settings available in your Site Settings to enable the use of SSL on your site. Figure 7-7 illustrates the settings available to the Host account for an individual site. In addition to enabling the use of SSL on your site, the systems administrator for your hosting provider must store the SSL certificate on the web server.

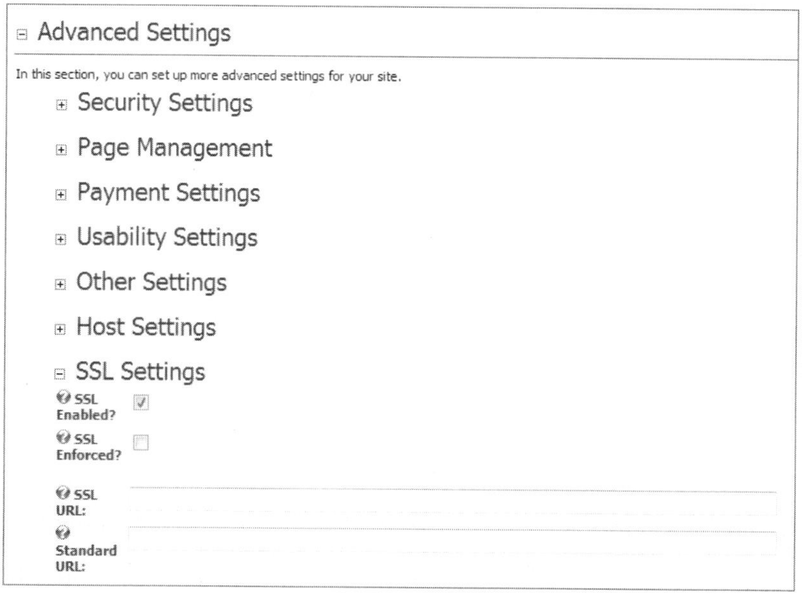

Figure 7-7

# Custom Design Considerations

DNN automatically includes a default skin, MinimalExtropy. Throughout the book, we've used this skin to demonstrate the functionality available in DNN. For personal and organization websites, as demonstrated in Chapters 5 and 6, respectively, a unique design may be important, but a unique look for your DNN site is even more important for a small business. Carrying your company's brand into your website will help to reinforce the brand equity you have created with your product and more traditional marketing materials. As you evaluate alternatives to the default skin package, you have two options: to purchase a commercially produced skin or to purchase a custom skin package developer for a custom website design.

This section reviews some of the design considerations that you should make before purchasing a commercial or custom skin package. Some of the considerations we'll review include layout options, navigation structure, containers, and dynamic content from tokens.

## *Layouts and Skin Variations*

Each individual skin in a skin package can control navigation structure, pane layout, and style guides. In a CMS, less is more as it relates to the number of skins in a skin package. More skins give you greater flexibility, but you risk sacrificing consistency and ease of maintenance.

Although elegant design and flexible content management do not have to be mutually exclusive, there are trade-offs between complex design and flexible content management. Often as a site's design complexity increases, static images and prescribed content are necessary to maintain the integrity of the design. As a result, the ease of swapping in new content can diminish. You should consider this balance between form and function as you evaluate custom or commercial designs.

As a rule of thumb, a skin package should contain at least the following skins to pick from:

- ❏ **Home or Index**: The home page should orient your visitors to the options available in interior pages. It is important for your home page to establish trust with the visitors and give them a clear understanding of your information architecture. Additionally, the home page offers you a chance to establish your message and brand.

- ❏ **Sub or Interior**: A first-level interior page template will give you more room for content and should offer the visitors more focused information as they start to navigate to interior pages in your site.

- ❏ **Detail**: A detail page will provide you with a template for pages that require significant textual or detailed information. In addition to providing room for detailed information, you should make sure to include a breadcrumb or some way for users to navigate back to the home page or interior landing pages.

- ❏ **Admin**: An administrative skin is used in DNN to load page settings, module settings, and edit controls. To you as a site administrator, this skin should offer a single pane, since a single control will typically load on this page.

Figure 7-8 shows the Appearance section of Site Settings that allow you to specify a skin specifically for edit functions in DNN.

Figure 7-8

As you evaluate commercial skin packages or plan a custom skin package, review the number of panes available in a skin. Many commercial skin packages offer a wide variety of panes to choose from as you place content on your pages. This is advantageous in that it gives you a great amount of flexibility; however, it can also be detrimental to the look of your site because you, as the site administrator, will have to make design decisions as you implement content. To reiterate, understanding the balance between design integrity and content management flexibility can help you to pick a skin package that enables you to administer your site and content easily.

## Consistent Navigation Elements

Consistent and predictable navigation is essential to guide your visitors though your site. Additionally, it can create trust with your users as your navigation structure and navigation elements serve as a guide for your site visitors. If visitors become confused or disoriented in your site, they are more likely to exit or restart their search. For a small business and e-commerce site, keeping your customers engaged in your site will help create sales and ensure that your site is a valuable resource for your customers.

There are a number of ways to provide predictable navigation on your site. The following list includes a few elements that you may want to include in your skin:

❑   A global navigation menu gives users a reference point and helps to ensure that visitors' navigation doesn't lead them to dead ends.

❑   Secondary navigation menus are often found on interior pages. Secondary navigation should be used to inform visitors of their options as they drill into your page structure. Typically, secondary navigation should allow for the addition and subtraction of pages without affecting the design of your site.

❏    Universal navigation elements used outside of your menu can reinforce a consistent message or action for your site visitors. In an e-commerce site, you would want to consider a way for customers to access their shopping cart or the checkout pages. Additionally, having a consistent place for visitors to look to find pages like Contact Us or Frequently Asked Questions (FAQs) can reinforce trust with your customers.

Brick-and-mortar retail businesses have entire industries based on consumer traffic patterns in stores. This same care and analysis can be applied to website traffic.

# Dynamic Content to Include

DNN skins can also render dynamic content using tokens or objects. The implementation of these tools is extensively documented in other books, such as *Beginning DotNetNuke Skinning and Design* (Wiley, 2007) and the *DotNetNuke Skinning Guide* (Wiley, 2007). For you to be an informed DNN administrator, it is important to understand there are a number of elements that a skin developer can include that will provide you with dynamically generated content. Some of the more widely used elements are listed in the following table:

**Dynamic Content Elements**

| Token Name | Description |
|---|---|
| [BANNER] | Displays banner images with links created in the Vendor activity. |
| [BREADCRUMB] | Displays the navigation path to the currently selected page. |
| [COPYRIGHT] | Displays the copyright information provided in the Site Settings. |
| [CURRENTDATE] | Displays the current date. |
| [LOGO] | Displays the image specified as the logo in the Site Settings. The logo also serves as a link back to the Home Page specified in the Page Management section of Site Settings. |
| [PRIVACY] | Displays a link to the privacy information for the portal. This content is localized and can be managed through the language editor. |
| [TERMS] | Displays a link to the term and conditions information for the portal. This content is localized and can be managed through the language editor. |

# Tracking Traffic with Google Analytics

If you plan to use a site traffic tool like Google Analytics, you will need to verify your site with the tracking software. In the case of Google Analytics, you will be provided a few lines of code to include in your site. This code can be included in a module applied across your site or you can embed the code in each of your skins. Both ways will yield the same result. We'll review the addition of this code to a module applied to all pages. If you are considering a custom skin package, this may be something you request to be included in the skin package.

## Including Tracking Codes in a Module

DNN includes a series of settings that will allow you to place a module on a page yet keep the content hidden from visitors. By now, you are most likely familiar with restricting content by using permissions.

This approach doesn't work for exposing the code to Google or other tracking software because the code needs to be visible to the software as it indexes your website's content.

To create a module that is visible to tracking software but invisible to visitors, perform the following steps:

1. Add a Text/HTML module to the bottom-most pane on your page.

2. Edit the text of this module and clear the content completely.

3. In the Module Settings, expand the Advanced Settings and paste the code given to you by Google Analytics into the module footer.

4. Also in Advanced Settings, select the Display Module On All Pages option.

5. Finally, in Page Settings for this module, disable the container by deselecting the Display Container check box.

Keeping the content of this Text/HTML module empty of content, disabling the container, and placing the code in the footer will make the code visible to tracking software but invisible to site visitors.

## Key Traffic Metrics

The reports provided by site traffic software like Google Analytics can be powerful tools to gain an understanding of your website visitors' traffic patterns and the popularity of your content. There is a long list of reports provided by these traffic trackers, so it is important to understand some of the key reports provided and what these reports mean to you as a small business owner.

The primary reports a website traffic tracker will provide include how many visits your site received and how many pageviews (the number of pages viewed by these visitors) your site received over a span of time. It is important to analyze the trends of these statistics to understand whether your website is gaining or losing popularity. As you analyze your visitors' activity, it is valuable to review the number of visitors you have in comparison to the number of absolute unique visitors. If the number of visits and unique visitors are both growing, this means you're reaching a broader audience; however, if the number of unique visitors declines in proportion to the number of total visits, this may mean your visitors are returning more frequently, but you're seeing visits from the same visitors. This isn't all bad, because it means the visitors you do have are loyal and are returning. These metrics are all subject to the goals of your site.

After reviewing the trending statistics for your website, you might start to become curious about why your site is gaining, losing, or not changing in popularity. The next places to look are the traffic sources for your website. Google Analytics reports on the sources of traffic in three segments: direct traffic, referring traffic, and search engines. In addition to traffic sources, you'll be able to see the frequency with which keywords are used to create traffic to your site. Visits from one source are not any better or worse than another, but again, you may want to track these statistics in relation to goals for your site. For example, if you send a direct mailing with your website address featured, you may want to see how your direct traffic responds.

The third area to analyze in your site traffic is the efficacy of the content on your site. What are the most commonly visited pages on your site? How long are visitors staying on your pages? Which pages are visitors first visiting? From which pages do they typically leave your site? These are the types of questions reports on content can provide. Bounce rate is an important report to review for your entrance pages or those pages on which you'd expect visitors to first land. It tells you the percentage of visits to a page resulting in one-page visits or visits in which the visitor leaves your site from this page.

# Administering Content

With the initial site setup and configuration complete, we'll now discuss the most important part of your website: the content. Planning the content of your website addresses two elements: the page structure and the modules you place on your page. Next, we're going to review a site map that will accommodate the content we plan to implement on the Smelly Soaps website. With a site map in place, we'll focus on implementing three modules that are helpful toward building a small business's website: the Store module(s), the FAQ module, and the Feedback module. You can apply the module implementation from earlier chapters to include the Blog, New Feed (RSS), Announcements, Events, or Gallery modules. Taking the concepts learned in earlier chapters and applying them to a small business will give you more options for administering content and can help to build your site's search engine ranking.

## Planning Your Page Structure

For our small business example, we'll create a website to sell the soaps of our fictitious small business, Smelly Soaps. On our website, we want to provide users the ability to see a wide variety of our soaps, grouped by category. In addition to seeing our categorized products, we'll feature soaps on the home page and display a list of the most popular soaps. The main focus of our website will be to sell our soaps and provide customers a place to see our full offering of soaps. In addition to selling soaps on the website, we want to make sure that our customers feel they can always contact us with questions or concerns.

The following table outlines the pages required to accomplish these goals. Additionally, we've mapped modules to the corresponding pages. With this site map created, we'll continue by configuring the modules to fit the needs of our business.

**Site Map Plans**

| Page | Modules/Content | Other Considerations |
|---|---|---|
| Home | ❑ Text/HTML module to welcome visitors to the site | The catalog modules will point to the Store page for full details about the products. |
| | ❑ Store Catalog module set to show featured products | |
| | ❑ Store Catalog module set to show popular products | |
| Store | ❑ Store Catalog module set to show a category view | |
| | ❑ Store Menu module to show a list of product categories | |
| | ❑ Store Mini-Cart module to allow users to check out from the store | |
| Your Account | Store Account module to provide users a place to review their orders | |

## Site Map Plans

| Page | Modules/Content | Other Considerations |
|------|-----------------|----------------------|
| Store Admin-istration | Store Admin module to administer products, categories, and store configuration options | The page will not be included in the menu and only visible to administrators. |
| FAQs | FAQ module to provide site visitors a way to gain answers to their questions | |
| Contact Us | Feedback module to allow visitors to communicate with us directly | Contacts module will be visible to only administrators. |

This plan is relatively basic, but it should give you an idea of a potential setup of your business's website. As you become more comfortable with administering your content, you may find the need to add more content and additional pages to your site.

# Administering Your Store

The Store module will allow us to set up a robust e-commerce tool and give our customers a place to shop for soaps and even complete purchases through our website. The Store module is composed of five modules, each serving a specific function. Before we go into detail about each of the modules included in the Store module, it is important to understand the way these modules integrate with each other. In our Store module implementation, we used Store version 2.01.09.

Next, we'll briefly review some of the hand-offs required for the Store module to function best for our website. The five modules included in the Store module are: Store Account, Store Admin, Store Catalog, Store Menu, and Store Mini-Cart.

The Store Catalog module is the hub for each of the other modules included in the Store module. It is important to consider this module first as you begin to create the store on your website. The Store Catalog can be configured in a number of ways and, as we build out our store, we'll configure it each way to fully utilize the module. For now, it is important to understand that the Store Catalog will display lists of products or the details for specific products. As we implement this module, we will set up specific types of lists for our soaps. As you set up Store Catalog modules to display lists of products, you'll also need to specify where the product details should be displayed.

The Store Admin module should not be visible to your customers. It will serve as the place for you to add, edit, and delete products and their categories. Additionally, in the Store Admin module you'll specify the details about your store, including your payment-processing service (referred to as a payment gateway), shipping, and tax information. Once you have your store set up, you'll process orders from this module as well.

The Store Account and Store Mini-Cart modules work together to provide your users a shopping cart and checkout workflow as they shop on your website. The Store Menu module provides a navigation menu for your users to filter your products by category. The menu will work in tandem with a Store Catalog module to display the products of the category selected from the menu.

With a high-level understanding of each of the modules' basic functions, we'll now set up our store to sell soaps. By setting up the Store module for Smelly Soaps, we'll get a full understanding of the configuration options available to make your small business site function for e-commerce.

# The Store Admin Module

The first step in implementing the modules included in the Store module is to place the Store Admin module on a page visible to only Administrators or other roles you wish to give access. As mentioned earlier, we've created a page specifically for this module and made it visible to only Administrators. Since the Administrators will be accessing this module to review orders and add products, we want the page to be easily accessible. So, we've included it in the menu and as a child page of the page we'll use as the main hub for all shopping, titled Store.

With the Store Admin module added to a page, we'll start by providing information about our e-commerce store. In the Store Info section, we've defined a name for our store, a description, and keywords. To utilize this information, we've enabled the SEO Feature setting. By enabling this, setting, the title, description, and keywords will be used to give our page more information to search engines. Figure 7-9 illustrates the SEO information we've defined for our store.

Figure 7-9

Next, we set some of the vital information for our store. By defining an e-mail for the store, our customers will receive order confirmation e-mails from an e-mail address tied to the store rather than the site administrator's e-mail address. In addition to some of the identifying information about our store, we should choose the page to use as the hub for shopping and checkout. In Figure 7-10, we have set the Store page to be the hub for shopping and the Store Account to be the page in which customers check out. These settings assume that we've created the pages we intend to use for these functions.

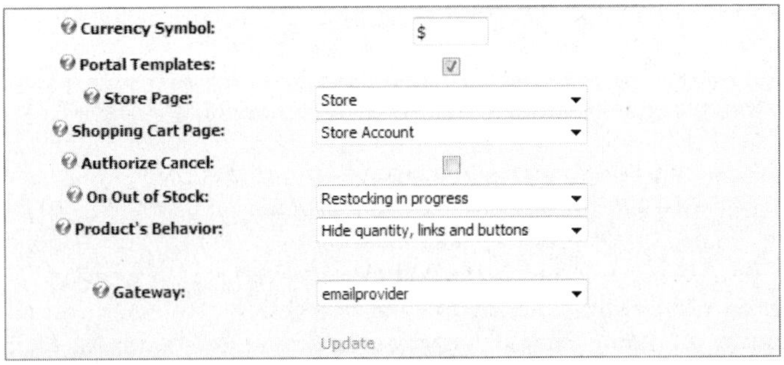

Figure 7-10

The last, and possibly most important, setting for our store's information is the Gateway. There are three options for order processing. We'll use "emailprovider" to keep our setup simple, but the Store module also allows you to integrate your store with PayPal and Authorize.Net as payment processors. To integrate with one of these processors, you'll need to create an account and the payment collection will all be completed with these gateways. Figure 7-11 illustrates the options for gateway providers. Using the e-mail provider, our customers will receive an e-mail confirming their order and indicating that we'll follow up with them in person to arrange payment.

**Figure 7-11**

The Store Administration module also allows you to setup tax and shipping information. Since your tax and shipping information will vary from ours, you can use the setup in Figure 7-12 as an example. The Tax Administration and Shipping Administration are found in the Store Info section of the Store Administration module.

|  | ⊟ Tax Administration | | | |
|---|---|---|---|---|
| Enable Tax: | | ✓ | | |
| Tax Rate: | 6.50 | | | |
|  | Update Tax Settings | | | |
|  | ⊟ Shipping Administration | | | |
| Description | Min. Weight | Max. Weight | Cost | Delete |
| Small Shipping | 0.00 | 15.00 | 3.00 | ▢ |
| Medium Shipping | 15.01 | 30.00 | 6.00 | ▢ |
| Large Shipping | 30.01 | 45.00 | 9.00 | ▢ |
| Bulk Shipping | 45.01 | 100.00 | 12.00 | ▢ |
|  | | | | Add |
|  | Update Shipping Rates | | | |

**Figure 7-12**

Once your Store Info is complete, you can manage your products, categories, orders, and reviews in the other sections of this module. We have created three product categories for our soaps: Bar Soap, Body Washes, and Hand Soaps. In the product categories, we provided a title, category description, and sort order. Figure 7-13 illustrates the setup for the Body Washes category. To administer the categories in your store, navigate to the Store Administration module and click on the Categories link. In the Categories section, you will see a list of any existing categories and have the ability to Add Categories or edit the existing categories.

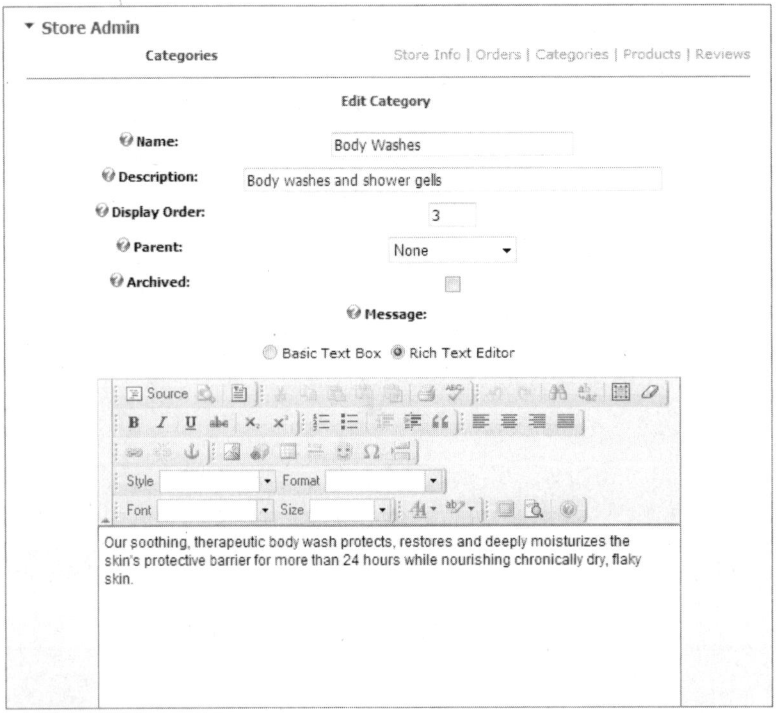

**Figure 7-13**

We have a number of products in each category, as do most e-commerce stores. In Figure 7-14, we have created a new product listing for a body wash. To add products to your store, navigate to the page with the Store Administration module and click on the Products link. From this section of the Store Administration module, you can filter your products by Category to review existing products or add a product by clicking Add Product. Since your product listings are most likely different from our soaps, it is important to understand the following fields:

❑   Model Name is the title of your product.

❑   Summary is used in the product description used in product lists.

❑   Unit Price is the price of your product.

❑   Shipping Weight is important if you calculate shipping costs based on weight.

❑   Quantity is valuable to include if you want to track inventory in your store. As products are ordered, the quantity will be decremented, and if the product is out of stock, it can be disabled from ordering. The specifics on how out-of-stock products are handled are configured in the Store Info section of the Store Administration module.

❑   Featured is important to use if you have a Store Catalog module set to list featured products. In our store, we'll highlight featured products on the Home page.

❑   Description is the detailed information for your product and is displayed on the Detail display page. The description of the product is not illustrated in Figure 7-14 but is located on the same screen.

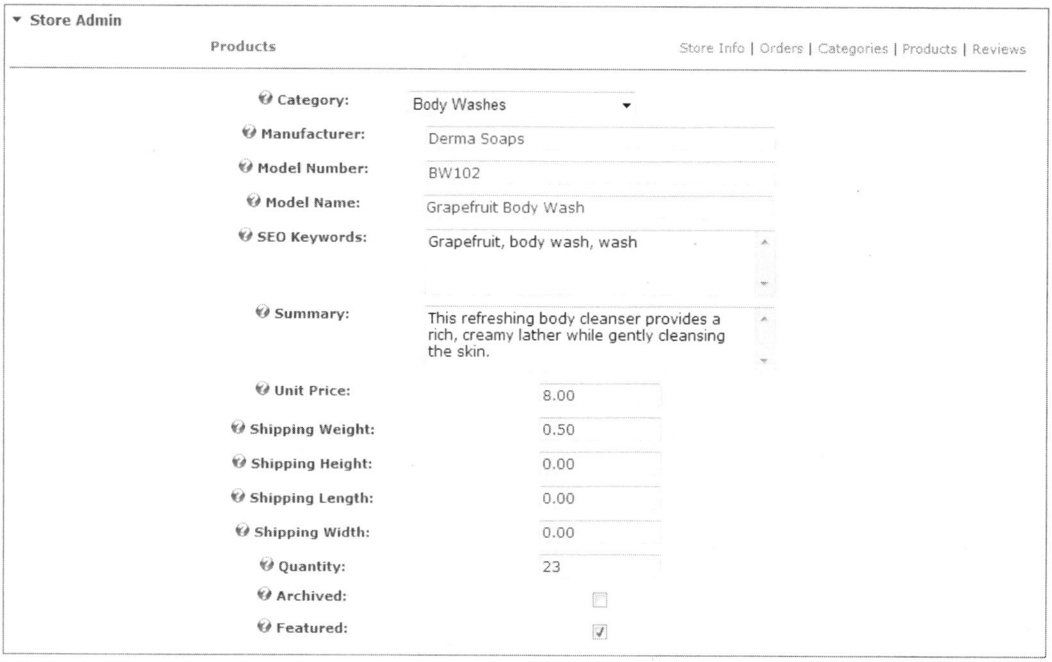

Figure 7-14

The next section of the Store Administration module to review is the Order History section. The Order History is located by clicking the Orders link in the Store Administration module. In this section, you can find the orders placed in your store and track their progress through the order process. As the store administrator, you control the status assigned to orders. Figure 7-15 illustrates a number of orders with a status of Processing in our store.

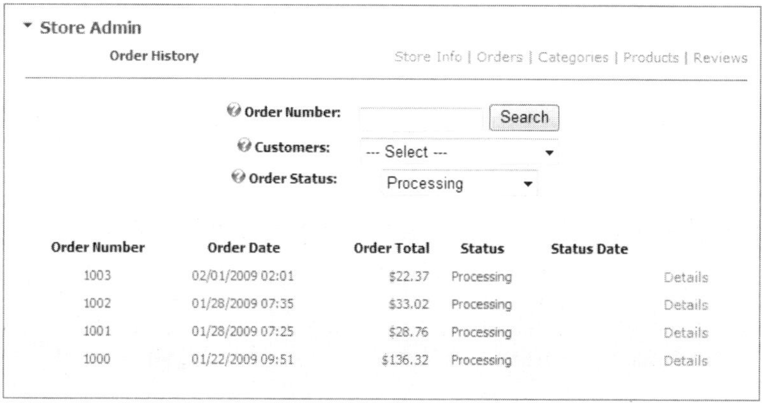

Figure 7-15

Each order will start with a status of processing. As we call customers to arrange payment, we'll manually advance the status. You can also reference orders by order number or customer name.

If you allow reviews to show with your product details, you can also moderate the reviews by customers in the Store Administration module. To locate the Reviews of your products, click on the Review link in the Store Administration module. This can be important, as you may want to regulate especially malicious reviews. Figure 7-16 illustrates a rave review of our Lavender Smelly Soap.

**Figure 7-16**

# The Store Catalog Module

With the fundamentals of our store configured, we can now start to display our products across our site. Since the five modules included in the Store module work together, there are integration points that need to be established in the modules. As you saw in the Store Administration module, we needed to indicate the pages contain our Store and Shopping Cart. We specified here that the Store page would be identified as the hub for our products. To start, we'll place an instance of the Store Catalog module on the Store page.

In this instance, we'll configure the module to display Category Products and also to display Product Detail information. Since this module is going to act as our hub, we'll allow other instances of the Store Catalog and Store Menu to populate products and product details here. In Figure 7-17, we have completed the setup of this Store Catalog module. To modify these settings, we chose Settings from the modules actions menu and navigated to the module-specific settings.

The Store Catalog can display products in a variety of ways based on different criteria. Each display has common settings related to the display of products in this display. Additionally, you need to identify the page in which you want product details to display.

---

### Templates Explained

Templates are a common feature included in a number of modules. We have seen templates used in the Announcements module earlier. The Store module uses templates again to give site administrators additional flexibility. To utilize templates, you need to be comfortable with modifying HTML code. If you feel comfortable doing this, you can create HTML for the layout of your display and inject the dynamic content using tokens defined by the module developers.

---

Figure 7-17

With a Store Catalog module set to display product lists and product detail information passed in from other modules, we'll apply the Store Catalog in a number of other places on our site to give customers a few options to find our soaps. We've placed the Store Catalog on the Home page twice. One instance is set to display Featured products, the other is set to display Popular products. For both of these modules, we've set the Display page to be the Store Page. Figure 7-18 illustrates the display of our featured and popular products.

Within the module settings for each of these modules, there are additional settings we have selected to control the format of our product listings without modifying the template for our display. We customized the width of our columns and the number of columns and rows to display our product listing.

A secondary action for this module is the ability to add products to your catalog from the actions menu included in this module. This allows you to add products directly to your catalog without having to access the Store Administration module.

## The Store Menu Module

The Store Menu module is a straightforward module in terms of setup and functionality. This module displays a list of the categories you have defined for your products. There are two settings in the module. First, how many columns of categories do you want to display? In our store, we want the menu to act like a vertical menu, so we'll display one column of categories. The second setting is to pick the page in which we want the products to display.

We'll place the Store Menu module on the Store page and have the product listings for a category display on the same page since the Store page has a Store Catalog module set to display product listings and product details. Figure 7-19 illustrates the completed setup of the Store Menu on our Store page.

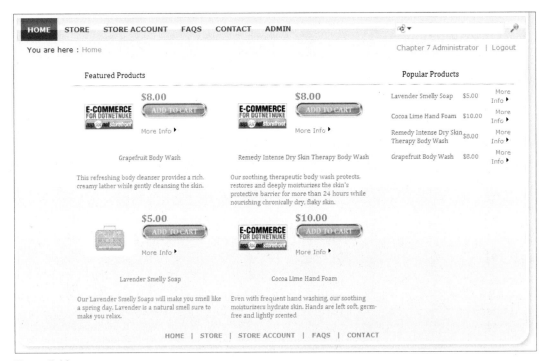

Figure 7-18

Figure 7-19

## *The Store Mini-Cart Module*

The Store Mini-Cart module gives your customers a way to place orders in a shopping cart without proceeding to the Store Account page. When customers do proceed to check out, they will be directed to the My Account page, which has the Store Account module. When customers have products in their basket, the Store Account module will allow them to review their order and proceed to check out. In Store Catalog modules set to display a list of products, the default display template allows users to add a product to their cart. Figure 7-20 illustrates products added to the Store Mini-Cart when customers choose Add to Cart.

**Figure 7-20**

It is a good idea to add the Store Mini-Cart to any page in which you allow users to view product lists. By doing this, your customers will receive feedback from your site that their purchase has been placed in the shopping cart.

To proceed to the Store Account page, the user can either click Buy Now from the product details or View My Basket from the mini-cart.

## The Store Account Module

The Store Account module is used as your customers' shopping cart and for Checkout activity. We have created a page specifically for this module, called Store Account. Because we want our customers to feel confident about the data they are sharing at checkout, we can use the DNN setup for SSL to secure the page separately from the rest of the site. Another option provided by the Store Account module is to secure only the checkout process. Figure 7-21 shows the ability to force SSL at checkout. This setting is located in the Settings for the Store Account module.

**Figure 7-21**

This would allow your site to use the SSL only when customers proceed past their shopping cart and on to checkout. Once your customers proceed to checkout, they will be prompted for a user account. After creating an account or logging in to the site, the customers can create and save a number of billing and shipping addresses. By default, the Store Account module will use the registration address. This is the address information collected in the profile. As a result, it may be valuable to require a valid profile at login and require address information from your users. This setup was documented in Chapter 6.

# Additional Content Options

Providing your customers a level of trust as they shop your e-commerce site is important to converting traffic into sales. There are a number of technical solutions you can implement to provide visitors a sense of security. Earlier we reviewed the use of SSL on pages. In the Store module, you can also secure the checkout process using SSL. As you review the design of your site, creating a predictable menu and page structure for users will allow them to easily navigate your site. These solutions will help to establish trust, but often customers need to feel reassured that there is someone on the other side of the online transaction.

Next, we'll implement two more core modules, FAQ and Feedback, to enable users to receive answers to their questions and reach out to us.

## The FAQ Module

Small business websites often post Frequently Asked Questions (FAQs) to avoid repeatedly having to answer the same questions. DNN's FAQ module enables you to manage your questions and answers without having to build static HTML content for your FAQ page. We have created a page specifically for FAQs and included it in our global navigation. More typically, this page might be included in a page footer or in a less prominent position on your site.

Although the implementation of the FAQ module is simple, it fits our needs well. Each question and answer can be assigned a category. For Smelly Soaps, we've created three categories: Shipping, Billing, and Product Information (see Figure 7-22).

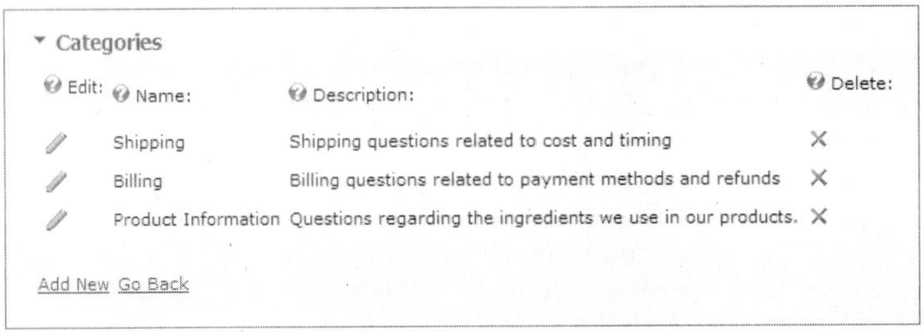

Figure 7-22

These categories provide us a way to group questions. As we create categories, we can provide a description for the category. Categories and their descriptions could provide us a way to direct our customer's questions as they are looking for answers. These fields are both available to be used in the configuration of FAQ display.

After defining the categories for our questions, we want to define the settings for our questions. Again, we encounter templates, giving us the ability to customize the display of our FAQs. There are a list of tokens which can be used to bring in content directly from your questions and answers. We'll use the default templates, and sort our questions by Date (newest first).

With the required setup complete, we can begin adding questions and their corresponding answers. Both the questions and answers are rich text fields, meaning that we have the ability to use the Rich Text editor to create content without needing to know HTML. Figure 7-23 illustrates the creation of a FAQ for our soaps. To add a new FAQ, select Add New FAQ from the module's actions menu.

Figure 7-23

This is a great tool for FAQs because you may want to provide links to other web pages or documents along with the answers to questions. As you add FAQs, your list of questions will begin to grow. As your list grows, you may want to resort the FAQs by popularity to make them more relevant. Figure 7-24 demonstrates a more complete list of FAQs.

## The Feedback Module

As its name implies, the Feedback module can be used to compile feedback from your customers. This module is initially designed to create a place for visitors to send feedback and also for site administrators to post the feedback of their users. For our store, we're going to use the module for a slightly different use. We'll use the module to allow users to submit feedback, but we won't display the feedback and simply use the module as a way for visitors to contact us with their suggestions and questions. The module can allow you to display the results of custom feedback, but for our implementation we're going to use it as a one-way communication tool. The functionality of the module will allow us to provide predefined subjects for the feedback and to route messages by category. This is especially valuable as inquiries come in because our customers will be able to direct their messages to the correct place without our intervention.

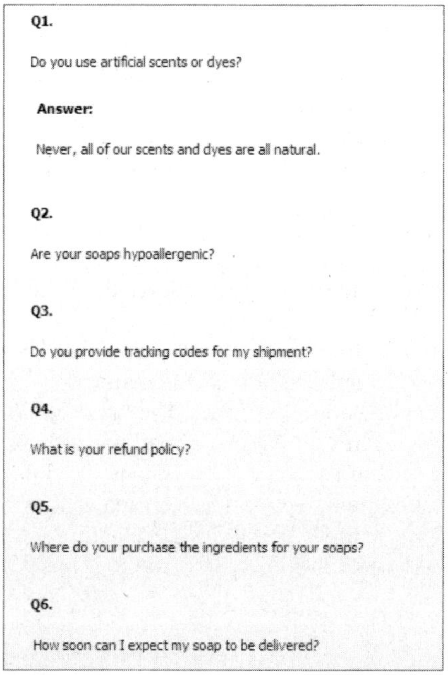

Q1.

Do you use artificial scents or dyes?

**Answer:**

Never, all of our scents and dyes are all natural.

Q2.

Are your soaps hypoallergenic?

Q3.

Do you provide tracking codes for my shipment?

Q4.

What is your refund policy?

Q5.

Where do your purchase the ingredients for your soaps?

Q6.

How soon can I expect my soap to be delivered?

**Figure 7-24**

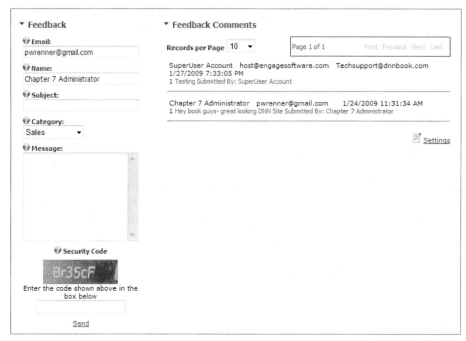

**Figure 7-25**

We created a page specifically called Contact. On this page, we may want to add other contact information, such as mailing address, phone number, and business hours. When you add the Feedback module to a page, two modules are placed on the page: Feedback and Feedback Comments. The Feedback module allows your visitors to send a message. The Feedback Comments module lists the most recent submissions. Figure 7-25 illustrates the Feedback module placed on our Contact page in the RightPane. The Feedback Comments module is only visible to Page Editors.

We're going to make this module visible only to Administrators and use the Feedback module to send only e-mail messages. If you want to post the feedback from your customers, the Feedback Comments module allows you to moderate the feedback and manage the list of feedback submissions.

To configure the Feedback module to intelligently route submissions to different e-mail addresses, we'll need to complete two tasks. First, we'll need to create a list of categories for the submissions. Each category has two fields: Name and List Value. The Name is displayed to the user, and the List Value can be used as an e-mail address. When an e-mail address is used as the List Value, it can be used as the Send To: address for the feedback submissions. As shown in Figure 7-26, we have created three categories, Sales, Billing, and Tech Support, each with specific e-mail addresses attached. To create your categories, navigate to the Feedback Lists action in the Feedback module's Actions menu. Within the Manage Feedback Lists page, you can toggle between managing Categories and Subjects.

Figure 7-26

Next, in the Module settings, we'll need to tell the module to use the List Value as the Send To: address when messages are categorized. By making the Category List Visible, and enabling Use Category Value as Send To:, our Feedback module will route inquiries to the appropriate e-mail address. In addition to Category lists, you can define a list of subjects or allow visitors to enter their own subject, just as in a normal e-mail message. We're going to allow users to Edit the Subject of their message. Additionally, we'll require a name with the message and Use Captcha. Using Captcha can help prevent malicious programs from scouring your site and submitting junk messages using the Feedback module. In Figure 7-27, you can see the completed setup of the Contact page. We have also included a Text/HTML module to provide our site visitors more information about our business.

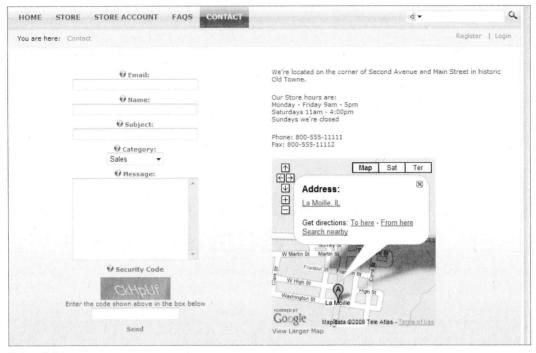

Figure 7-27

# Summary

Using the core functionality of DNN, we've implemented a robust website tailored to a small business. With some thoughtful decisions and carefully planned setup, DNN can make administering and maintaining a website for your business or e-commerce site easy. The requirements of your small business website may be more sophisticated and complicated than some of our previous implementations, but, using the core features available in DNN, you'll be able to create a site that is easily managed and full of robust functionality for your customers.

By reviewing design considerations, you can feel confident shopping for a commercially available skin package or contracting for a custom developed skin package. The design can impact the user experience and the administrative functions for your site. With a better understanding of some of the key considerations, you can assess what you find valuable to your website.

Using modules provided by the DNN core project teams, you have the ability to implement a product catalog, complete with inventory tracking and order processing. By adding the Feedback and FAQ modules, you can give your users an easy way to connect with you and reinforce trust with your customers.

# Advanced Portal Administration

One of the fundamental features of DotNetNuke (DNN) is the ability to manage multiple websites under a single installation of the software. This feature is valuable for a range of reasons. For the technical staff of a large organization or an enterprise solution, the ability to manage a single application while creating and managing numerous websites can result in consolidation of responsibilities and a more centralized web environment. For a marketing department, the ability to apply consistent design elements through skin packages to multiple websites can facilitate continuity and extend a branding message. For web administrators, having a consistent set of tools to manage content can help to ease administrative tasks.

Regardless of your role in an organization, understanding the power of a multi-portal environment can help you to maximize your implementation of DNN. Along with added sophistication comes greater complexity. In this chapter, we'll review at a high level the structure of websites built in DNN to gain a better understanding of the implications to creating multiple websites, or portals, in a single instance of DNN. By reviewing these implications, you'll gain an understanding of how you can capitalize on DNN's powerful content management framework.

This chapter discusses the following topics:

- ❏ Environmental considerations for implementing multiple websites
- ❏ Managing multiple portals within a single instance of DNN
- ❏ Managing files in DNN using the File Manager
- ❏ Leveraging the provider model to satisfy unique needs for your organization

## Evaluating Your DNN Environment

From the start of your implementation of DNN, it is important to consider the general plan for your web environment and determine the direction you may go with your websites(s). In previous chapters, we've evaluated a single website for a specific usage of DNN. In this chapter, we'll continue to expose the power of DNN by reviewing your DNN environment in its entirety, discussing the implications of a multi-portal implementation. DNN is a powerful web platform and scales well, but careful planning will ensure that you start your DNN implementation moving in the right direction. The first decision in determining the direction of your web environment is the number of instances of DNN your organization will require.

One instance of DNN can house multiple websites. Determining whether a single instance of DNN with multiple portals is appropriate will depend on a number of factors. The alternative to a single instance with multiple portals would be a separate instance of DNN for each website. If you have the luxury of making this choice, consider the following factors:

- ❑ Shared file system and database
- ❑ Roles and responsibilities of your website administration
- ❑ Downtime or failure isolation
- ❑ Software upgrades and version compatibility

The following sections review some of the factors in more detail. Many of these factors are interrelated, and the weight you place on these factors will vary with your intended use of DNN. You may also identify additional considerations important to you, but this list is intended to get you started as you evaluate your DNN environment.

## Shared File System and Database

The installation process for DNN will automatically create a file structure on your web server and a table structure in your database. Within an instance of DNN, there are files that will be shared across websites and files that are specific to an individual site, or portal. Figure 8-1 illustrates the typical file structure created when you install DNN.

Each portal within your instance of DNN will have a separate directory in which to store files, skins, and containers specific to the portal. Figure 8-2 demonstrates the subdirectory created for each portal within an instance of DNN. All the directories and files outside of the Portals folder are shared across the portals within your instance of DNN. These shared directories are all the files that the DNN application uses to run a website. When using a single DNN for multiple websites, each website uses the same files but has its own individual portal directory for content.

Modifying files within the shared directories will result in a change for all websites. The DesktopModules directory is a prime example of a folder with files shared across all portals. Because the modules installed in a single instance of DNN are shared across each portal, the markup and underlying code and style sheets (module.css) are shared by all portals. Figure 8-3 shows the files located in the Announcements module's directory in DesktopModules. The markup provided in the user controls (.ascx files), the resource files located in the App_LocalResources directory, the module.css style sheet, and the SQL scripts are shared by all the portals in this instance.

| Name | Date modified | Type |
|------|---------------|------|
| admin | 1/17/2009 3:00 PM | File Folder |
| App_Browser | 1/17/2009 3:00 PM | File Folder |
| App_Code | 1/17/2009 3:00 PM | File Folder |
| App_Data | 1/17/2009 3:00 PM | File Folder |
| App_GlobalResourc... | 1/17/2009 3:00 PM | File Folder |
| bin | 1/17/2009 3:00 PM | File Folder |
| Components | 1/17/2009 3:00 PM | File Folder |
| Config | 1/17/2009 3:00 PM | File Folder |
| controls | 1/17/2009 3:00 PM | File Folder |
| DesktopModules | 1/17/2009 3:00 PM | File Folder |
| Documentation | 1/17/2009 3:00 PM | File Folder |
| images | 1/17/2009 3:00 PM | File Folder |
| Install | 1/17/2009 3:00 PM | File Folder |
| js | 1/17/2009 3:00 PM | File Folder |
| Portals | 1/17/2009 3:00 PM | File Folder |
| Providers | 1/17/2009 3:00 PM | File Folder |
| Resources | 1/17/2009 3:00 PM | File Folder |
| 403-3.gif | 12/10/2007 1:53 PM | GIF Image |
| Default.aspx | 8/22/2008 7:40 PM | ASP.NET Server ... |
| Default.aspx.vb | 11/7/2008 2:07 AM | Visual Basic So... |
| development.config | 9/25/2008 7:12 PM | XML Configurat... |
| DotNetNuke.ico | 12/10/2007 1:53 PM | ICO File |
| DotNetNuke.vstem... | 12/24/2008 4:27 PM | Visual Studio Pr... |
| DotNetNuke.webproj | 12/10/2007 1:53 PM | WEBPROJ File |
| ErrorPage.aspx | 6/4/2008 5:20 PM | ASP.NET Server ... |
| ErrorPage.aspx.vb | 6/2/2008 2:53 PM | Visual Basic So... |
| favicon.ico | 12/10/2007 1:53 PM | ICO File |
| Global.asax | 12/10/2007 1:53 PM | ASP.NET Server ... |
| KeepAlive.aspx | 12/10/2007 1:53 PM | ASP.NET Server ... |
| KeepAlive.aspx.vb | 3/12/2008 4:04 PM | Visual Basic So... |
| logo.gif | 12/10/2007 1:53 PM | GIF Image |
| release.config | 9/25/2008 7:12 PM | XML Configurat... |
| SiteMap.aspx | 12/10/2007 1:53 PM | ASP.NET Server ... |
| SiteMap.aspx.vb | 11/25/2008 2:10 PM | Visual Basic So... |
| spacer.gif | 12/10/2007 1:53 PM | GIF Image |
| web.config | 9/25/2008 7:12 PM | XML Configurat... |

Figure 8-1

Figure 8-2

---

**Localized Content**

Most modules include a subdirectory to store resource files (`.resx`). These files are used to localize content for your instance of DNN. If you modify these files directly in the file system or through the Host Language editor, the changes will affect all portals. DNN allows administrators to create portal-specific versions of resource files to facilitate localized content specific to a portal.

The use of resource files is an example of content shared across portals with an additional level of flexibility for the individual portals to interject their own version of the content.

---

| Name | Date modified | Type | Size |
|---|---|---|---|
| App_LocalResources | 1/17/2009 2:40 ... | File Folder | |
| Announcements.ascx | 11/18/2008 1:3... | ASP.NET User C... | 1 KB |
| EditAnnouncement... | 11/18/2008 1:3... | ASP.NET User C... | 6 KB |
| Settings.ascx | 11/18/2008 1:3... | ASP.NET User C... | 6 KB |
| module.css | 11/18/2008 1:3... | Cascading Style... | 1 KB |
| DNN_Announceme... | 11/18/2008 1:3... | MANIFEST File | 1 KB |
| 03.01.00.SqlDataPr... | 11/18/2008 1:3... | SQLDATAPROVI... | 8 KB |
| 03.03.00.SqlDataPr... | 11/18/2008 1:3... | SQLDATAPROVI... | 6 KB |
| 03.03.01.SqlDataPr... | 11/18/2008 1:3... | SQLDATAPROVI... | 1 KB |
| 03.03.02.SqlDataPr... | 11/18/2008 1:3... | SQLDATAPROVI... | 6 KB |
| 03.03.04.SqlDataPr... | 11/18/2008 1:3... | SQLDATAPROVI... | 3 KB |
| 03.03.05.SqlDataPr... | 11/18/2008 1:3... | SQLDATAPROVI... | 3 KB |
| 03.04.00.SqlDataPr... | 11/18/2008 1:3... | SQLDATAPROVI... | 12 KB |
| 04.00.00.SqlDataPr... | 11/18/2008 1:3... | SQLDATAPROVI... | 11 KB |
| 04.00.01.SqlDataPr... | 11/18/2008 1:3... | SQLDATAPROVI... | 1 KB |
| Uninstall.SqlDataPr... | 11/18/2008 1:3... | SQLDATAPROVI... | 3 KB |

**Figure 8-3**

In addition to the shared directories and files outside of the individual portal directories, the host has a file directory. This directory is named `_default`, and it is used to store the files available to all portals. It also stores the Skins, Containers, Page Templates, and a number of other shared files available to all portals. Figure 8-4 demonstrates the `_default` directory for an instance of DNN with multiple portals.

**Figure 8-4**

As with the file system, the database tables created for your portals in DNN are shared across all websites in your instance of the application, but individual records are also specific to an individual site. Most records created in your DNN database tables will be identified with a specific portal. However, a single database stores all of the records within your instance of DNN.

### *Implication of a Shared File System and Database*

Since the files in your file system and the records in your database will be shared across a single instance of DNN, you'll want to consider the exclusivity or isolation required for your websites. If an upgrade to your software is desired for one portal, will you want to upgrade all your portals? If you want to keep upgrades separate, then separate installations of DNN may better suit your needs.

In contrast to an individual instance of DNN for each site, there are benefits to a single version of DNN for multiple websites. By keeping all your portals in a single instance of DNN, you will be able to maintain a single set of extensions and skin packages. If you administer multiple sites, having a single version of the DNN framework and extensions can aid in general maintenance. As a host to multiple websites, a single instance of DNN can allow you to dictate the extensions available to the portals in your instance.

By saving skin packages at the host-level, you can distribute consistent branding to each of your portals. Additionally, the host account can prescribe the tools that portal administrators can use in managing the content on their sites. Again, this gives portals within a single instance of DNN some continuity and consistency. As a change is made to a skin in your host skin packages, the change can be made available to each of the portals. This prescribed style and content approach can be heavily leveraged in an enterprise implementation.

Looking ahead, you should also consider your future need to segregate a portal from a multi-portal instance of DNN. It is easier to separate an individual portal from a single instance of DNN than to consolidate portals from multiple instances into a single instance later. To separate an individual portal from a single instance of DNN, a copy of the file system and database can be applied to a new server or a new directory on your server. The portals sharing this instance can be deleted upon establishing the new instance of DNN, while protecting the portal you intend to isolate. The process of consolidating instances into a single installation of DNN would require significant SQL scripting and, in reality, would not be advised regardless of your expertise.

The final consideration for your DNN environment is downtime and mitigating the scope of data corruption across your websites. As the axiom goes, "If something can go wrong, it will go wrong." Planning for downtime or the potential for data corruption should be an important consideration for any web environment. If a single website has more volatility or susceptibility to potential data corruption, are you willing to share this risk across your other websites? Within a single instance of DNN, all sites share each others' risks.

# Managing Multiple Portals

As you evaluate your hosting environment and its implications for a multi-portal installation of DNN, it is important to fully understand the concepts related to administering multiple DNN portals. Next, we'll review the concept of portals within DNN in more detail so that you fully understand the features available to the host administrator.

The term "portal" is not unique to DNN. A web portal is another term for a website or a collection of web pages. A technical distinction between a portal and a website is that a portal is a collection of information personalized or disseminated to a group of users. Regardless of whether your website is a public Internet, private intranet, or semi-private extranet site, we'll use the term "portal" synonymously with "website." The aggregation of content and ability to tailor content to specific users are both inherent in the DNN platform, so each website in DNN is a portal.

Each installation of DNN has at least one host, or master, portal. In addition to this master portal, you have the ability to create two types of subportals: parent and child portals. Functionally, parent and child portals are the same. The only difference between parent and child portals is that a parent portal has a unique domain name, and child portals reside under the domain name of a parent portal. Before we go into too much more detail about creating parent and child portals, it is important to understand how the multi-portal feature works in DNN.

# How Multiple Portals Work

For any website, your domain name will need to be pointed at the web server in which your site resides. The software on your web server will determine how to handle the requests for your domain name. In the case of DNN, Internet Information Services (IIS) handles the requests and directs the requests to the appropriate websites on your server. In a typical web hosting arrangement, each domain pointed to your web server would need its own account for the physical directory created on the web server. For a website created with DNN, numerous domain names can be pointed to the same physical directory on your web server. Once the requests are directed to DNN, the routing is handled through a feature called *portal aliases*. Figure 8-5 illustrates the process of routing domain names to separate portals using DNN.

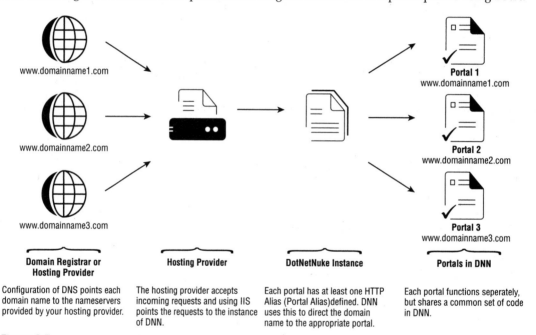

Figure 8-5

## Portal Aliases

Since a variety of domain names can point to the same website in IIS, DNN needs a way to determine which portal in your installation is being requested. The portal alias, also referred to as an HTTP alias, allows DNN to present the correct portal from the request without having to set up separate websites in IIS for each domain name.

Using the host account for your DNN instance, you can administer the portal alias through the Site Settings for each portal. The process for adding an alias is as simple as clicking Add New Alias (see Figure 8-6).

SuperUser Account  |  Logout

▼ ● **Portal Aliases**

❓ **HTTP Alias:**  www.dnnusersguide.com

Add New Alias  Cancel

**Figure 8-6**

In addition to adding the HTTP alias to the Site Settings for your portal, there are a few assumed requisite setup tasks required in your DNS and IIS settings. First, to complete the required DNS setup, your domain name will need to be directed to the IP address of the servers on which your site is hosted. Next, you'll need to add a host header to the DNN website in IIS.

## Using Portal Aliases

Next, we'll review a typical use case for portal aliases in a DNN environment. In our example, we'll demonstrate moving a DNN site from a testing domain address to a production domain address. There are other implications to moving to a live or production environment, such as URL mapping, but for the sake of this demonstration, we'll step through the process of creating a staging website in DNN and moving the site to a production domain upon going live. This example can also translate to moving from a local development environment to a live, hosted environment.

In our example, we have a test site located at a fictitious URL, `http://test.dnnusersguide.com`, which we're using to stage a site prior to launching the site. The web server already has DNN installed and is communicating with a test database. To move this staging site to our production environment, we first will need to define the new URL as a portal. This is important to do prior to pointing our live domain at our production servers, because even if IIS is configured correctly, the site will redirect to the old alias. With the portal alias defined for our live domain, we simply need to complete the standard DNS configuration changes by changing the nameserver location to the IP address of our live domain and adding the domain to our Host Header in IIS.

# Creating Additional Portals

Adding websites to your DNN instance can be easy. After you have evaluated the implications to hosting multiple portals in a single instance of DNN, the creation of new portals is straightforward. As we discussed earlier, there are two types of portals: parent and child. Next, we'll walk through the process of creating each of these. Parent and child portals function in the same manner within your instance of DNN, but the setup varies slightly, as a parent portal requires IIS configuration.

## Adding a Child Portal

A child portal resides within the parent portal's domain name. Upon creating your child portal, a new folder with the portal's ID will reside in the Portals directory of your DNN instance. Additionally, the child portal creates a directory in the root level of your DNN instance with a separate `Default.aspx` file.

---

### Handling Child URLs

This additional `Default.aspx` file is used to handle the URL requests for your child portal. The child's version of the `Default.aspx` file has code that rewrites a request for `http://www.dnnusersguide.com/child` to look something like `http://www.dnnusersguide.com/default.aspx?alias= childportal`. Since the original request for `/child` could be a folder in your main portal, DNN needs a way to recognize the request as the child portal.

---

To create a child portal, you'll need to be logged in as a super user, or Host account. As a super user, you can view the portals in your instance of DNN through the Host menu in the Portals page. In the Portals page, complete the following steps:

**1.** Click Add New Portal. The Add New Portal page will appear, as shown in Figure 8-7.

Figure 8-7

**2.** Change the Portal Type to Child.

**3.** The Portal Alias will assume the parent portal's domain. Add the name of the child portal after the forward slash.

**4.** Give your portal a site title, description, and keywords. The title is the only required element.

**5.** Choose a portal template. By default, the Default Website portal template will be the only template listed.

**6.** Create a Portal Administrator account in the Security Setting section.

**7.** Click Create Portal.

That's it. You've just created a child portal. The site will function just as the master portal does, with segregated pages, users, and content.

## Adding a Parent Portal

Parent portals exist within their own domain or as a subdomain of another domain (for example, http://subdomain.dnnusersguide.com). The setup of a parent portal in DNN is similar to a child portal; however, there is a slight difference in the creation of the portal in DNN, and there are additional steps to directing your domain name to the new portal.

By following the steps described in creating a child portal, you'll notice the only difference in creating a parent portal is that you'll need to select Parent instead of Child as the Portal Type and define the full domain as the Portal Alias for your site, as demonstrated in Figure 8-8.

**Figure 8-8**

In addition to adding your domain to the Portal Alias field, you'll need to complete the process of directing your domain name to your instance of DNN by configuring your DNS entry and directing IIS to the file system of your website. The configuration of IIS for your websites is covered in detail in Chapter 2. To configure DNS, you must work with either your domain name registrar or your website hosting providers.

## Configuring Portal Settings as the Host

As the host of multiple portals within your instance of DNN, you have a number of configuration options to control the function and features of your portals. Chapter 3 reviewed the Host Settings for your implementation of DNN. As you administer multiple portals, the relevance of the additional settings available to super user accounts will depend on the relationship you have with the portals within your instance of DNN. As discussed in Chapter 3, most of the settings will throttle the portals within your instance by defining settings like Page Quota, User Quota, and the allowed Disk Space.

By administering Premium Module, you can provide additional value to your portals by either providing or restricting the modules used on individual portals. As we discussed earlier, an instance of DNN shares all the modules installed. Using the Premium Modules feature, you can control which module a portal has available. This feature could be used as a way to produce revenue or recoup the costs of modules purchased by the host if payment is required before a module is made available, but it can also be a way to only provide relevant modules to each portal. Providing a full list of modules installed in the instance can be overkill for specific portal administrators. Administering premium modules can also be a way to prescribe or determine the features particular portals will use. Figure 8-8 illustrates a host administrator explicitly granting a portal access to specific extensions. These settings are located in the portal's Site Settings. Only super user accounts have access to the Host Settings illustrated in Figure 8-9.

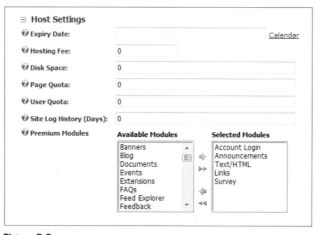

Figure 8-9

All the modules/extensions available to the portals will be listed in the Available Module list. The host can chose from this list of modules to provide selected modules for an individual portal. As you can see in Figure 8-10, the portal administrator now has a refined list of modules to administer content on their portal.

Figure 8-10

# Managing Files on Your Server

As we discussed earlier, DNN both shares and segregates files between portals within a single instance. Many of the shared files are outside of your control as the host administrator. Some of the files are segregated to give the control to the individual portal administrators. Additionally, there are files that you, as the host administrator, can manage at the host level to share across portals while controlling in one place.

Next, we'll review some of these shared files and discuss managing files as an administrator of multiple portals. After reviewing the files stored and managed across portals, we'll review managing files through the File Manager.

# Files Stored by the Host

DNN's File Manager enables you to fully manage directory structures and files without having direct access to your file server. Portal administrators have access to their own portal folders, and host administrators have access to all folders in their installation to perform maintenance.

Each portal has its own directory, which corresponds with its portal ID. For example, the master portal (Portal 0) in your installation of DNN has its own directory and can be referenced in your installation by appending /Portals/0/ to your URL. The host also has a directory (_default), which can be referenced in your installation by appending /Portals/_default/ to your URL.

### Referencing Host Files

As mentioned previously, the host has a directory in which to store files shared across all portals. The most notable use for this directory is for the host to provide skin and container packages to all portals. Figure 8-11 shows the choice that administrators have for locating skin and containers in the Appearance section of their Site Settings. The radio buttons provide a control for the administrator to pick from skins (and containers) located in the host's directory (/Portals/_default/Skins/... ) or located in their portals specific directory (Portals/0/Skins...).

**Figure 8-11**

This feature is provided in a number of ways throughout your portals as a way for you, as the host, to provide content to your portal administrators. Host administrators can also provide specific skin and container packages to individual portals by manually adding a skin or container package to an individual portal's Skins directory.

# File Storage and Management

The File Manager enables portal administrators to upload, edit, delete, and organize the files in their portal's directory. The File Manager offers an alternative to FTP or direct access to the file system. Additionally, the File Manager allows you to manage folders (subdirectories), files, folder security, and file permissions. To access the File Manager for your portal, you can either navigate to the Files icon in the Common Tasks of your control panel or access it by going through the Admin menu to the File Manager page.

The File Manager provides the following three folder options for storing your files:

❑ Standard – File System

❑ Secure – File System

❑ Secure – Database

Each file storage option provides a different level of security for your files.

## Standard - File System Storage

The Standard – File System folder is the most typical storage type for files in a file system. You can use this option when you are not concerned about access to your files. Any files you provide publicly can be accessed by anyone who knows the file path of your files. This shouldn't be a concern for files you're linking to directly on your site.

The files in your file system are stored and can be managed just as you would typically manage files on your PC. The root directory for your portal is located in a folder in DNN referenced as /Portals/[your portal number]. As we walk through the management of files in the Standard – File System folder, we'll reference the master portal, Portal 0.

Figure 8-12 illustrates the file organization of our portal. When we refer to files in the root directory of a portal, we are referring to files located in the top, portal-specific folder. If we placed an image (image.gif) at the root level for our portal, the file would be located in /Portals/0/image.gif. In previous chapters, we created additional folder structures in our portal to organize content more granularly.

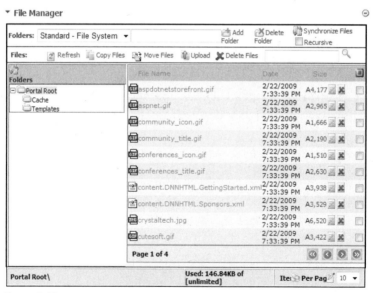

Figure 8-12

Next, we'll review the process of adding files to the directories in your portal and cover the nuance settings of the File Manager. By understanding these features, you'll be able to more effectively manage files on your file system using the File Manager.

First, we'll start by adding files to the root of our portal, as demonstrated in Figure 8-13. Adding files through the File Manager is a two-step process: select the folder and then select the file, but the actual clicks necessary have a few more intricacies.

1. First, select the folder, in the left navigation pane, to which you wish to add files. When adding the root directory, select Portal Root.

2. Once you have selected the folder, click Upload in the top toolbar.

3. You will be prompted to locate the file locally on your computer or network. Choose the file locally, and click Open.

   You'll notice that above the browse option, the full path to which you will be saving the file is mapped.

4. Once the file is listed next to the Choose File button, click Upload File. Figure 8-13 illustrates steps 1–3 just before the file is uploaded to the site. Upon clicking Upload File, your file will be stored on your file server and listed in the File Manager.

**Figure 8-13**

The file will now be stored in your portal.

As you may have noticed as you uploaded a single file, there is a check box in the Upload activity that allows you to decompress ZIP files. If you have a number of files you wish to upload to the same folder, you can select a compressed (.zip) folder from your local drive, check Decompress ZIP files, and the files will be extracted from the .zip package and stored individually on your file system. Additionally, the .zip package will be stored in the folder on your file system. Figure 8-14 illustrates the ability to upload a folder of compressed files.

**Figure 8-14**

Next, we'll add subdirectories in our portal and add more files from the root to a subdirectory. As you can imagine, as you add files to your portal's root directory, referencing these files later can become challenging. The File Manager allows you to create subdirectories within your portal's root folder. To add a subdirectory, complete the following steps, as illustrated in Figure 8-15:

**1.** From the list in the left navigation, select the folder to which you want to create a subdirectory.

**2.** Enter a name for your new folder in the field next to the Add Folder icon.

**3.** Click the Add Folder icon.

**Figure 8-15**

Folders with subdirectories now will be listed in the File Manager with an expand (+) icon.

If you do have FTP access or direct access to the file server, you can manage files directly on the server. If you want to administer the files later using the File Manager, there are two settings that will help you to keep your views in synch. In the top-right corner of the File Manager is an icon labeled Synchronize Files. When you click this icon, files in the folder you have selected will synchronize with the file system so that any changes made directly to the file system will be reflected in the File Manager. The Synchronize Files option allows you to synchronize the files recursively in folders below the folder you have selected. "Recursively" merely means that the synchronization will step through each folder below the selected folder, not just a single folder (think cascading or a waterfall effect).

## Secure – File System Storage

The Secure – File System option in the File Manager prevents users from typing in a URL that links directly to a file in the file system by hacking or guessing the name and file path of your files. A folder created in a Secure – File System folder is still stored in the file system, but the filename has `.resources` appended when it is uploaded. Since the file has `.resources` appended, IIS will restrict direct access to this file from a browser.

Creating secure files is done by creating a secure file system directory. This is done in a similar fashion to creating a subdirectory in your portal's file system, but prior to creating a folder, you'll pick Secure – File System from the Folders drop-down list (see Figure 8-16).

Once you have created a Secure – File System folder, you'll notice that the folder is listed in the Folders list in the File Manager with a padlock icon (see Figure 8-17).

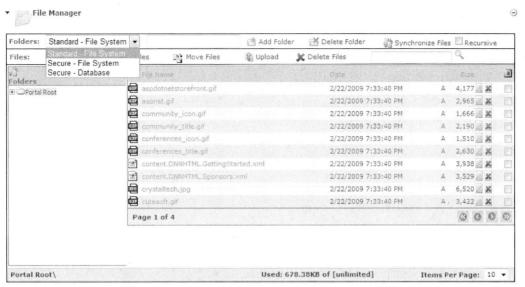

Figure 8-16

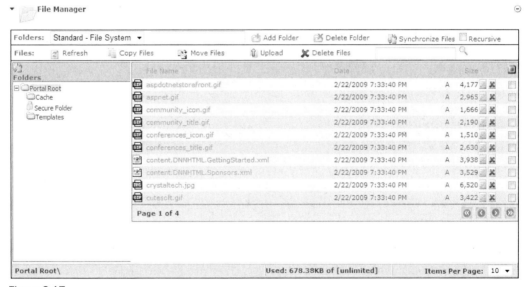

Figure 8-17

With files stored in this secure folder, you can no longer directly reference the file through the file path. To reference the files stored in a secure folder, you can create links by browsing the server by using the interface provided by DNN's rich text editor (FCKEditor). When editing content using the rich text editor, you can create a link to files on your site's file system using the link icon (looks like a chain link). In Figure 8-18, you can see how a secure file is referenced by locating the file on the site through the FCKEditor's Link Gallery. Also notice that the folder is marked with a padlock to indicate that it is stored securely.

---

**Creating Links to Secure Files**

The link path created in referencing secure files uses the page titled `LinkClick.aspx`. The file is recalled from the file system using a query string (for example: `/LinkClick.aspx?fileticket=y45r4JA-moE%3d&amp;tabid=37`). This allows the file to be referenced without IIS restricting access to the file.

---

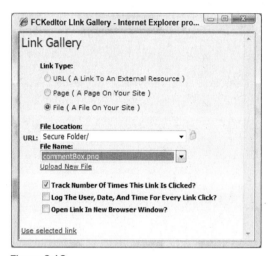

Figure 8-18

## Secure – Database Storage

Storing files in the database is similar to secure storage in the file system, but the files are stored in a column in the database for your instance. To an administrator, creating a Secure – Database folder is the same as creating a Standard or Secure – File System directory. The only difference is that the folder is marked with a database icon to indicate the files are stored in the database (see Figure 8-19).

Before you begin storing all your files in the database, consider the performance impact of larger files. Because the files will be retrieved from the database, the process can be slower than retrieving files from the file system.

## File Manager Permissions

As the administrator, there are levels of permissions you can set within your File Manager. Understanding these permissions can help you to manage the files on your file system effectively as well as give you the opportunity to distribute the responsibilities for uploading files. The File Manager functions just as any other extension on your site functions. As the administrator, you can place the File Manager module on a page and grant or restrict View and Edit permissions at the page or module level. However, to modify files using the File Manager, the administrator needs to grant Edit rights explicitly to the folders in which users of specific roles can add files.

Figure 8-20 demonstrates a page specifically created for the File Manager. Registered Users have View and Edit rights, but, as Figure 8-21 demonstrates, they do not have write permissions to any of the folders. The File Manager has an additional level of permissions that control the ability of users to view (or have access to) the files in a specific folder and that allow users to write (or add) files to specific folders.

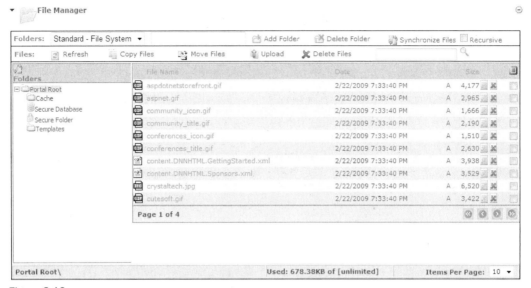

Figure 8-19

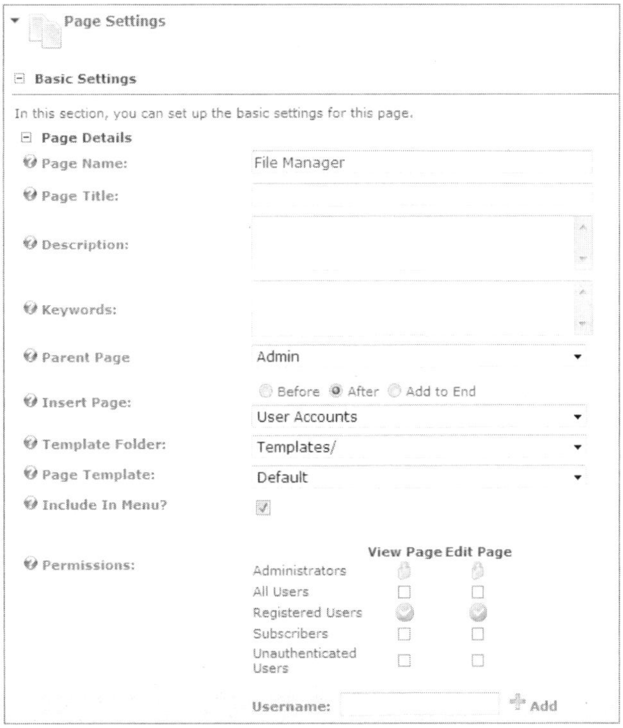

Figure 8-20

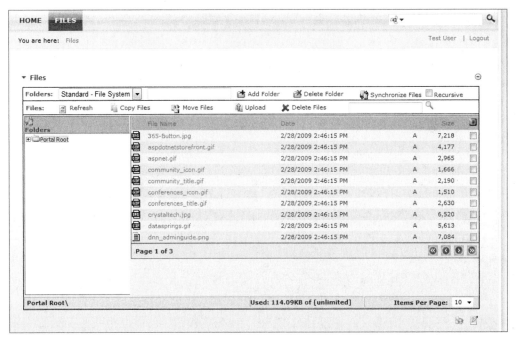

**Figure 8-21**

Administrators can grant roles two levels of access to the files on a site. By default, All Users have the ability to view the files on your file system. Placing the File Manager on a page visible to All Users isn't a very realistic scenario, but as you create links to the files on your files system, the View Folder permissions will control whether users can access the files referenced. As you create subdirectories, there may be folders that need to be restricted to a specific group of users. In Figure 8-22, only users in the Board Members role are able to access files in the Board Meeting Minutes folder. As files from this folder are referenced across the site, only users in the Board Members role will be able to access the files.

If you have additional content managers adding content to your site, you may wish to grant them the rights to upload files to your file system. When you grant Write to Folder permissions to a role, users in that role will be able to upload files to the folder to which they have write permissions. In Figure 8-22, board members have write permissions to the Board Meeting Minutes folder. Figure 8-23 demonstrates how a user in the Board Members role would be able to add files to the Board Meeting Minutes folder through the FCKEditor. They would have the same access in other modules across the site to which they have edit rights and in which the module references the file system.

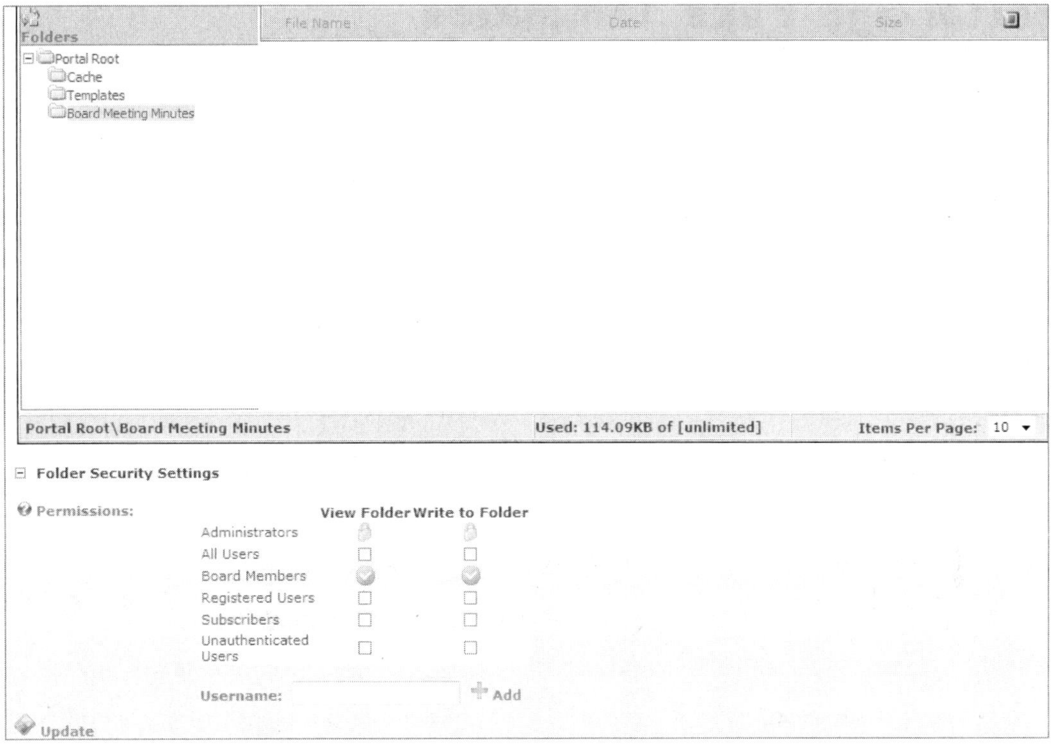

Figure 8-22

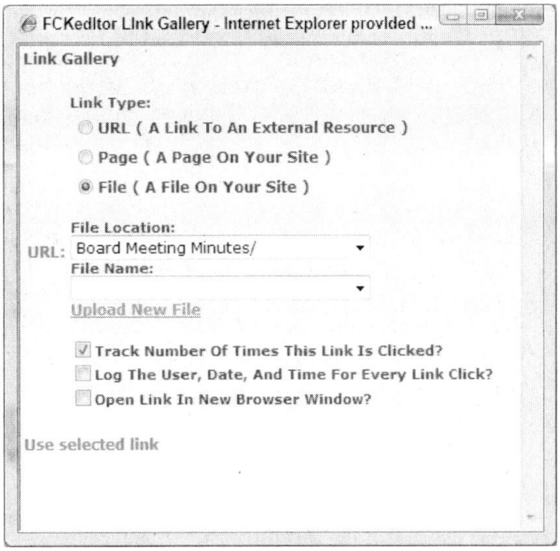

Figure 8-23

# Portal and Page Templates

As the administrator for an enterprise implementation of DNN, there are times when you may want to create a template to use as the starting point for new pages or even entirely new sites.

Templates are XML files with predefined values that translate to settings and configuration of your DNN page or portal. The templates created for pages and portals are different, but the process for creating templates is similar.

The possibilities for using templates can be endless, and with an understanding of this concept, you'll be able to effectively roll out new pages or websites quickly and control the setup for which you want to maintain consistency.

---

### Templates and the IPortable API

The core DNN framework provides an API named `IPortable` that allows modules to be imported and exported within a portal. This interface is used in the framework to import and export pages and portals using templates.

The effectiveness of the template will depend on the modules' use of the `IPortable` interface. This is important to note because as you implement pages or portals using templates, the content and settings loaded with the template will be determined by the implementation of the `IPortable` interface by the module developer.

In cases of modules not using this interface, DNN will recognize the module to be placed in a pane, but the module-specific settings and/or content may not be loaded completely.

---

For more information on the XML and the full features of templates in DNN, the Portal Template document explains the full features and is available for downloading at `www.dotnetnuke.com/Support/Documentation/DownloadableFiles/tabid/478/Default.aspx`.

## Portal Templates

A portal template can dictate a number of properties for a portal, including Title, Description, Site Settings, and Appearance. Additionally, you can use a portal template to import roles, pages, modules, and content into your portal.

The host administrator is the only user who can create portal templates. This is logical because the host is the administrator to all existing and new portals. To create a portal template, navigate to the Portals page in the Host menu. At the Portals page, you can create a new template from an existing portal by performing the following steps:

1.  Click Export Portal Template. The Export Template page appears, as shown in Figure 8-24.
2.  Select the portal from which you wish to create a template.
3.  Give the template a name.

4.  Give the template a description. The description can be helpful to provide information about which pages, skins, and modules are used in the template.

5.  Determine whether content will be imported with the template. If you do not include content, the settings, pages, skins, and modules will be included, but the modules will be void of content.

**Figure 8-24**

Figure 8-25 illustrates the creation of a portal template from our personal site created in Chapter 6. Once you have exported the portal to a template, an XML file will be created in the /Portals/_default/ folder. The file will have the name you provided for the template, with an extension of .template (see Figure 8-25).

**Figure 8-25**

With the template file created, you will be able to create new portals by selecting it as the Template, as illustrated in Figure 8-26.

## *Page Templates*

When creating new pages, you might have noticed that a blank Text/HTML module is placed in the ContentPane. This is accomplished by using the default page template provided by DNN. Page templates enable you to replicate pages with similar content and layout. Also, page templates can be used to provide site administrators a starter kit of pages to ensure consistency in the pages of like type.

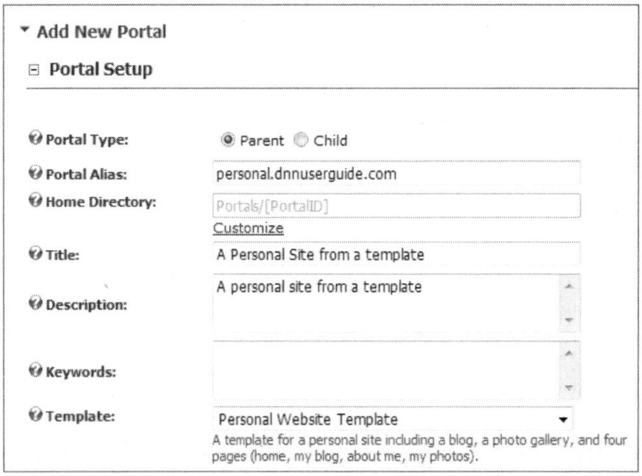

**Figure 8-26**

To start, we'll review the default page template provided by DNN. Like portal templates, a page template is an XML file that dictates the page details, settings, module, and content for a page. The following is the code used to create the default page template:

```
<portal version="3.0">
  <description>Default page template with just an HTML/Text module</description>
  <tabs>
    <tab>
      <panes>
        <pane>
          <name>ContentPane</name>
          <modules>
            <module>
              <title>Enter Title</title>
              <cachetime>0</cachetime>
              <alignment>left</alignment>
              <color />
              <border />
              <iconfile />
              <alltabs>false</alltabs>
              <visibility>Maximized</visibility>
              <header />
              <footer />
              <startdate>0001-01-01T00:00:00.0000000+11:00</startdate>
              <enddate>0001-01-01T00:00:00.0000000+11:00</enddate>
              <containersrc>
              </containersrc>
              <displaytitle>true</displaytitle>
              <displayprint>true</displayprint>
              <displaysyndicate>false</displaysyndicate>
              <inheritviewpermissions>true</inheritviewpermissions>
              <modulepermissions>
                <permission>
```

```
                            <permissioncode>SYSTEM_MODULE_DEFINITION</permissioncode>
                            <permissionkey>EDIT</permissionkey>
                            <rolename>Administrators</rolename>
                            <allowaccess>true</allowaccess>
                        </permission>
                    </modulepermissions>
                        <definition>DNN_HTML</definition>
                        <moduledefinition>Text/HTML</moduledefinition>
                </module>
            </modules>
          </pane>
        </panes>
      </tab>
    </tabs>
  </portal>
```

If this code makes your head spin, don't worry; you can use page templates without understanding the XML. At the very least, review some of the high-level names used for the nodes of this XML. If you are unfamiliar with XML, put aside the fear of code and just review some of the names of each element. To start, the code identifies the first <pane>, the ContentPane, in which a module is going to be placed. This makes sense. The default page template places a module in the ContentPane. Next, it gives the module a <title>, "Enter Title." The remaining elements of this code match a number of the settings you are already familiar with in the Module Settings. If you look closely, you could probably match each element to a setting in Module Settings. Later in the XML, the permissions for the module are applied in the <modulepermissions> elements. The final section defines which module is placed in the pane. In this case, the module definition tells the page to use the Text/HTML module.

You don't need to know XML to create templates. Understanding the inner workings of the template can help you to better utilize this feature, but for the most part DNN does the work for you.

## Creating and Using a Page Template

To create a page template, you first need to build a page that will serve as your template. Our sample page contains three modules: a Text/HTML module, with content describing our corporate philosophy and mission statement; a Text/HTML module, left blank for division managers to insert their division mission statement; and a Links module, with relevant links to important information. This could be a very useful template for managers to create their pages for their division in a corporate intranet site.

With our three modules placed on a page, and page permissions and settings configured, we'll export this page as a page template.

1.  Open the control panel and under Page Functions, choose Export.

    The choices for a page template are similar to those for a portal template, but in this case the Folder is the folder specific to your portal. Unless you have multiple directories of templates, you can use the default directory "Templates."

2.  Define the name for your template. By default, it is going to be the name of the page from which you create the template.

3. Give your template a description. This will provide administrators with a clue about what is included in the page.

4. Include content. In our example, we'll include content to bring forward the links and corporate philosophy statement.

5. Click Export.

The page template file is now saved in the Templates folder in our portal's directory. This template can be used in two ways: to create a new page or to replace an existing page. When you create a new page from a template, you will simply need to locate the template folder from the Templates directory and name your page. All of the page details can be assumed from the page template.

You can use the page template either by creating a new page by selecting the Add function in the Page Functions menu and then selecting the template in the Basic Settings (see Figure 8-27), or by selecting Import from the Page Functions menu and then selecting Create a New Page as the Import mode (see Figure 8-28).

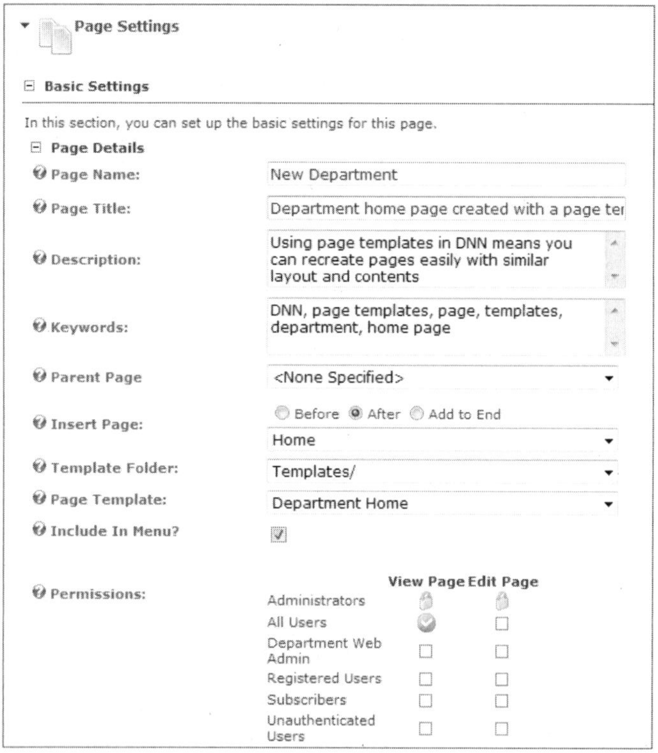

Figure 8-27

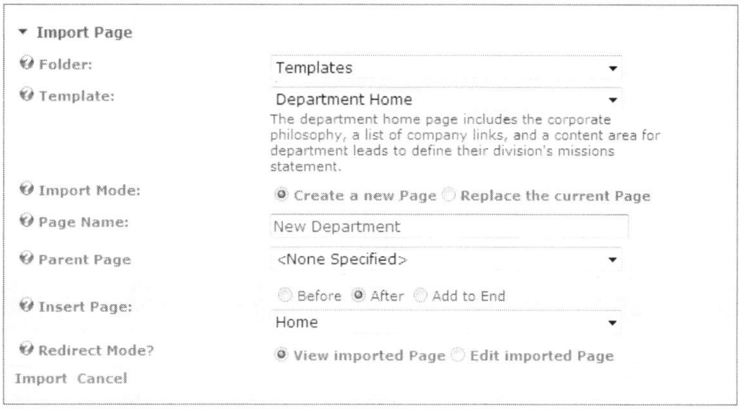

**Figure 8-28**

As a host administrator, you may want to provide the same set of page templates to multiple portals. As we just demonstrated, page templates are stored in the Templates directory for a specific portal. If you have access to the file system, you can copy the template files and paste them into each portal's Templates directory.

# Distributing Content Management Responsibilities

Chapter 4 discussed the various settings used to create web pages. In an environment where there is a single administrator, the page editor is the site administrator, so granular implementation details may not be as relevant as an environment in which you have multiple content administrators. If you intend to use DNN to share content management responsibilities with multiple people, granting full administrator responsibilities may not be ideal. Next, we'll review some of the more subtle settings available in creating content that will be important considerations for distributing content management responsibilities.

## Page Edit Permissions

When you give a user or group of users Edit permissions to a page, the users will have Edit rights to all child pages of the page to which you have granted access. This can be used to your benefit to allow users to create child pages without having to explicitly create the pages and grant them edit permissions. A typical use case for this feature would be the example of a softball league website we built in Chapter 6. In this example, each coach was the page editor for his or her team's landing page. If a coach was particularly ambitious, he or she could create a full range of child pages under the page to which we gave them edit permissions. This feature, in coordination with page templates, can be extremely powerful in distributing content management responsibilities.

## *Copying to Descendents*

There are two features in Page settings that have additional implications for child pages. Similarly to applying page creation permissions, applying permissions to child pages as well as to the page to which you have granted access, allows users with edit rights to a page to apply permissions and designs to child pages.

Even if you explicitly restrict permissions on a child page, these permissions could be overridden by using an option in Page Settings called Apply Permissions to Descendents. The Apply Permissions to Descendents option allows the permissions of a single page to be applied to all child pages. Similarly, another option, Copy Permissions to Descendents, allows users with edit rights to a page to apply a skin and container selection to all child pages (see Figure 8-29).

**Figure 8-29**

These features are valuable in making group changes to page permissions or skin design selections without having to touch each page's settings. As you grant Edit rights to pages, this setting should be considered because users with edit permissions to a page with child pages (descendents) will be able to manage the permissions of descendent pages.

## *Using Referenced Modules*

There are two ways to use referenced modules on your site. As you add modules to a page, one of the options is to Add Existing Module. Add Existing Module is an option in the control panel that allows you to pick a module that already exists on another page. This feature can be useful when you want to use a single module to provide the same content across multiple pages. The other way to create referenced modules on your site is to apply a single module to all pages in your site. The module is created only once but is referenced on every page of your site. To apply a module on all pages, navigate to the Advances Setting section of the module's settings. Figure 8-30 illustrates setting a module to be referenced on multiple pages.

Creating referenced modules can be extremely powerful when you want to apply global banners or footer content without having to modify the skin files. Along with this powerful feature come content management considerations. As you create referenced modules, it is important to consider that users with Edit rights to a referenced module can affect the display of the content across all the pages on which the module is referenced. Again, this feature can significantly reduce duplicate content administration, but as you distribute content management responsibilities, the control of your content can be diluted and not as isolated as you might think when you're using referenced modules.

Figure 8-30

# Leveraging the Provider Model

The provider model is an important feature in DNN that allows functionality in the framework to be swapped in and out without disrupting the core code base of DNN. As an administrator, how this model works is not as important as how this model can work for you. The following table lists the uses of the provider model in a standard implementation of DNN. Mapped to the provider type is the standard provider implemented with DNN.

**Provider Implementations**

| Provider | Standard Provider |
|---|---|
| Membership | DotNetNuke ASP.NET Membership Provider |
| Logging | DotNetNuke Database Logging Provider |
| Navigation | DotNetNuke DNN Menu Navigation Provider |
| | DotNetNuke DNN Tree Navigation Provider |
| | DotNetNuke Solpart Menu Navigation Provider |
| HTML Editor | DotNetNuke Fck HTML Editor Provider |

*Continued*

**Provider Implementations** *(continued)*

| Provider | Standard Provider |
|---|---|
| Caching | DotNetNuke File-Based Caching Provider |
| Profile | DotNetNuke Profile Provider |
| Scheduling | DotNetNuke Scheduling Provider |
| Search | DotNetNuke Search Indexer Provider<br>DotNetNuke Search Provider |
| Data | Microsoft SQL Server |
| Authentication | Default DotNetNuke Forms Authentication<br>DNN_LiveIDAuthentication<br>DNN_OpenIDAuthentication |
| Friendly URL | FriendlyURL |

In DotNetNuke 5.0, super user accounts can install providers in the same manner as other extensions, as described in Chapter 3. Previously, the providers used in DNN were not installable, and the modification of providers was manual. In the future, the installation of providers will be automated. When a provider solution is provided as an installable extension, the providers can be easily swapped out for new tools. Figure 8-31 shows the list of provider extensions found in the Extensions page in the Host menu.

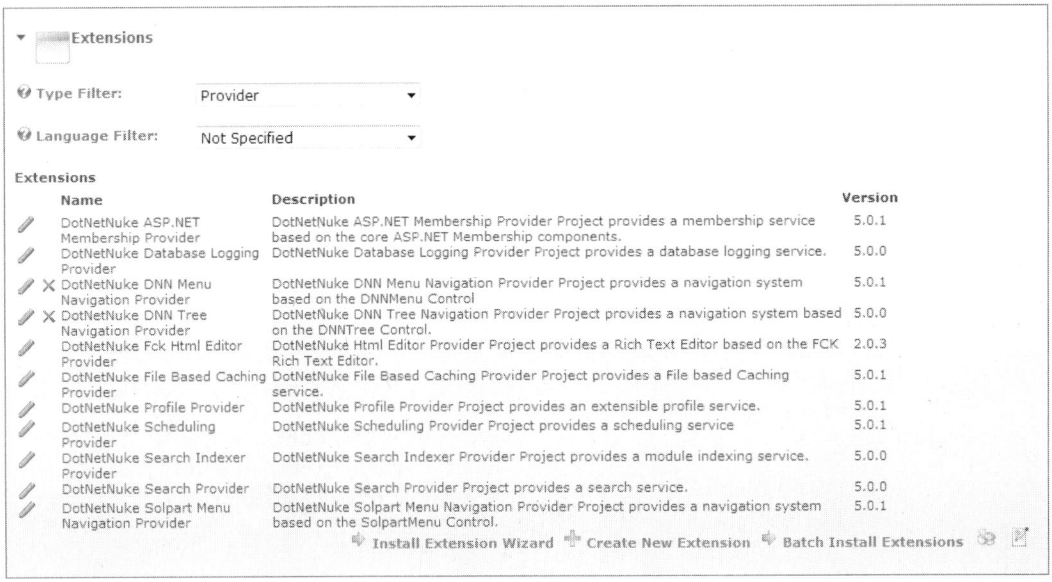

Figure 8-31

240

As a savvy DNN host administrator, you can use the power of the provider model to your benefit by implementing other providers for some of these features. Some of the most frequently modified providers are URL rewriting, user authentication, and the HTML editor.

The Friendly URL provider allows you to modify the way that the URLs are presented to the user. One of the most common complaints about database-driven content management systems is that URLs are messy. The Friendly URL provider and other providers for URL rewriting allow you to modify the way that URLs are presented to the user. Some third-party URL providers also allow for more sophisticated rewriting logic to be applied.

The Authentication provider enables you to allow visitors of your site to log in with a username and password. However, you can plug in different authentication providers that will allow users to log in with common authentication mechanisms such as Microsoft's Live ID (formerly Microsoft Passport), or Active Directory, a common authentication system within corporate environments.

The FCKeditor is the standard HTML editor in DNN. The HTML editor providers give you control over content formatting. Any module using the HTML Editor will provide users the ability to create HTML without knowing the markup language. Each editor provides other options and features to create rich text without knowing difference between a <b> tag and a <strong> tag.

# Summary

This chapter reviewed how to leverage the ability to manage multiple websites under a single installation of DNN. This feature is one of the most attractive features of DNN. As a site administrator, it is important to understand how your portal fits into the DNN application as a whole. For a host administrator, DNN offers a number of tools to make managing multiple portals easier. The ability to host multiple websites in a single code base can provide efficiencies and complexities. With a firm understanding of the implications of managing multiple sites, you can better leverage the power of a DNN implementation.

After reviewing the relationship of portals in a single instance of DNN, and considering the way that files and database tables are shared, we reviewed some of the administrative tools available to make the most of your enterprise installation of DNN. In the next chapter, we'll look at what's next for you as your DNN environment functions as a live content management system.

# Your Website Is Up and Running — Now What?

Now that you have your DotNetNuke (DNN) website up and running, this chapter covers some of the items you need to know in order to keep things running smoothly. We'll talk about portal health as well as the backup, restoration, and upgrading processes for a DNN website. This chapter also discusses how to use the files generated from the backup and restoration processes to configure multiple environments for use in testing and staging content for your production website.

After describing the various types of environments that you might have for your website, we'll wrap up the book by getting into some of the advanced administration functionality within DNN.

This chapter discusses the following topics:

❑ Opportunities to improve the performance of your live DNN site

❑ Backing up and restoring your website so that you can confidently upgrade DNN and extensions on your site

❑ Various website environments you may want to consider as you manage your websites

❑ Various tools that DNN provides to make the most of your site

❑ Features and settings in DNN to help distribute the management of your content

## Portal Health

Checking the "health" of your portal is an important part of maintaining a good website. Knowing how big your database currently is, how many users and pages your portals have, and which modules are being used on your site are important aspects to understanding the overall health of your portal. DNN provides some of this information through the Host ⇨ Dashboard page. First implemented in version 04.09.01, this page provides a number of items that can be useful when monitoring the health of your website.

# Database Health

Database health is an important aspect of maintaining your DNN website in order to ensure the validity of your content and the performance of your website.

## Database Size

If your database becomes too large, the performance of your website can be greatly impacted. A common database size for a simple DNN website will be less than 100 MB. If you have a very active site with a lot of users and content being posted, the size of your database may be much larger. If you are using SQL Express for your database, size can definitely become an issue, as SQL Express databases are limited to 4 GB.

You can check the size of your database files by going to the Host ⇨ Dashboard page and clicking on the Database Server link on the left side of the module. As shown in Figure 9-1, you will see a Database Files section that lists the files that your database consists of and the size of those files.

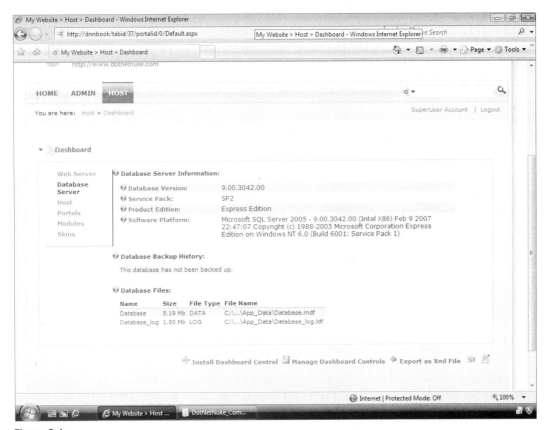

Figure 9-1

A common culprit to a large database can be the EventLog table in the database. This is information that DNN stores regarding events that occur on your website, such as users registering and logging in, and even errors that occur on the site. The data in the table should be pruned automatically by DNN, but if that pruning fails to occur, the table may grow large and cause performance problems. You can manually prune the data when logged in as a super user. From the Event Viewer page, simply click on the Clear Log option.

### Database Backup History

Another important aspect of the Database Server page on the Dashboard page is the Database Backup History. You can see in Figure 9-1 that this database has not been backed up. Maintaining backups of your site and database is important to maintaining the health of your database. You can read more about the backup process later in this chapter.

## Pages and Users

You can monitor the number of pages, roles, and users that your portals have on the Portals portion of the Dashboard page. Here, you will find a listing of the portals in your DotNetNuke instance, along with the preceding information. This information can be very useful in analyzing the activity on various portals within your instance.

## Modules and Skin in Use

One way to improve the performance of your DNN instance is to uninstall modules that are not in use on your portals. In order to figure out which modules and skins are being used on your portals, you can use the Dashboard ➪ Modules page. Here, you will find a listing of the modules that are installed for your DNN instance and the number of instances for each module. The module instances are the number of times the modules are being used on pages. As you can see in Figure 9-2, there are a number of modules that aren't being used and could potentially be uninstalled from your DNN instance.

The Skins section of the Dashboard page shows which skins are currently being used, allowing you to delete any unused skins. While skins are not as big of a deal for performance on your DNN instance as other factors, it is recommended that you clean up unused skins from time to time to prevent them from being used if they are not meant to be.

# Backing Up Your Website

An important part of the maintenance of any website is making sure that you have the ability to recover from a disaster. A disaster can come in many forms, sometimes self-inflicted, other times not. It is common for people first learning DNN to shoot themselves in the foot by doing something that they didn't intend to, or didn't understand the repercussions of. Having a backup of your website files and database will allow you to recover more quickly from such an incident.

Backing up your website and database also provides you with a means to setting up multiple environments. It is common practice to have both a production website and a testing website. We'll cover more about environments later in this chapter, but the process for setting up a test environment usually consists of backing up and restoring your production website on a different web server, sometimes on your own computer.

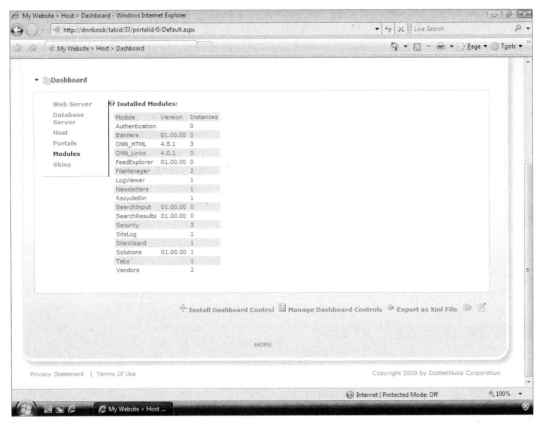

Figure 9-2

# When to Back Up

There are many times when you should back up your DotNetNuke website. We'll cover some of these scenarios and why they are important.

## Scheduled Backups

It is important to have a scheduled backup in place that you can fall back on if something goes wrong with the normal operation of your website. A common schedule for backups on a regular Internet site is either weekly or daily. If the content on your site changes frequently, you will likely want a more frequent backup process. If you're updating the content on the site only every few weeks, then having a daily backup might be overkill. In active websites, daily backups will usually suffice, but in some cases more frequent backups may be necessary. The length of time since your last backup, as well as when you are doing a restore, will determine the amount of data lost since that last backup.

## Upgrading DotNetNuke

DNN provides somewhat frequent updates, offering new functionality and bug fixes with each release. While DNN is designed to be upgradable, and upgrades are easy to manage, as you will see later in this chapter, it is always important to back up your website and database prior to performing an upgrade.

Because DNN is so flexible, it is possible that a customization to your website may cause a problem with an upgrade. If an upgrade fails, you want to be able to restore your site to the previous state. In most cases, you will upgrade DNN without a problem, but the time that it does fail, you will be glad you have a backup ready to go.

## When Installing/Upgrading/Uninstalling a Module

Another important time to back up your website is when you are making major changes to a module, such as installing a module, upgrading a module, or uninstalling a module from your DNN instance. These actions are not the act of putting a module on a page within DotNetNuke, but the process, as a super user, of managing extensions. In all these processes, it is possible that the module is executing a SQL script to add or remove information to or from the database. If something fails during this database access, having a backup makes correcting the problems easier. As with upgrades to DNN itself, most installations/upgrades/uninstalls for modules will work fine, without issues, but when something does go wrong, the backup will save you a lot of headaches.

# How to Back Up

How you back up your website and database will differ slightly, depending on your hosting environment. This section discusses some elements common across most environments.

## Backing Up the File System

An important part of backing up your website is to have a good organization system. If you ever need to recover from a previous backup, you want to be able to find it. Having a backup directory, perhaps at c:\backups\, can be a good start. You can paste the copy of your DotNetNuke directory into this backup directory and then rename that pasted folder to be DotNetNuke_##_##_####, where you replace the # signs with the current date. That way you know what is what in your backup directory.

Depending on how you are performing this part of the backup process, either locally or remotely, the time this will take may vary. It will also depend on how big your website is. The more files that have been uploaded to your website, the larger the contents of the directory will be, thus increasing the amount of time it takes to back up the files.

### Local File System Backups

Backing up your file system when you have access to the operating system on a server, or your local computer, is easy. Simply copy the contents of the directory where your DNN website exists, For example, using the examples in this book, that would be c:\inetpub\wwwroot\dotnetnuke. If you browse to c:\inetpub\wwwroot\, you can simply right-click on the DotNetNuke directory and choose Copy, and then paste it into the backup directory. If you are using SQL Express for your database, you've also just backed up your database at the same time, as the database exists in the App_Data directory inside of your DotNetNuke directory. This makes the restoration process easier later on.

### Remote File System Backups

If you're not using your desktop PC as a local web server, you likely have FTP access to the files for your website. You will need to connect to your website using an FTP application such as WS_FTP and copy the contents of your website's directory to your backup directory on your computer. Copying the files via FTP will likely take longer than if you were accessing them locally, but don't let that deter you.

### Backing Up the Database

Backing up your database can be the easiest part of making a backup of your website, although it can also be the most difficult part if you aren't familiar with some of the necessary tools. Here, we will talk about a few of the ways to back up your database.

#### Local Database Backups

The easiest backup process for the database will be possible if you are using SQL Express in its default configuration for DNN. If that is the case, the database resides in the `App_Data` directory inside of your DNN website folder. If you've backed up your file system, you've already backed up your database as well. If you want to back up the database individually, you can simply copy the contents of this `App_Data` directory to your backup directory.

If you aren't using SQL Express, and instead are using SQL Server 2000, 2005, or 2008, you will have to back up the database using the tools that SQL Server provides. For SQL 2000, that means using the Enterprise Manager application you likely used to create the database initially. For SQL 2005 or 2008, the tool provided is called Management Studio. The process for each application is similar. Once you are connected to the database server through the tool, you can navigate down through the tree views to the databases node and find the database being used for your website.

Once you've located the database, right-click on the database and choose the Backup option. This will walk you through the process of backing up the website, ultimately creating a .BAK file that can be used when restoring the database.

With SQL Server 2000, 2005, and 2008, you can set up maintenance plans on your database to perform a number of tasks on a scheduled basis, including regular backups. This is a good thing to do daily or weekly, depending on the level of activity on your website.

> *For more information on how to back up your database, refer to the article "Backing Up and Restoring Databases in SQL Server" at* `http://msdn.microsoft.com/en-us/library/ms187048.aspx`.

#### Remote Database Backups

If you're using a third-party hosting company, check to see what kind of backup plans they offer. The process for these plans may differ by provider. One scenario would be that you can access the database server remotely using either Enterprise Manager or Management Studio, depending on the version of SQL Server, and you could do backups using that software.

The more likely scenario is that the hosting provider will have a SQL management tool that is accessible via a web interface, allowing you to run backups using this tool. Check with your hosting provider to see what they provide for backups. As with a local backup process, it is a good idea to try to set up backups on a scheduled basis so that, if you do run into problems with your website, you have recent backups available. You will probably find that low-cost hosting providers do not provide scheduled backup services, so you will need to manually back up your database on a set schedule.

## How to Restore

As with conducting a backup, the process for restoring your website files and database will differ, depending on how your website is configured. We will first cover the basics of restoring a site that apply to both local and remote scenarios, then we will discuss the local process for restoring your website and database, followed by information about restoring your site on a remote server. Restoring your DNN website to a previous backup shouldn't be something that you have to do frequently, although this can be a very useful process to master. Knowing how to restore your website can come in handy to get your website up and running quickly if something goes wrong. It can also be useful if you are setting up a test environment before upgrading your production website. We talk more about environments later in the chapter.

## The Basics

The process of restoring a website will potentially impact you in a few different areas. It is important to understand what this impact will be on your particular website. The restoration of a website will cause you to lose any data that has changed on the website since the time that the last backup occurred. Of course, this is assuming that you are using the last backup for your restoration. It's possible that you might be going to an older backup. For a lot of websites, this won't cause any issues, as their content may not change frequently, but on a website that is active, such as a community forum, this may be more of an issue. You should keep this in mind when planning your backup processes. Backing up more frequently will help to minimize the amount of potential data loss.

Another area of impact will be how your website is accessible to its visitors during the restoration process. You likely don't want visitors to be accessing the contents of the site during any of the restoration process, so you will want to take the website down while you are going through the process. There are a number of ways you can disable your site. We will cover a few simple ways. If you are looking for more advanced configuration options for IIS, check out www.iis.net.

### Disabling Your Website

The first, and often easiest, way to disable your website is simply to shut it off. You can do this either through IIS by "stopping" the website, or by stopping the application pool in which the website runs. If you have direct access to the web server on which your site is hosted, these can both be done through the Internet Information Services Manager, available from the Windows Control Panel under Administration Tools. If you are on a hosted server and only have a web control panel, you should have an option there to stop the website. The downfall to simply stopping your website is that the visitors to your site will likely get a 404 or other error message stating that the server is unavailable. This may or may not be a big concern for you. If it is, try the next option.

You can also disable your website during the restoration process by using a file called app_offline.htm. This is a HTML file that you can create in the root of your DNN website to bring the site down. This file is not a DNN-specific item; it will work on any ASP.NET 2.0–based website. Whatever contents you put in this simple HTML file will be displayed to the visitors of your website. Providing a simple "This website is currently undergoing maintenance" message is usually a sufficient way to notify the visitors that something is occurring and that they can visit the site later. The name of this file is important; it should be app_offline.htm, not app_offline.html. Once you are ready to turn your website back on, you can simply delete the app_offline.htm file.

### Creating a New Site in IIS

A more advanced option for doing a restoration of your website would be to restore the backup of your site as another website in IIS. This can be a useful way to do a restoration so that you can test out the restoration before making it visible to your site's visitors. This is a more advanced topic than we will get into for this book, but if you are comfortable with IIS, you can go through the process of configuring a new website and restoring the contents of your backup on this site. Once you are done testing, you can simply change the IIS sites around to point to the proper folders on your web server for the newly restored site.

## Restoring the Files

The process of restoring the files for your website will vary somewhat, based on the kind of access you have to your web server. If you can access the server directly, copying the files around for the restoration process will be easy. If you only have FTP access to the site, the files will take a little more effort and time to restore.

### Restoring Local Files

If you have desktop access to the web server on which your website is hosted, we recommend that you perform the following steps to restore the files for your DNN website:

1. Locate the files from the backup of your website.

2. Find the location of the folder where your website exists on the web server. (In Chapter 2, we configured this location as `c:\inetpub\wwwroot\dotnetnuke`.)

3. (Optional) Delete the contents of the folder located in the previous step. You would do this *only* if you are sure that you have a backup of the directory ready to use.

4. Copy the contents of the backup directory into your directory found in `step 2.folder`. If you are prompted to overwrite any files, click Yes, or Yes to All.

One thing you may or may not have to do is to reconfigure the permissions on the files in the DotNetNuke directory. It is easy enough to do this, so we recommend setting up the permissions again each time just to be sure that they get applied properly. For a refresher on how to configure permissions, refer to Chapter 2.

> **SQL Express Users**
>
> If you are using SQL Express for your database, the files for the database are in your DotNetNuke directory, in a folder called `App_Data`. This comes in handy during the database portion of the restoration process, but it might cause a problem when you copy the files over during the file process of the restoration. You might run into a problem where you can't overwrite the database files because they are in use. If that is the case, you can go into IIS and stop the application pool that your website is running under. This will free up the files from any processes that are currently using them. If you are running Windows XP, you will need to restart IIS in order to reset the application pool. You can do so by right-clicking on the top node in the tree view in IIS and choosing the Restart option.

### Restoring Remote Files

The process for restoring the files on a remote web server is similar to that for a local server; you just don't have the same easy access to the files as you would if you were logged in to the server itself. In some cases, a website hosting provider will offer backup restoration services as part of your hosting contract. If so, you can attempt to have them perform the restoration for you. If this isn't an option, you can perform the following steps to restore the files to your remote server.

1. Find the files that you are going to be using for the restoration process. If they are currently on the web server in a backup directory of some sort, you should connect to the server and download the files.

2. Connect with your FTP client to your website's root folder.

3. Upload the contents of your backup folder to your website's root folder. This process may take a while, depending on how many files you have to upload and the speed of your Internet connection.

4. Reconfigure any file permissions, as you did during the initial installation process (refer to Chapter 2). You will likely perform this through your web hosting control panel.

### *Restoring the Database*

Another important step for restoring your website is to restore the contents of your database. If you are using SQL Express, you likely have already completed the process. As mentioned previously, the files for SQL Express reside within the DotNetNuke directory. So, by restoring the contents of the directory, you also restored your database files.

If you are using SQL Server 2000, 2005, or 2008, however, the restoration process is going to be a bit more complex.

### Restoring the Local Database

You should open up your database management tool, either Enterprise Manager for SQL Server 2000 or Management Studio for SQL Server 2005 and 2008. From here, you will need to locate the database for your DNN website. Right-click on the database and choose the Restore option. You should have a list of options in the window that appears, enabling you to choose from the recent backups for your DNN database. If you don't have these options, or if you are restoring a database on a new SQL Server, choose the Device option, and then locate the backup file for your database.

Once you've chosen the appropriate backup that you want to restore, you can proceed with the restoration process. The process should replace the contents of your existing database with the contents of the backed up database.

### Restoring the Remote Database

The process for restoring a remote website and database is similar to the process for restoring a local database. Some hosting providers allow you to connect to the database from a remote connection, using the same tools you would for a local database. If that is the case, you can use the process described in the preceding section. If that is not the case for your hosting account, you will likely have a web interface, similar to the web hosting control panel, or even within that control panel, that allows you to manage your databases. You will need to contact your hosting provider to see what they provide for the management and restoration of your database.

# Upgrading DotNetNuke

One of the great benefits of DNN is that there are frequent releases of the software that provide new features and fix bugs, and these releases are almost always compatible from version to version. Before you decide to perform an upgrade, it is a good idea to know which version of DNN your site is currently running. You can find this out by logging in as a super user (host) and going to either the Host ⇨ Host

Settings page, the Extensions page, or the Dashboard page. DotNetNuke should be listed as an extension, along with the version number.

If you have the ability to do so, we highly recommend that you try to upgrade your DNN site in a test environment before you try to upgrade your website in a production environment. We will talk more about the various environments in a later section; the following upgrade information is applicable to any environment that you are upgrading.

## Deciding When to Upgrade

Because DNN has frequent releases, you might find that you don't want to upgrade your website every time a new release comes out, and in many cases we would agree with that decision. While DNN strives to put out quality releases every time, it is not possible to cover every website and server's configuration in testing of a release before it comes out. As a result, there are cases when a release might actually break websites that it is applied to. We generally recommend waiting at least a couple of days, if not a week or two, after an upgrade comes out before you apply the upgrade to your website.

There are even some cases in which upgrading is not recommended. When a major release comes out, we will usually hold off on upgrading to that major release until we are sure that it is stable and won't cause our websites any problems. How do you know if this is going to be the case, if you should upgrade to a release? The best way to determine if a release is going to work for you is to test it out. Upgrade a test version of your website and make sure that the site still functions as expected after the upgrade has been applied. This might not be possible if you don't have a test environment configured. If that is the case, we generally recommend that you read some of the forum posts in the Install It forum at DotNetNuke.com (www.dotnetnuke.com/Community/Forums/tabid/795/forumid/107/scope/threads/Default.aspx) to see what issues people might be running into with a new release.

When considering whether to upgrade your version of DDN, you should consider the following questions:

❑    Are there new features in the latest version of DotNetNuke that you need on your website? If not, then perhaps an upgrade won't be beneficial

❑    Are there security updates available in the new release of DotNetNuke that would make your site more secure? If so, you should strongly consider an upgrade

❑    Are you experiencing performance problems with your website that have been addressed in the new release? If so, an upgrade would likely be a good idea

In order to answer these questions, you'll need to know what is in the new release of DNN. You can check out the Change Log for each version by visiting support.dotnetnuke.com. This website is the tracking system for all releases of DNN and contains a list of known bugs, as well as a change log for each version of DNN that highlights which bugs have been fixed and which new features have been added.

## Disabling Your Website during an Upgrade

The previous section "Disabling Your Website" discussed disabling your website during the restoration process so that visitors don't access the dynamic aspects of the site while you are in the middle of changing things around. The same goes when you are upgrading your DNN website. Although you don't have to disable your site for an upgrade, using one of the methods discussed previously is highly recommended.

# Deciding Which Package to Use

When a new release of DotNetNuke occurs, you will find a number of packages available for download from DotNetNuke.com. During the installation process, you used the _Install package. It would make sense that you would then use the _Upgrade package to upgrade your instance of DNN. Most of the time, that will be the case; you will use the `DotNetNuke_Community_XX.XX.XX_Upgrade.zip` file, where *XX.XX.XX* is the version number you are upgrading to. If you are upgrading from a version of DNN that is older than 04.06.02, you will need to use the _Install package to perform the upgrade. We will cover upgrading using both of these packages in the next few sections.

# Performing an Upgrade

If you've skipped to this section without reading about backing up and restoring your DNN instance, be sure to read those sections before continuing with the upgrade process. An important part of the upgrade process is to back up your website completely before attempting an upgrade. If you don't perform the backup prior to an upgrade and something goes wrong during the process, you may not be able to correct the errors that occur and get your website running properly again. Please always back up the files and database.

## Using the Upgrade Package

The process for using the Upgrade package for DNN is pretty straightforward, and makes for a very quick upgrade for your website.

1. Back up your files and database.

2. Download the Upgrade package from DotNetNuke.com.

3. Extract the contents of the ZIP file into a folder on your computer, or on the web server if you are working directly on the web server.

4. Once you've extracted the files, you can simply copy these files over the files in your website's folder. We used `c:\inetpub\wwwroot\dotnetnuke\`. This will replace all the files that are necessary to replace for the upgrade but won't overwrite any of the files you've uploaded for your portal that exist in the `c:\inetpub\wwwroot\dotnetnuke\portals\` folder.

5. Once the files have been completely copied, navigate to your website.

In our case, we would go to `http://dnnbook/`. DNN handles the upgrade process once you've copied the new files over the original files. It will compare the version of the database with the version of the files and, if necessary, execute any processes necessary to complete the upgrade. In general, these processes will include SQL scripts that will be run on the database to make any necessary changes to the structure and data within the database.

If you disabled your site using the `app_offline.htm` file or simply by stopping your website in IIS, you will need to enable the site before the upgrade process will run. Keep in mind that the upgrade process will run on the very first request for the site after the files have been copied over. If you left your site live during the copying process, it's possible that someone else may hit the site during that time and fire off the upgrade before all the necessary files are in place. It is also possible that once you enable your website, someone else will make the first request, before you get a chance to. They will likely see the upgrade screen, which in most cases will not make any sense to them. When an upgrade occurs and the first request is made, you should see a screen similar to Figure 9-3. This will tell you which version you were running, as well as which version your site was upgraded to. The upgrade process will run, and you should see a success message and then a link to take you back to the website.

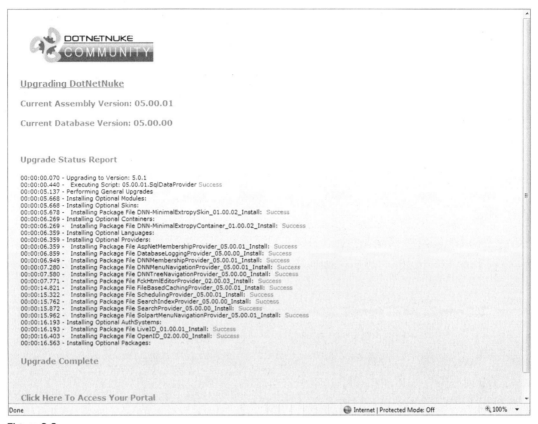

Figure 9-3

If you don't see the upgrade screen and aren't sure whether the upgrade completed, you can always log in as a super user (Host) and check the Extensions page to confirm which version of DNN your site is running.

If something fails to run properly during the upgrade process, you should see an error message on the upgrade screen. It is those times when something fails that you will be glad that you have a backup of your files and database so that you can restore the previous copy of the site. If you failed to make a backup, you may or may not be able to successfully recover from whatever occurred during the upgrading process.

If something fails to install properly during the upgrade, you can always try to run the upgrade again by restoring the backup and performing the upgrade steps again. Sometimes this will be all that is necessary to successfully upgrade, although at other times you might have to do some investigating and testing to figure out why an upgrade failed, both of which are outside of the scope of this book. The best source for free help, if you need assistance with tracking down an upgrade problem for your DNN site, are the Forums at `forums.dotnetnuke.com`.

### Using the Install Package

Using the Install package to perform an upgrade is the way that upgrades used to be done, prior to the solidification of the Upgrade package. The process is for the most part the same, although there are a few files that you need to be careful with when copying the contents of the install package over the contents of your DotNetNuke folder.

The benefit of using the Install package over the Upgrade package is that the Install package has all the latest modules, whereas the Upgrade package contains only the files necessary to upgrade DNN, not all the new module versions. You can manually download the new module versions from DotNetNuke.com, and in general that is the recommended process, rather than using the Install package.

To perform the upgrade using the Install package, complete the following steps:

1. Back up the files and database for your DNN instance.

2. Download the Install package from DotNetNuke.com.

3. Extract the contents of the ZIP file into a folder on your computer, or on the web server if you are working directly on the web server.

4. Once you've extracted the files, simply copy and paste those files over the files in your `c:\inetpub\wwwroot\dotnetnuke\` folder. *You do not want to copy the APP_DATA folder and the WEB.CONFIG file.* If you copy these files over, you run the risk of losing important information about your website. This will replace all the files that are necessary to replace for the upgrade, but it won't overwrite any of the files you've uploaded for your portal that exist in the `c:\inetpub\wwwroot\dotnetnuke\portals\` folder.

5. Navigate to your website.

As you can see, the only difference between the Upgrade and Install packages for the actual upgrade process is that you do not want to copy the `web.config` file and the `app_data` folders from the downloaded Install package. The rest of the process is the same: enable your website and access the site in a browser.

# Upgrading Extensions (Modules and Skins)

Over time, you will find that there are new features that you would like to implement on your website. Some of these new features will come through new extensions, and some will come from enhancements to existing extensions. We covered the extension installation process in Chapter 3. The process for upgrading an extension is exactly the same as the process for initially installing the extension. It is managed by a super user (Host) on the Host ⇨ Extensions page.

From this page, you can choose the module actions for the Extensions module and choose Install Extension Wizard. You will choose the file for the new version of the module you would like to upgrade, and DNN will walk you through the Installation Wizard. The difference between the initial installation of the extension and the upgrade is that DNN will run only the SQL scripts that are necessary to upgrade from the current version to the new version of an extension. This comes in very handy because you should be able to easily upgrade your modules without losing the existing content for the extensions on your website.

> ### Always Back Up before Installing, Upgrading, or Deleting Extensions
>
> A very useful step when installing DNN extensions is to back up your files and database prior to beginning the installation process. In most cases, the installation/upgrade/delete processes will work without problems, but if something fails, having a backup of your site will save you time to recover the data. Even the most experienced DNN users have been burned by a failed process while working with an extension. Having that backup ready to go will make your life far easier in case of such an event.

Before you install a new extension, or upgrade an existing extension, we definitely recommend you go through the process in a test environment first. In some cases, upgrades to extensions will change the way they format content. Upgrading a test environment first will allow you to see if that is the case for the extensions you are upgrading or installing, without having to frantically fix things on your production website. This will better prepare you for upgrading the production site.

# Setting Up Multiple Environments

Throughout this chapter we've talked about having multiple environments, mainly for use when testing upgrades for DNN and extensions, as well as when installing new extensions. Setting up a development environment is not a complex process; if you were able to set up DNN, you will likely be able to set up other environments as well. Before we get into the process of how to set up additional environments, we will talk about a few different types of environments that you might configure.

## Types of Environments

You can set up your DNN website in the following types of environments:

❑ **Production environment** — If you've made it this far into the book, you likely already have a production environment configured. A production environment is the website that your customers are accessing, and should be backed up regularly.

❑ **Staging environment** — A staging environment is one that is configured to test out the content for a website before moving it to your production site. Because DotNetNuke doesn't have any workflow and approval capabilities built in, it is common to have a staging environment configured that is used to prepare and format content. You can bypass the need to have a staging environment by having pages on your DNN site that are only accessible to content administrators, on which they can format and prepare content. When the content is ready for production, it can be moved from these inaccessible pages to pages that are accessible to your website's visitors.

A staging environment is generally configured by taking a backup of your production website and either restoring it as a different website on the same server, for example `http://staging.dnnbook/`, or configuring it as a new site on a totally different web server.

❑ **Testing environment** — A testing environment, as its name suggests, is used for testing purposes. It should be a playground in which you can install new extensions and upgrades to the

DNN platform before you even think about putting them into your staging or production environments. A testing environment should regularly be set up from a recent backup of your production environment; that way you are closely testing how your site may react to the addition of extensions or DNN upgrades. Use a test environment liberally, install modules that you think you might need on your production site, and see if they work and provide the functionality you are looking for. If they do, you can then look at installing them in the production environment, after you back that environment up, of course.

❑   **Development environment** — A development environment can be extremely useful if you are developing custom modules for your DNN websites. This type of environment might be a backup of your production environment, like the other two types, or it might even be a clean installation of the DotNetNuke Source package. Extension development is outside of the scope of this book. Check out the *Professional DotNetNuke Module Programming* book, also from Wrox, for more information on development and configuring your development environment.

A common property of all these environments is how they are configured. If you already have a production website running, you can make a backup of that website and restore it as a new website to create any of the other types of environments. A few steps in this process differ from the backup/restoration processes.

## Configuring a New Environment

The process for setting up additional environments is a mix of the installation process and the process for restoring a backup of a website. Following are the steps required for configuring your new environment; for some of the more detailed information for some of the steps, we point you to the appropriate chapter in this book. This process can also be used if you are moving a website from one web server or hosting provider to another. The following steps assume that you already have the DNS entries for your new URL configured with your domain registrar.

1.   Configure the portal alias for your new environment.

You can configure the portal alias when logged in as a super user by visiting either the Admin ➪ Site Settings page or the Host ➪ Portals page. You should add the URL that you will be using to access your new environment as a portal alias for your website.

This is an important step in the process. If you fail to do this before moving on to the next step, or do it incorrectly, you likely will not be able to access the new environment but will instead be redirected to a different website address, likely back to your production environment. This can cause a problem if you don't realize which site you are on when you log in and start changing things. You should always be aware of the URL of the website that you are logged in to.

---

### Changing Your Portal Alias in the Database

If you are accustomed to making changes to data in a database, you can modify or add a new portal alias by working with the PortalAlias table in your DNN database. Any changes made to the data in this table will be loaded the next time your website starts. You can also reset the site to force a reload of this information.

---

2.   Back up your production environment (see earlier in this chapter).

3.   Extract the contents of your backup to the new directory's location (see Chapter 2).

4. Configure the file permissions for the new location (see Chapter 2).

5. Configure your website in IIS, using the new URL you defined in step 1 as the portal alias (see Chapter 2).

6. Restore the database as a new database in SQL Server (see earlier in this chapter, assuming that you aren't using SQL Express).

7. Configure the SQL user account for your new database and the `web.config` connection strings (see Chapter 2, assuming that you aren't using SQL Express).

8. Access your new environment with the new URL.

# Rotating Content Using Banners

DNN enables you to use rotating banners for advertising and to manage advertising clients, known as *vendors*. By using banners, you can generate revenue from your website or simply rotate content on your site when users visit different pages. DNN provides a number of ways to incorporate banners on your site. Each approach uses the same basic concepts, but the mechanism for implementation varies. After explaining the basic concepts, we'll discuss some implementation strategies and considerations.

Rotating content using banners comprises two related functions: placing the banners and managing the banners. You can place banners on your site using either the Banners module or by incorporating the Banner skin object into your skin. We'll discuss some of the considerations for implementing each approach later in this section. You can manage banners by using the Vendors page. The Vendors page is located in both the Admin and Host menus. The Vendors page allows you to create accounts for each advertiser on your site and manage the banners associated with each vendor account. Next, we'll review the process of establishing a new vendor account. Once we have a vendor account created on our site, we'll implement the banners for our single vendor using the Banners module to show how the placement of banners works in tandem with the management of the advertising client's (vendor) account.

## Managing Vendor Accounts

The first step in managing the advertisers on your site is to create an account for their banner advertising. This account can be used to manage contact information and banner advertisements, and review reports on impressions (the number of times a banner appears on your site). To create a vendor account, navigate to the Vendors page in the Admin menu.

---

**Vendors at Portal or Host Level**

It is important to note here that both the super users (Host) and portal administrators can manage vendors separately. Upon placing banner advertising on your site, you'll have the choice of selecting banner advertising from the Portal (Site) or Host vendor list. We'll review the considerations for this feature in more detail later in the section. In the following example, we'll be implementing banners for vendors managed by the portal administrator.

---

The first thing you'll notice is that the Vendors page is similar to the one used to manage user accounts. Vendors and users share a number of traits. Like users, vendors can be authorized or unauthorized. Unauthorized vendors' banners will not be displayed on your site, but you can retain the account for later use in case the vendor decides to advertise again on your site. Additionally, vendor accounts have profile-like information you can collect and store with their account. As shown in Figure 9-4, we have created an account for a fictional advertiser on our site. The fields in Vendor Details are all required, as indicated by the asterisks. The fields in Address Details are fixed, and you can toggle the requirement for these fields on and off as is relevant to your site.

Figure 9-4

## Vendor Relationships

After creating the vendor's account, you can start to define the relationship with the vendor. The next time you access the vendor's account, three new sections will appear in their account information: Vendor Classification, Banner Advertising, and Affiliate Referrals. A vendor can either be a banner advertiser or a referring affiliate. Banner advertisers are vendors for which you wish to track the referrals your site is generating for their advertisements. Referring affiliates are vendors for which you wish to track the referrals to your site from a link on their site. The following example will quickly explain the setup for a referring affiliate.

---

### Tracking Affiliate Referrals

When you create a vendor account in the Vendors activity, the vendor is assigned a unique identification number. To track referrals to your site using the Affiliate Referral feature, you'll need to pay attention to the identifier for your vendors. When you create or edit a vendor account, the URL in your browser will clue you in to the

*Continued*

---

identifier for your vendor's account. The identifier will appear in your URL similar to
`/VendorId/1/Default.aspx`.

With the identifier captured, you can track the referrals to your site by including
`?AffiliateId=#` (# being the vendor identifier) in the URL you provide your affiliate.

## Managing Banner Advertisements

Next, we'll add banners to the vendor's account. Expand the Banner Advertising section of the vendor's account to expose the Add New Banner action. Each banner will have a name, type, and group for identification and categorization. As described in the following table, the remaining fields in the banner define how the advertisement will look and function on your site. In Figure 9-5, you can see an example of a new banner.

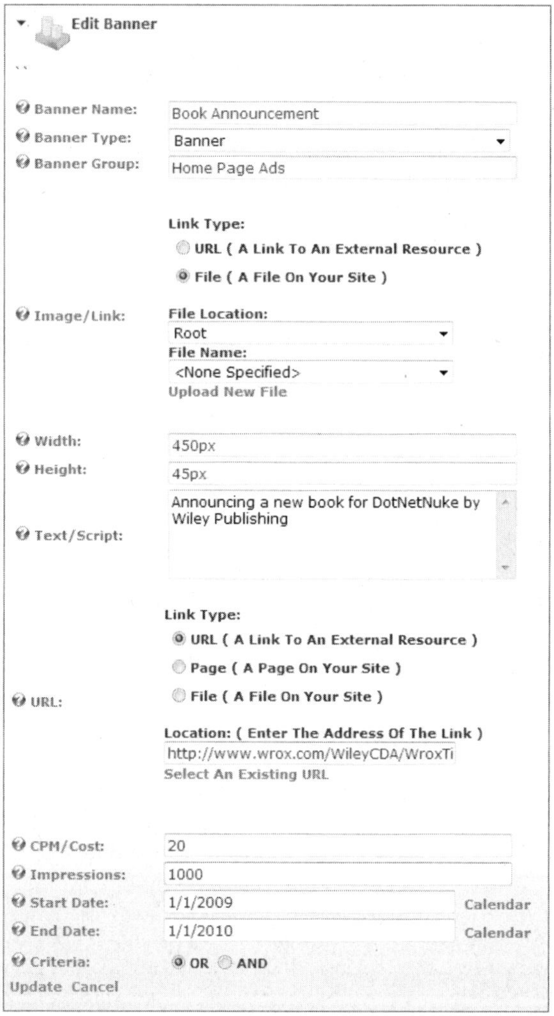

Figure 9-5

**Banner Advertisement**

| Field | Description |
|---|---|
| Banner Name | The name or description for the advertisement you are creating. Make sure to use a descriptive title to make identification easier. This is only visible to editors of the Vendors page. |
| Banner Type | You can use Banner Type to classify the advertisements. When you place banners on your pages, you'll display banners from a specific type. Typically the banner type is determined by the size and dimensions of the banner on your page. |
| Banner Group | The Banner Group is a subclassification given to your banners to further organize banners. As you type into this field, the existing groups will appear as they match your input. To use existing groups pick from the suggestions. To create a new group, specify the new name. |
| Image/Link | This is the image used in the banner advertisement. If the image is stored on your file system, use the File selection. If the image is stored on an external file system, link to it using the URL selection. |
| Width | The width of your banner in pixels. |
| Height | The height of your banner in pixels. |
| Text/Script | The text associated with your banner. In image banners, this will be used as the Alt text, for Text banners this is the content of your advertisement. |
| URL | The URL used for your banner when visitors click on the advertisement. |
| CPM/Cost | The cost per impression. This value is used in relation to the number of impressions you define in the next field. If you leave the Impressions field empty, it will act as a fixed rate. |
| Impressions | The number of impressions from which the cost is calculated. |
| Start Date | The start date for this banner. |
| End Date | The end date for this banner. |
| Criteria (OR/AND) | The criteria for which you base the expiration of a banner. For example, the banner should expire after 10000 impressions OR by a specific date. |

# Banner Placement

After creating the banner advertisement for your vendor, you can place it on your pages. As mentioned earlier, you can place banner advertisements either by using the Banners module or by incorporating the Banner skin object in your skin. Using the Banners module gives the page editors more flexibility in the placement of the banners on their page. Using the skin object can give the portal administrator control over the placement and use of banners on all pages using the skin.

Using the Banners module gives the module administrator a number of configuration options for the display of banners on the page. The first decision is whether to pull banners from the Portal's or Host's vendor accounts. Figure 9-6 shows the setup of a Banners module set to display two advertisements at a time. You can see that the Banners module will display two 450px banners horizontally. To accomplish this display elegantly, we need to make sure that the banner advertisements created in the vendors' accounts are 450px wide and 45px tall.

Figure 9-6

To use the Banner skin object, you need to fully understand the concepts of creating or modifying the skin package. Without going into these details, it is important for portal administrators to know that this option exists and that, as the portal administrator, there are settings you control to facilitate the use of the Banner skin object. Figure 9-7 shows the Basic Site Settings to determine whether the Banner skin object should use the Host or Site vendor account.

Figure 9-7

## Other Uses for Banners

Banners can be an effective tool to generate revenue on your site and track advertising impressions. If your website isn't used to directly generate revenue from advertising, you can still use the Banner and Vendor features to rotate content on your website. The Banners module is often used to rotate page titles or header images. You could also use this functionality to rotate testimonials, quotes, showcase your portfolio, or randomly rotate a corporate message on your site.

The setup for an internal use of the Banner functionality is similar to the setup we just completed, but you may not require all the additional tracking features for revenue and impressions. For a vendor, you can simply create yourself as a vendor in the system.

# Token Replacement

Token replacement is available in the Text/HTML, Form and List, and Newsletters extensions. This feature allows you to pull dynamic elements into your content. The following table lists all the available tokens in DNN currently. Some of these tokens are more relevant than others for a Newsletter, and some are specific to only the Form and Lists module.

**Available Tokens**

| Token | Description | Example |
|-------|-------------|---------|
| **Portal-Related Tokens** | | |
| [Portal:Currency] | Each portal has a default currency set in the Site Settings. | USD, CAD, EUR |
| [Portal:Description] | The portal description as defined in the Basic Site Settings. | "A website for amateur bull riders to discuss new rodeo techniques." |
| [Portal:Email] | The e-mail address of the administrator for your portal. | admin@dnnuserguide.com |
| [Portal:FooterText] | The text you provide in the Copyright field of Basic Site Settings for your portal. | Copyright 2009 Wiley Publishing |
| [Portal:HomeDirectory] | The root, or home, directory for the portal. Since each portal has their own home directory, this token lists the path to this folder using a relative path. | /Portals/0/ |
| [Portal:LogoFile] | The filename of the logo used for your portal. | Logo.jpg |
| [Portal:PortalName] | The title used for your portal as defined in Basic Site Settings. | DNN Users Guide Test Site |
| [Portal:URL] | The URL defined as your first Portal Alias by the host. | www.dnnuserguide.com |
| [Portal:TimeZoneOffset] | The difference in minutes between your Portal Time Zone and Coordinated Universal Time (UTC). The Portal Time Zone is set in the Advanced settings for your portal. | -360 for US Central Timezone |
| **User-Related Tokens** | | |
| [User:DisplayName] | The display name of the user. | pwrenner |
| [User:Email] | The e-mail address of the user as specified in their user account. | |
| [User:FirstName] | The first name from the user's account | Patrick |
| [User:FullName] | The First and Last name combined from the user account | Patrick Renner |

*Continued*

**Available Tokens** *(continued)*

| Token | Description | Example |
|-------|-------------|---------|
| [User:LastName] | The last name from the user's account. | Renner |
| [User:UserName] | The username of the user. | prenner |
| [Membership:Approved] | A yes/no flag indicating if a user is authenticated. | Yes |
| [Membership:CreatedDate] | The creation date of the user's account. | |
| [Membership:IsOnline] | A yes/no flag indicating if a user is currently logged in to the site. | |
| [Profile:<Property>] | A wildcard token used to incorporate custom user profile properties. To use profile properties, <Property> should be replaced with the property name. If the user does not have a value for this property field, the token will be blank. | i.e. [Profile:Country] would return United States |
| **Page Related Tokens** | | |
| [Tab:Description] | The page description as specified in the Basic Page Settings. | |
| [Tab:EndDate] | The end date specified for a page in the Advanced Page Settings. | |
| [Tab:FullURL] | The full URL for the page in which you're using token replacement. | http://localhost/dnn5 /TokenReplacement/tabid /57/Default.aspx |
| [Tab:IconFile] | The icon filename for a page icon if specified in the Advanced Page Settings. | |
| [Tab:Keywords] | The keywords defined in your Basic Page Settings. | DNN, Tokens, Newsletter, Text/HTML, modules, Form and List |
| [Tab:PageHeadText] | The text used in the Page Header Text field in the Advanced Settings section of Page Settings. | |
| [Tab:StartDate] | The date set as the start date in the Advanced Page Settings. | |
| [Tab:TabName] | The title of the page. | |

**Available Tokens**

| Token | Description | Example |
|-------|-------------|---------|
| [Tab:TabPath] | The relative path to the current page. | //PageName |
| [Tab:TabURL] | The URL for the current page. | |
| **Module-Related Tokens** | | |
| [Module:Description] | Module Definition Description | |
| [Module:EndDate] | Module Display Until Date | |
| [Module:Footer] | Module Footer Text | |
| [Module:FriendlyName] | Module Definition Name | |
| [Module:Header] | Module Header Text | |
| [Module:HelpURL] | Module Help URL | |
| [Module:IconFile] | Module Path to Icon File | |
| [Module:ModuleTitle] | Module Title | |
| [Module:PaneName] | Module Name of Pane where the module resides | |
| [Module:StartDate] | Module Display from Date | |
| **Date- and Time-Related Tokens** | | |
| [DateTime:Now] | The current date and time. | 3/6/2009 2:30 AM |
| [DateTime:Now \| <format>] | The current date and time with a format as specified by you; the formatting uses standards defined by .NET. | i.e. [DateTime:Now \| MMMM] would return March |
| **CPU Performance** | | |
| [Ticks:Now] | CPU Tick Count for Current Second | |
| [Ticks:Today] | CPU Tick Count Since Midnight | |
| [Ticks:TicksPerDay] | CPU Ticks per Day | |

# Sending Newsletters

The Newsletters feature provides a simple tool to send e-mails from your site to users with an account on your site or to individual e-mail addresses. In this section, we'll review the features of the Newsletters feature and introduce token replacement, a powerful tool integrated in a number of places in DNN that allows you to pull dynamic content into your content.

Using the Newsletters activity, you can send one-off HTML or plain-text e-mails. In addition to sending e-mails from your website, you will receive a bulk e-mail confirmation from DNN with the results from your e-mail. The Newsletters activity sends a confirmation e-mail to the e-mail address listed as the FROM: address. This confirmation e-mail includes the number of e-mails attempted and the number successfully sent.

## Basic Settings

The Basic Settings for your Newsletters activity will determine the recipients, sender, and subject of your e-mail (see Figure 9-8).

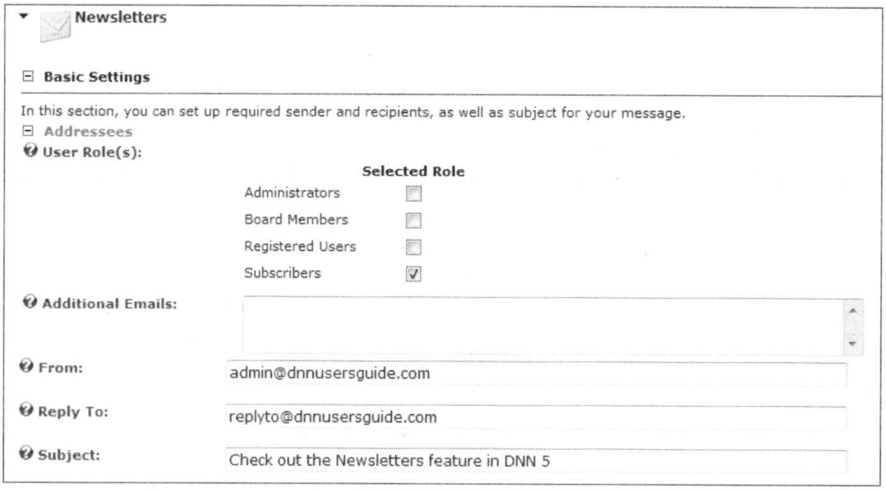

Figure 9-8

You can send e-mails to users in specific security roles or to individual e-mail addresses. To send e-mails to multiple recipients, simply separate their addresses with a semicolon. The Newsletters activity allows you to specify a separate From: and Reply To: e-mail address. The From: address will default to the e-mail attached to your user account. By default, the Reply To: address will be the same as the From: address. Additionally, you define the Subject of your e-mail in the Basic Settings.

## The Message of Your E-mail

The Message section of the Newsletters activity is the body of your e-mail. You can either use the Rich Text Editor or plain text to create the body of your e-mail. By using the Rich Text Editor, you have the same features available that you have when creating the rich text content on your site. If you use the Rich Text Editor, the content will be sent formatted in HTML. Consider the recipients of your e-mail as your decide whether to craft your message in HTML or plain text; while HTML messages can be more elegant, plain-text e-mails are more broadly accepted by e-mail services. Not all e-mail services will accept the formatting of an HTML message.

By using tokens, you can provide personalized content to each of the recipients in your e-mail. To use the tokens in your newsletter, simply place the token into the body of your message

---

**Sending a Personalized E-mail**

The following is an example of a personalized e-mail that you could send to each user in your portal to thank him or her for becoming a member of your site:

Dear [User:FirstName],

All of us here at [Portal:PortalName] ([Portal:PortalURL]) would like to thank you for your valued membership to our site. You have been a member since [Membership:CreatedDate].

Feel free to contact us at [Portal:Email] anytime with suggestions or ideas for what you'd like to see on our site.

Thanks,

[Portal:PortalName]

---

To use tokens in your message, you must also indicate to DNN that you want to interpret the tokens, and you must use the Send Method of TO: One Message Per Email Address (Personalized). These settings are described in the following section.

## Advanced Settings

The Newsletters activity allows you to configure a number of other features for your e-mail. As described in the following table, each of these settings is found in the Advanced Settings section.

**Advanced Settings**

| Setting | Description |
| --- | --- |
| Attachment | Allows you to attach a file to your e-mail message. The file must be stored in your portal's directory. |
| Replace Tokens | To use the tokens in your e-mail, you must tell DNN to look for them. By default, the Newsletter has token replacement enabled. |
| No duplicate addresses | When you activate this option, DNN will screen out duplicate e-mail addresses listed in your Addressees list. This will check for e-mails included from the User Roles and Additional Emails list. |
| Priority | Flags your message as High, Normal, or Low priority. Whether the priority of your message will be included with the message will depend on the e-mail service of the recipient. |
| Send Method: TO: One Message Per Email Address (Personalized) | Sends the e-mail individually to each addressee, replacing all available tokens. |

*Continued*

**Advanced Settings** *(continued)*

| Setting | Description |
|---|---|
| Send Method: BCC: One Email to Blind Distribution List (Not Personalized) | Sends a single e-mail to the sender, including all addressees as hidden recipients. |
| Send Method: RELAY: One Message Per Email Address (Personalized) | Sends all individual e-mails to a specific relay address. The token for users' mobile phone or fax number is required to complete the delivery, and a relay server (outside DNN) must be configured to complete the delivery. |
| Send Action: Synchronously | Sends your e-mails immediately upon the refresh of your page. This is appropriate for smaller e-mail lists. |
| Send Action: Asynchronously | Send your e-mails using the Scheduler activity. This is appropriate for larger e-mail lists. |

# Managing the Recycle Bin

When you delete a page from your portal or a module from a page, they are not permanently deleted from your portal. The deleted pages and modules are sent to the Recycle Bin. As an administrator, it is important to frequently monitor your site's Recycle Bin and delete modules and pages completely from your portal when you deem them obsolete.

DNN allows you to empty the entire Recycle Bin or permanently delete records one by one. Maintaining a manageable Recycle Bin can help the performance of your site as well as help avoid ambiguity as you search for content in the Recycle Bin. Next, we'll step through the process for permanently deleting pages from your site. The process for permanently deleting modules is the same as for permanently deleting pages.

1.  Navigate to the Recycle Bin in the Admin menu.

2.  Select the Page from the Pages List.

3.  Click the red "x" icon to permanently delete the page from your database.

Additionally, the Recycle Bin allows you to restore the modules and pages from the Recycle Bin to an active state on your site. When restoring modules from the Recycle Bin, it is a good practice to make a test page available and restore the modules back to your test page. This will allow you to review the content prior to making the content live on your site. Also, you can better control the pane in which the module is placed when you make it live again. Figure 9-9 illustrates restoring an inadvertently deleted module to our test page. From the test page, you can then move the module to its desired page by using the Advanced Settings section of the module's settings.

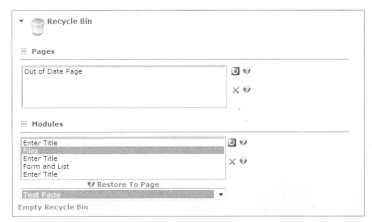

Figure 9-9

# Configuring User Settings

DNN enables administrators of the Users and Roles modules to configure the way users are managed on your site. The User Settings activity is found in both the actions menu of both the Security Roles and User Accounts modules. The User Settings is divided into three sections. Next, we'll review the settings in each of these sections to demonstrate how the settings can impact your site.

## *Membership Provider Settings*

The Membership Provider Settings are a read-only display of the configuration options provided by ASP.NET and set in the `web.config` file. Since these settings apply to all portals in an installation of DNN, they are not editable by the Portal Administrator.

Figure 9-10 illustrates the default settings of the Membership Provider Settings. The following code in the `web.config` file matches a number of these settings. The remaining settings are determined by the ASP.NET SQL Membership Provider.

```
<add name="AspNetSqlMembershipProvider" type=
    "System.Web.Security.SqlMembershipProvider"
connectionStringName="SiteSqlServer" enablePasswordRetrieval="true"
    enablePasswordReset="true"
requiresQuestionAndAnswer="false" minRequiredPasswordLength="7"
    minRequiredNonalphanumericCharacters="0"
requiresUniqueEmail="false" passwordFormat="Encrypted" applicationName=
    "DotNetNuke" description="Stores
and retrieves membership data from the local Microsoft SQL Server database" />
```

Figure 9-10

## Password Aging Settings

The Password Aging Settings are also read-only and are tied to the settings determined in the web.config file. The two settings in this section, Password Expiry and Password Expiry Reminder, are determined by ASP.NET Membership Provider defaults. To change these settings, you'll need to modify your web.config file to override the default values.

## User Accounts Settings

The User Accounts Settings are an increasingly important set of configuration options. In DotNetNuke 5.0, the ability to distribute the management responsibilities gave Administrators the ability to delegate responsibilities of the Users and Roles modules. The configuration of these settings can help to make the management of users easier and provide administrators of these modules with relevant information. We've segmented the settings into logical groups because a number of the settings in the User Settings are related.

### User Accounts Display Options

The first group of settings in this section determine which fields are displayed as columns in the list of users in the User Accounts module. Figure 9-11 illustrates enabling all the fields as columns.

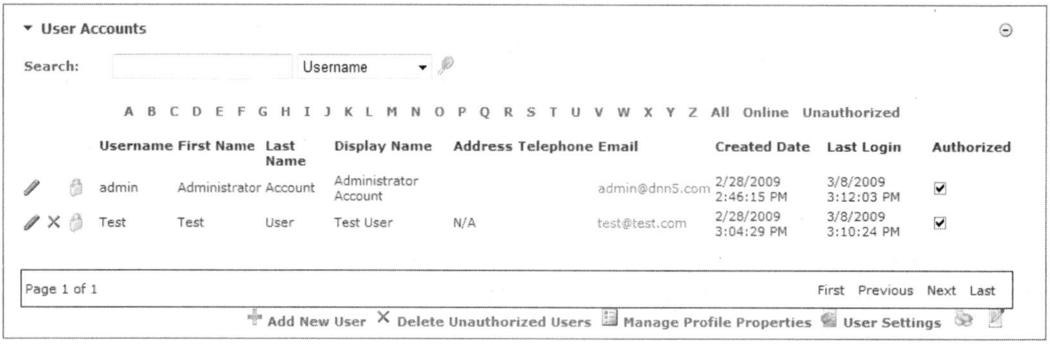

Figure 9-11

The next setting determines the Default Display Mode. This setting determines which users are listed when you first access the User Accounts module. Choosing All will return all users registered on your site. The list of users will be paged after 10 users (by default), and you can search by first letter of the username or by specific profile values. Choosing First Letter will return all the users with a username starting with the letter A. Choosing None will force administrators to start by searching for users or clicking on one of the links.

By default, the list of users in the User Accounts module will be displayed with a pager control. The page control will display the number of users set to display in the Users per Page setting. If you'd prefer to display all users, you can disable the paging control by enabling the Suppress Pager in Users Grid setting. The Users per Page, Suppress Pager in Users Grid, and Default Display Mode settings all control the way the user accounts are listed in the User Accounts module. The number of users on your site will affect the decisions you make for these settings. If you have a large number of users, for example, you'll want to avoid displaying All users as the Default Display Mode without using the pager control.

## User Account Display Options

The next group of settings determines the way that profile information is displayed to users on your site. Default Profile Visibility Mode determines the default value for the visibility of profile fields. User profile values can be displayed throughout your site, using a number of modules — for example, the Links module can create links to user accounts. If you link to user account information on your site, it is important to determine which profile fields are visible to all users.

Display Profile Visibility is closely related to Default Profile Visibility Mode. You can display to your users the visibility settings for their profile fields. Figure 9-12 demonstrates a user accessing their Profile information. When Display Profile Visibility is enabled, users can determine the visibility of each of the profile fields.

**Figure 9-12**

If you want to allow users to subscribe or unsubscribe to or from Public Roles, enable Display Manage Services. This will allow users access to the Manage Services activity in the User Account control. If you don't use Public Roles, you may want to hide Manage Services.

## Account Access and Creation

The next set of options determines the user experience during registration and login. There are three settings that allow you to redirect your users at some point in their visit to your site. Redirect After Login allows you to specify a page on your site to which authenticated users will be directed after login. This can be useful if you have a landing page specifically for members of your site. Redirect After Logout allows you to specify a page on your site to which users will be directed after logging out. You could use this setting to present users with a survey after logging out or a page thanking them for their visit. Redirect After Registration allows you to present your newly registered users information about the benefits of membership. This can be especially beneficial if your site's membership type is Verified (on the site settings page). The page you redirect users to after registration can give them more information about the Verification process.

Using CAPTCHA For Registration will require users to confirm their registration with a CAPTCHA code. CAPTCHA codes are useful for filtering out robots to keep them from registering fake users on your site, because CAPTCHA masks the text values with an image. Figure 9-13 illustrates the use of CAPTCHA during the registration process.

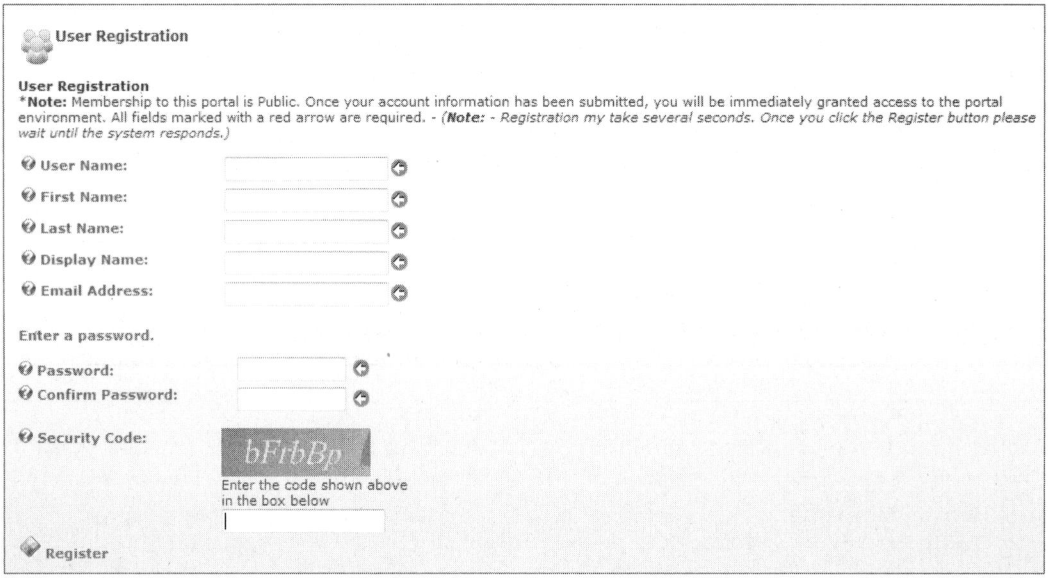

Figure 9-13

Display Name Format gives you the ability to automatically create a display name for your users. If you specify a format, users will not need to provide a display name during registration. To create a display name format, you can pull information like [FIRSTNAME], [LASTNAME], [USERID], [USERNAME], or hard-coded characters.

Email Address Validation allows you to provide your own custom regular expressions to validate e-mail addresses. This can be useful for corporate websites that require the e-mail address to have the corporate e-mail account as part of the e-mail address. Regular expressions are complex strings that allow you to restrict the format of text entered into a field.

---

**The Default Regular Expression Used in DNN**

The default regular expression used in DNN is `\b[a-zA-Z0-9._%\-+']` `+@[a-zA-Z0-9.\-]+\.[a-zA-Z]{2,4}\b`. This regular expression will allow e-mail addresses with a mixture of alphabetic and numeric characters, with the @ symbol before another mix of alphabetic and numeric characters and ending with an extension of only alphabetic characters.

---

If you have required profile fields, you can force users to complete these fields either during registration or before they can log in to the site. Require Valid Profile for Registration should be used sparingly because longer registrations can dissuade users from registering on your site. Require Valid Profile for Login will force users to complete their profile once they attempt to log in to the site. Unless your required profile fields change frequently, requiring a valid profile at login should force users to complete their profile when new properties are required, and not prompt them to change their profile upon each login.

Users Display Mode in Manage Roles determines how you manage users in a specific role. In the Manage Roles activity, you can see all users in a specific role. To add a user to the role, you can either search by username with a Text Box or choose the user from a drop-down list (Combo Box). If you have a large number of users in your roles, it may be better to use the text box to search for users, as the drop-down list will become a scrolling nightmare.

# Advanced Administrative Functionality

There are a number of changes to DotNetNuke 5 that provide ways to advance the management of your websites. The new permissions model allows you to deny permissions to specific roles/users, and you now have the ability to distribute some of the administrative functionality to other users of your portal without having to give them administrator rights to the portal, as you had to do in previous versions. You can allow users and roles to send newsletters, set up banners, and view site statistics; and you can manage the users and user settings for a portal. This functionality is provided through the abstraction of the administrative functionality into individual modules in DNN 5.

For example, to provide a user or group of users (a role) access to the Newsletters module, perform the following steps:

1. Create a new role called Newsletter Manager.

2. Add the users who should have access to this role from the Manage Roles page for the Newsletter Manager role.

3. Create a page called Newsletter Manager. You can do this at any level within your navigation, outside of the Admin and Host menus.

4. Configure the permissions for the page to be visible only to the Newsletter Manager role.

5. Place a Newsletters module on this newly created page.

Configuring the newsletter administration is as simple as that. You can do the same for any of the other Admin modules that DNN now provides, including the Recycle Bin, Users and Roles, Tabs (pages), Site Log, and even the Vendors module. The ability to delegate these tasks to users is a great step forward for the DNN platform.

# Summary

This chapter has been a hodgepodge of some of the administrative tools that DNN provides, things to think about, and actions to perform to keep your website up and running. We first covered some of the basics of using the Dashboard page to monitor your portal's health.

We then covered the extremely important topic of backing up your website and database. We can't stress enough the importance of backing up your database and files consistently. The simple process can save you hours of trouble if you run into a problem with your DNN sites. After backing up your website, you can restore that backup to create multiple environments to test things out before moving them to your production site. We walked you through the process of restoring a site and database, and then talked about the specifics of configuring multiple environments.

Next, we got into some advanced administration functionality that DNN provides. We showed you how to manage the banner and vendor functionality within DNN, for use with advertising or simply content rotation on your DNN pages. We also walked through the process of using the Newsletters module to send notifications to your users. The Newsletters module, like a few other modules, provides you with the ability to use the token replacement functionality.

After describing the Newsletters functionality, we covered the necessary information regarding the Recycle Bin, and the proper way to restore content that has been deleted from your site.

If your website has a large number of users, you will find the discussion on User Settings to be extremely helpful. We highlighted the functionality that the User Settings provides to a DNN administrator and what those settings control on the admin and public-facing portions of your site.

To conclude the chapter, we talked briefly about new functionality within DNN 5 that allows you to delegate some of the administrative tools that were available only to administrators in prior DNN versions.

We hope that this chapter, as well as the book as a whole, has proven to be a useful tool as you work with the DNN framework. Thank you!

# Index